IMAGES
of America

GLIMPSES OF MAINE'S ANGLING PAST

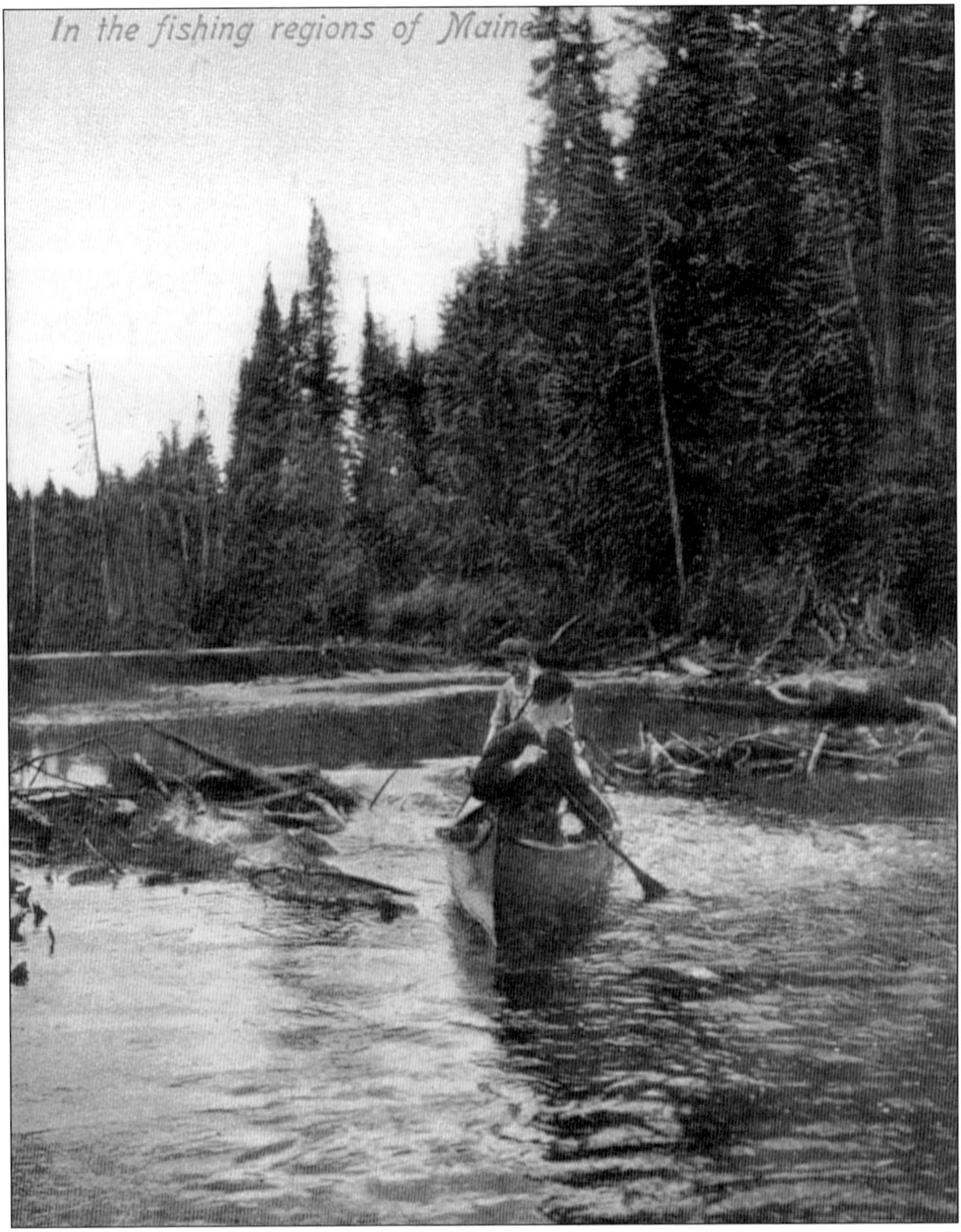

Before the days of automobiles, planes, speedboats, and dams, a canoe trip in the Maine woods was considered one of the most delightful outing excursions known in the great outdoors. This was a trip that combined paddling your own canoe, running rapids with the aid of a guide, and sled transportation through the forests. All sorts of men and women of all ages were drawn to the Pine Tree State to have the experience and the adventure.

Cover Image: This photograph was taken at East Outlet Dam, Moosehead Lake, prior to 1947. Note the long-handled net used for landing fish from the dam.

IMAGES
of America

GLIMPSES OF MAINE'S ANGLING PAST

Donald A. Wilson

ARCADIA
PUBLISHING

ISBN 978-0-7385-0407-0

Published by Arcadia Publishing
Charleston, South Carolina

Printed in the United States of America

Library of Congress Catalog Card Number: 99069378

For all general information contact Arcadia Publishing at:
Telephone 843-853-2070
Fax 843-853-0044
E-mail sales@arcadiapublishing.com
For customer service and orders:
Toll-Free 1-888-313-2665

Visit us on the Internet at www.arcadiapublishing.com

Dedicated to the guides, the sports, the camp operators, and the boat and equipment manufacturers who made it all happen.

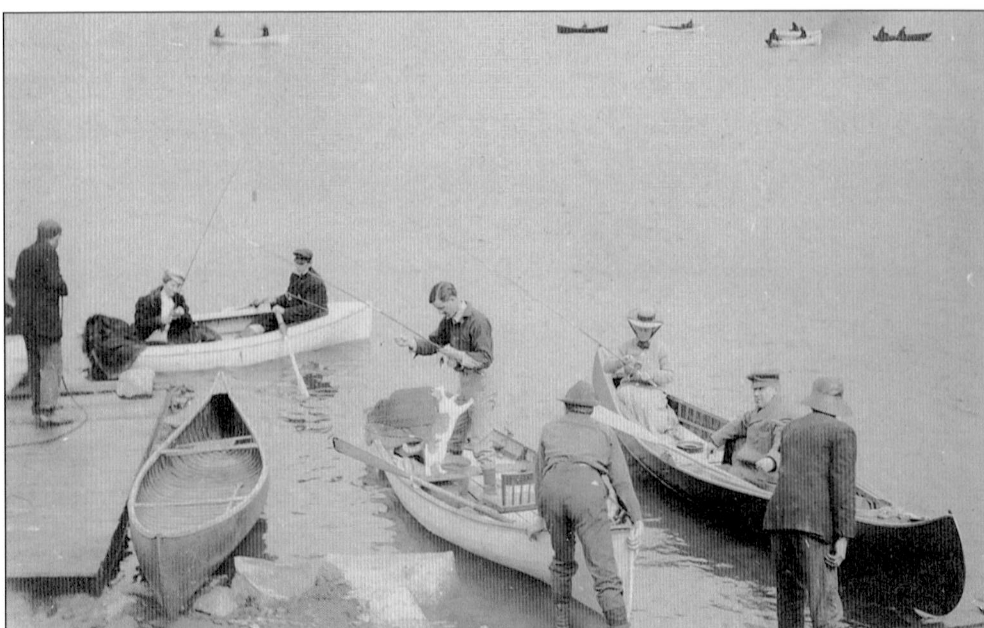

Guides and sports make ready for a day's fishing. Swan Lake in Waldo County once boasted "excellent salmon fishing." This was one of the areas where a private fish hatchery was located.

CONTENTS

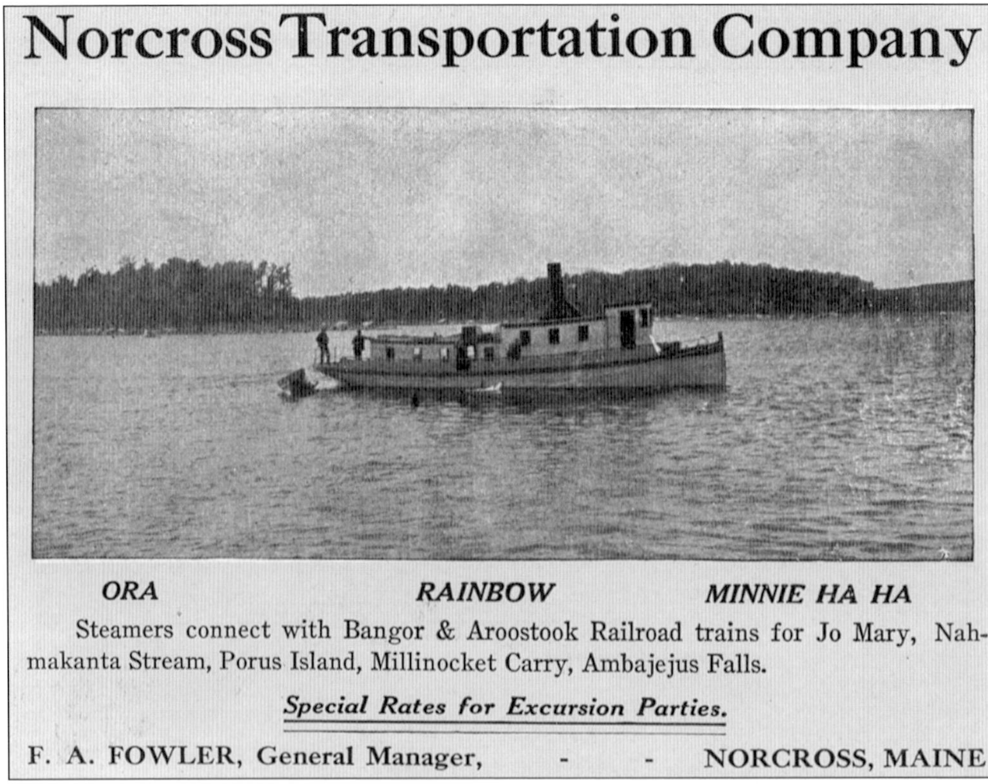

One of the many steamers that once existed in Maine, this one connected with the railroads to take sportsmen to the various camps and fishing grounds. (From *In the Maine Woods*, 1908.)

ACKNOWLEDGMENTS

Much appreciation goes to the Bangor & Aroostook Railroad Company, which granted permission to use selections of text as well as advertisements from *In the Maine Woods*, its yearly promotional publication produced for six decades. While I relied on limited sections of text for historical and statistical information, I borrowed freely from their advertisements as a supplement to my personal collection of photographs. I believe that the words of those who lived and worked at the time add tremendous insight to the topic and tell us about the past much better than any modern author could possibly do. The B&A information has greatly enhanced the text and assisted us all in having a glimpse of the past as they saw it . . . back then.

Other Publications by Donald A. Wilson

New Hampshire Fishing Maps (with Charlton J. Swasey), DeLorme, 1982
Smelt Fly Patterns, Frank Amato, 1996
Maine Aquatic Insects: Mayflies, Caddisflies & Stoneflies, Adventures in Angling, 1997

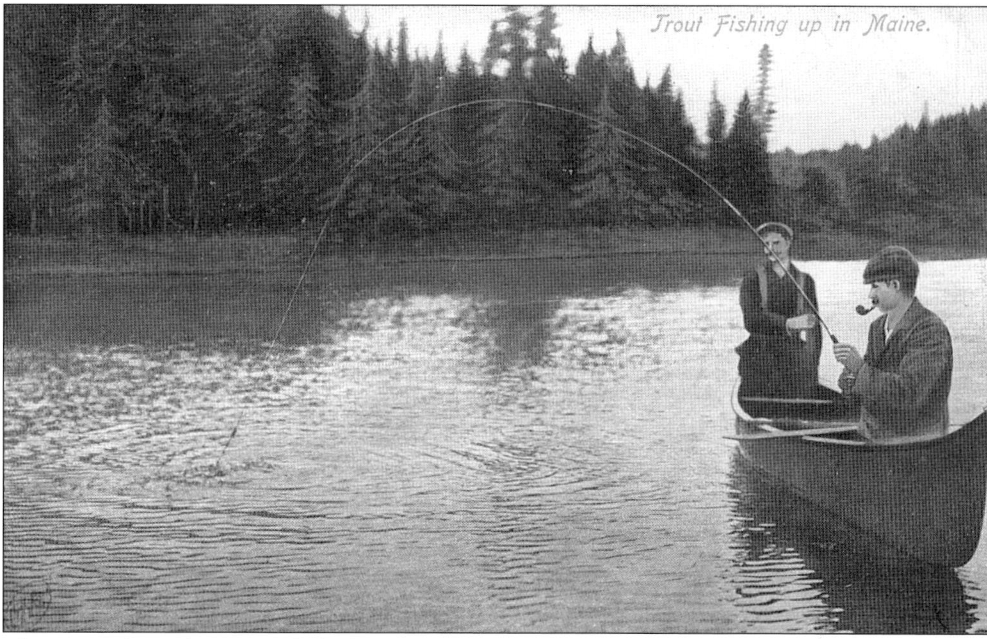

The sport plays a big one, while the guide steadies the canoe on one of the backwoods waters.

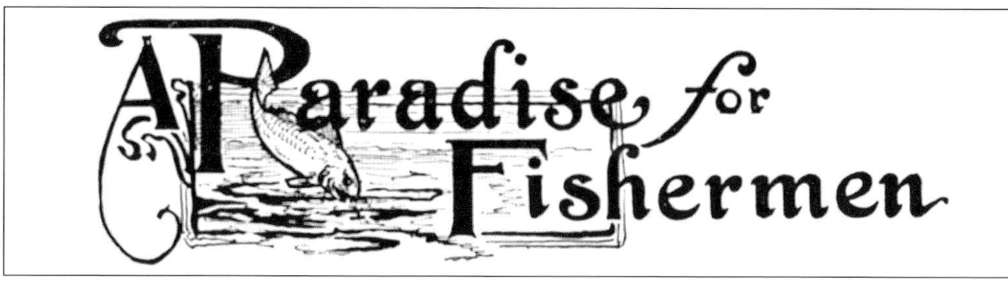

INTRODUCTION

Without airplanes, and with only a few roads, getting to Maine and the isolated fishing spots was no small matter in the early times. Only during the past five or six decades have travelers been transient and, as such, changed the concepts of fishing in wilderness areas forever.

Lumbering began in Maine in the early 1800s, and with it came an increased road network quickly followed by the railroads. There were four major lines in Maine: the Bangor & Aroostook, the Boston & Maine, the Canadian Pacific, and the Maine Central. All heavily promoted travel to Maine for hunting, fishing, canoeing, and pure relaxation. The railroad flyers, travel brochures, and publications were numerous and were filled with attractive advertisements and informative articles describing a sportsman's paradise.

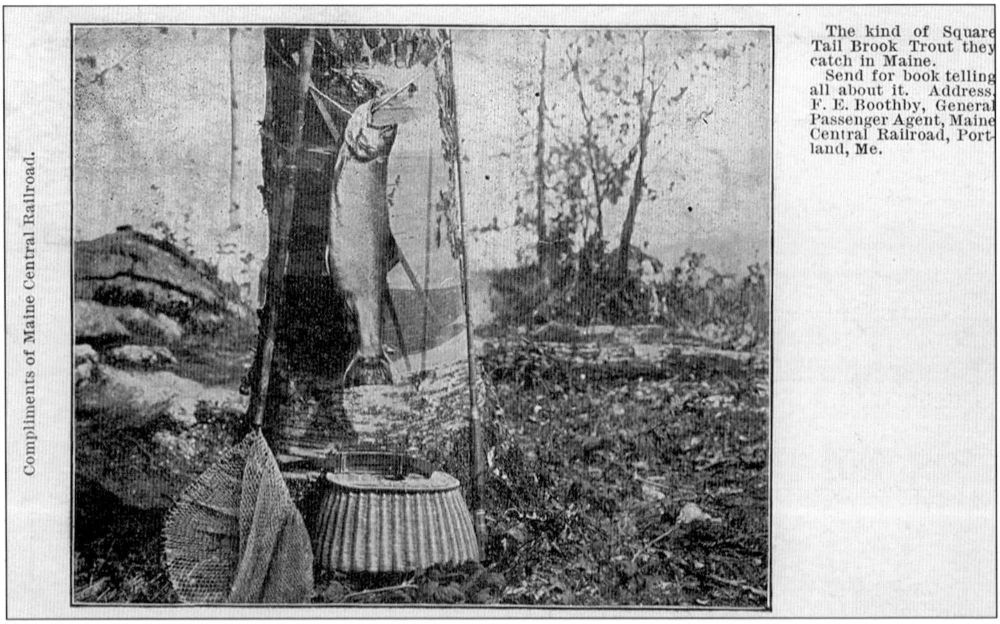

Railroads, stage lines, and lodging establishments all took advantage of trophy fish to entice sportsmen. This is a typical advertisement of that nature. While fish of this size were not caught by everyone, they were plentiful in many areas.

With the logging operations, literally hundreds of driving dams were built over the decades, creating ponds, diverting streams, and creating fish habitat, which did not previously exist. For years, these dams and their freshets carved out new pools and controlled water flows, such that water remained in many streams and ponds that would have otherwise dried up in midsummer. People arrived from all over the Northeast and beyond to stay for extended periods—weeks, sometimes months, occasionally the entire season. Huge establishments came into being, some accommodating thousands of sportsmen at any one time. They were self-contained, offering lodging, meals, boats and canoes, and guide services. An article appeared in the October 1896 issue of the *Maine Central* stating "one great cause for the increase in the number of sportsmen going to Maine, and that is the played-out condition of the Adirondacks. Half of the sportsmen have always previously spent their vacation in the Adirondacks, and a great many others have hunted in the various parts of the west, till they read the accounts of what can be found in Maine."

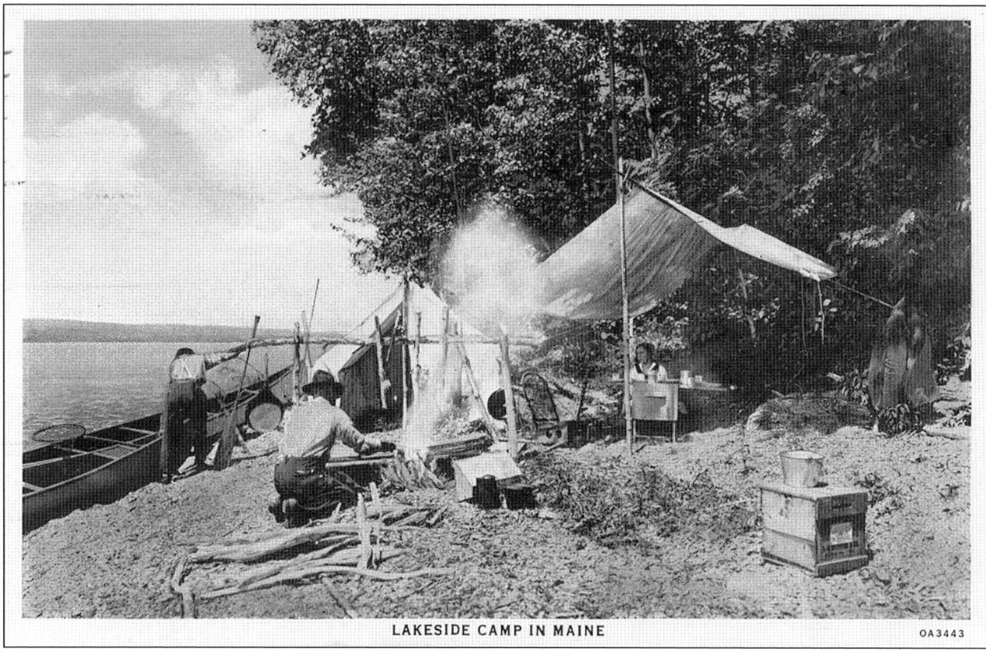

One guide takes care of the canoes and the fish, while the other prepares the meal. This was a typical setup with a cooking-dining fly and a tent for sleeping quarters.

From the resorts, sports with their guides branched out, taking side trips and canoe journeys that lasted for days, sometimes weeks. They camped as they went, fishing waters that saw few anglers in any given season. They commonly took the railroad or the stage to a remote location and then canoed back, stretching the return trip into days, exploring and fishing along the way. Lake fishing was preferred by some, from canoes at first, later from rowboats, and then from boats equipped with outboard motors.

This was an era, and it has passed. Today, the hotels are mostly gone, and people now fish for a few hours to a day or more and move on. The accounts left behind help us understand what once was; they may even lead us to wish that we had been there.

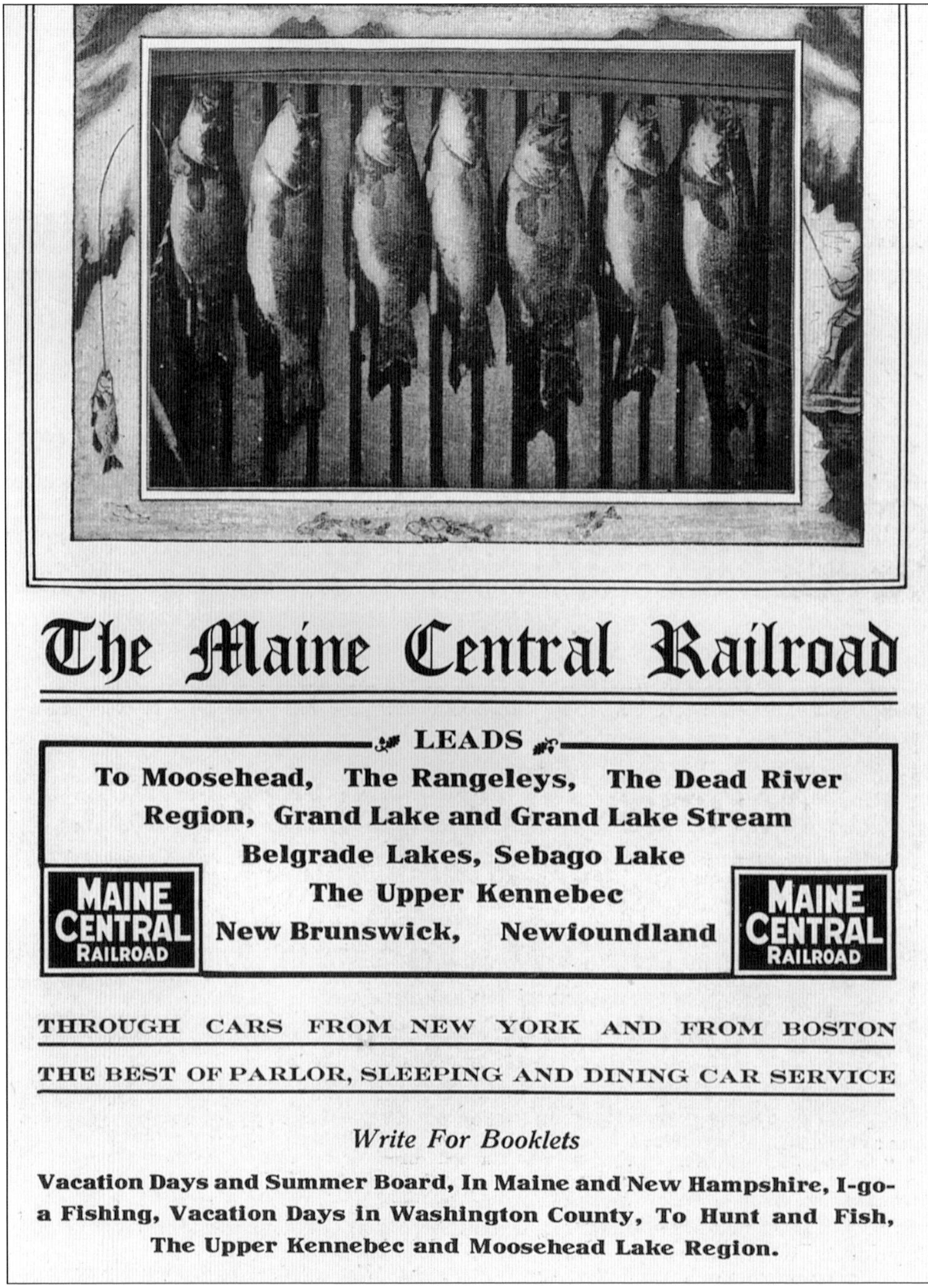

This is a Maine Central Railroad advertisement in a Bangor & Aroostook Railroad publication. There were four major lines in Maine along with several smaller lines, each serving a different area but all of them interested in a share of the tourist trade. They promoted fishing, hunting, and vacationing. (From *In the Maine Woods*, 1912.)

One

THE SEBAGO LAKE REGION

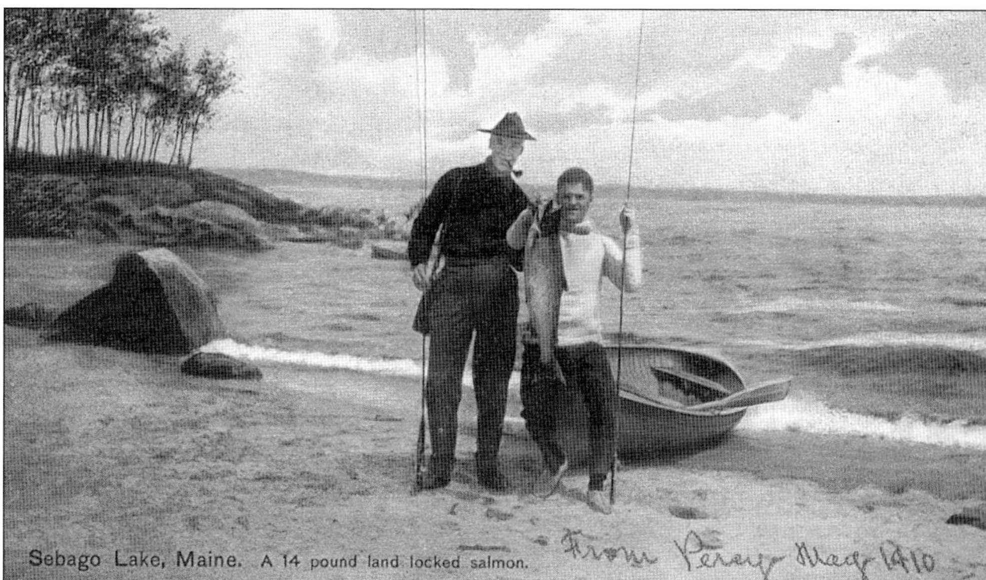

Fish of this size were once commonly taken at Sebago. In 1907, Edward Blakeley of Darien, Connecticut, established a new world record for landlocked salmon with a fish weighing 22 pounds, 8 ounces—a record that stands today. Stories exist of even larger fish having been taken in nets for spawning programs, up to 27 pounds or more, with a 35-pound fish caught in a weir in 1907. Sebago was one of the original river basins where salmon occurred naturally, the others being the St. Croix including West Grand Lake, the Union including Green Lake, and the Penobscot including Sebec Lake. Salmon have since been introduced to many Maine lakes; the first was probably Cathance Lake in Washington County in 1868. Today, some 300 Maine waters contain salmon populations.

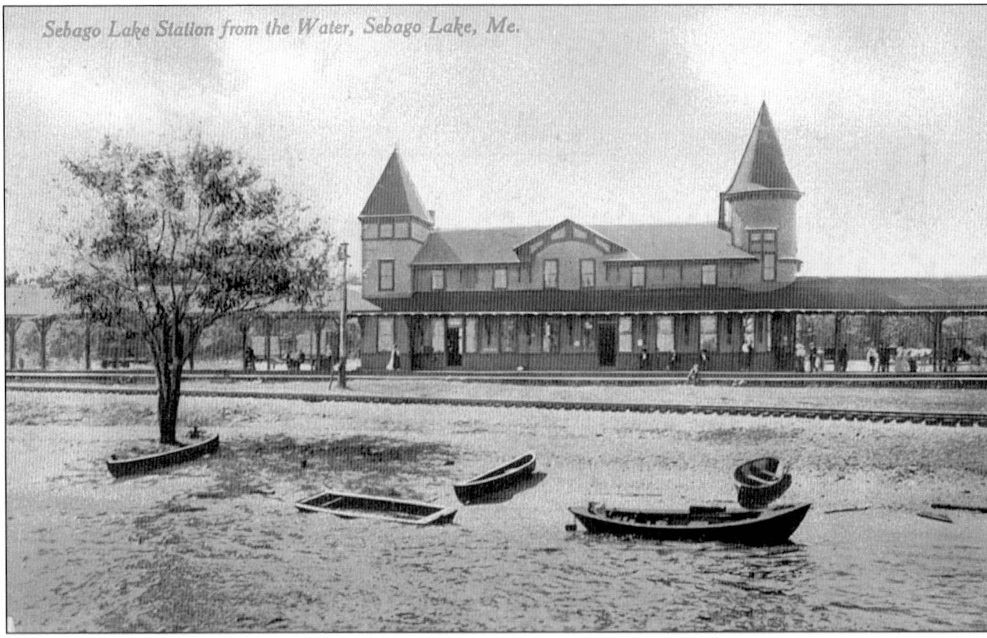

For the residents of Boston and vicinity, Sebago Lake was advertised as being the nearest of the large Maine fishing resorts, reached by a 16-mile ride over the Maine Central Railroad from Portland. From here, anglers could take a boat to other parts of the lake or beyond.

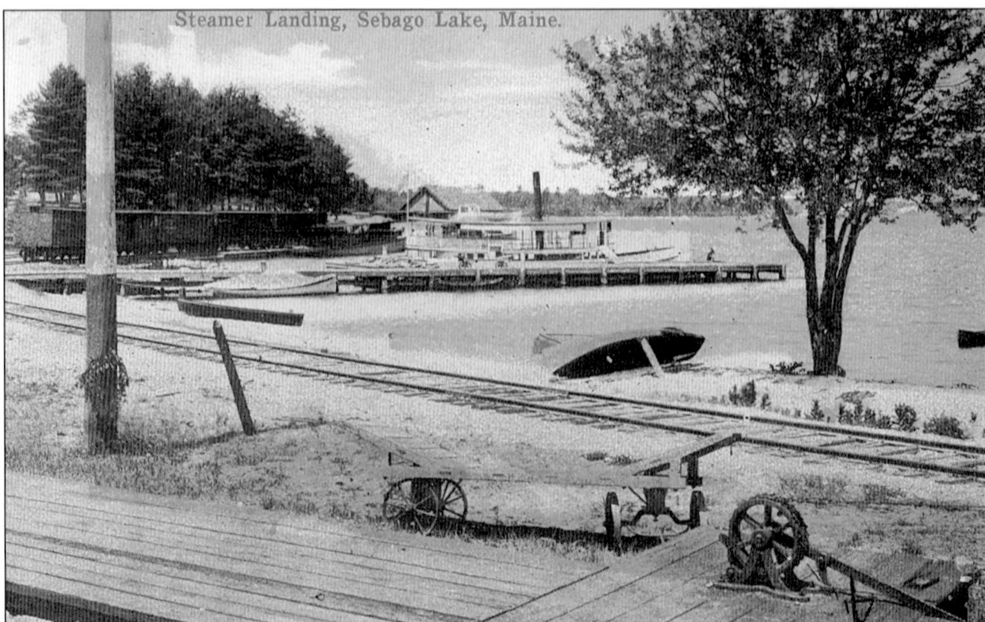

Across the tracks from the station was the boat landing. Steamers became active in 1847, sailing from the lake up the Songo River, through Songo Locks, continuing up Long Lake to Bridgton and Harrison. It is said that by 1912, the Sebago Lake, Songo River, and Bay of Naples Steamboat Company transported 38,000 passengers in a season. Anglers could travel with ease from the cities farther south to some of the best salmon fishing in the world.

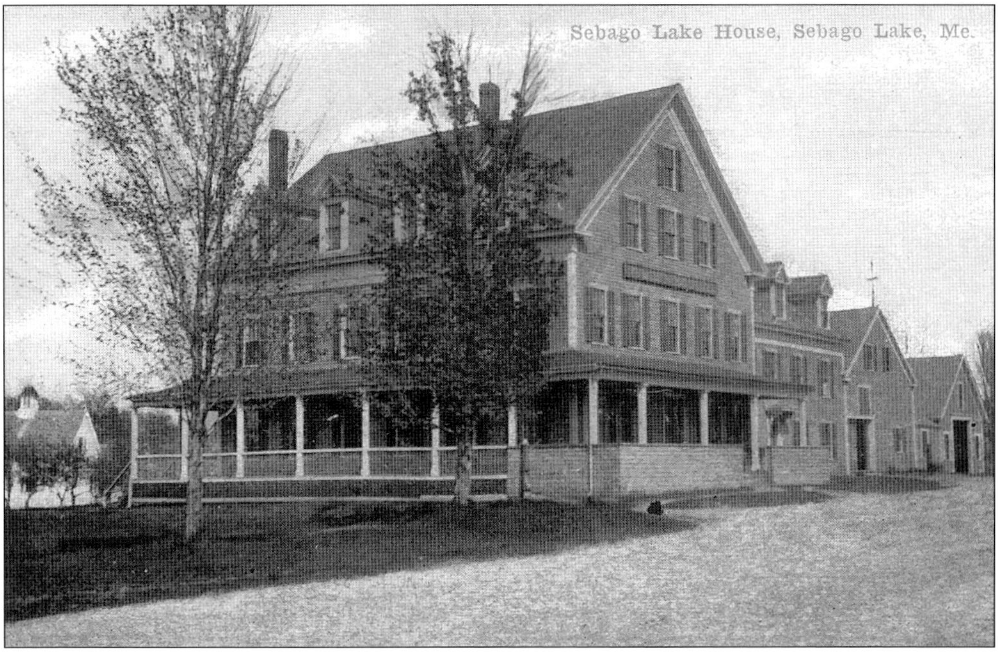

Near Sebago Station were several lodging establishments. The Sebago Lake House was only about a three-minute walk from the railroad station. It could accommodate 50 people and in 1909, charged $2 per day or $8 to $12 per week.

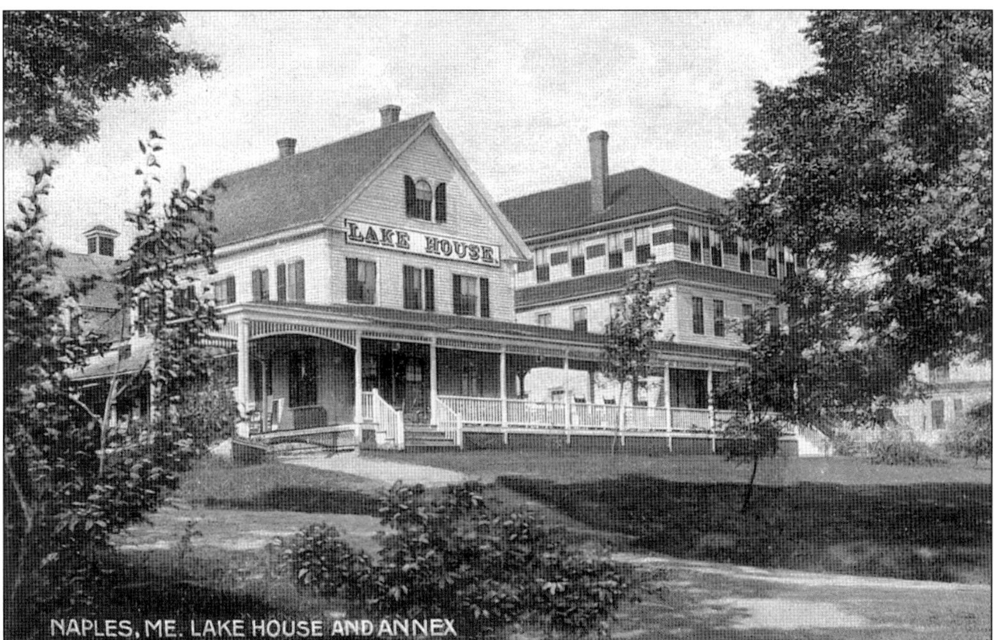

The Lake House was located at the north end of the lake and was an early resort frequented by anglers.

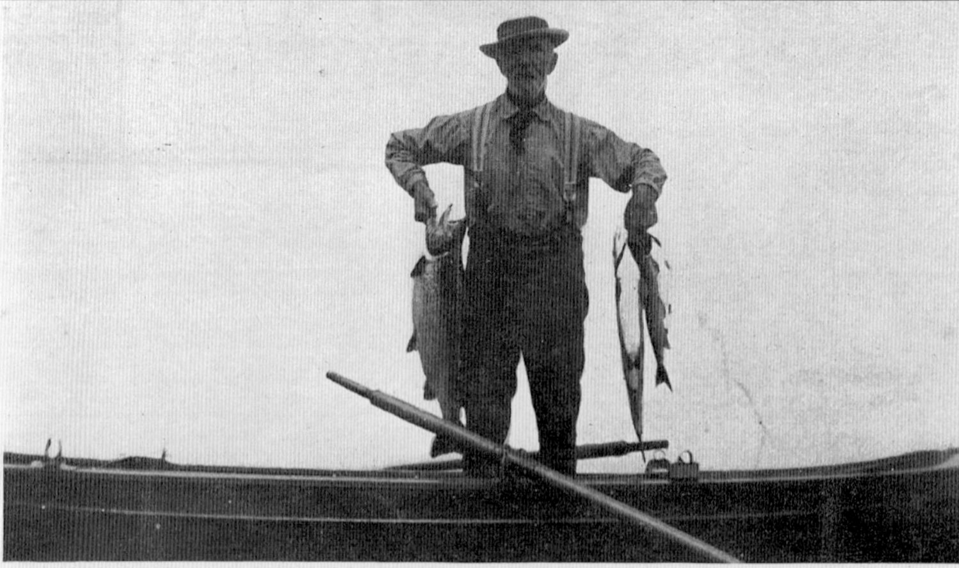

EAST SEBAGO, ME.
A GOOD CATCH BY GEO. E. FITCH, ONE OF THE OLDEST AND FIRST SALMON FISHERMEN ON SEBAGO LAKE, ME. WEIGHT OF FISH, 17, 10 AND 7 LBS.

Fishing at Sebago was advertised "by trolling with live bait (shiners or minnows) on a single hook or archer spinner, silver soldiers, blue backs, white bait, phantom minnows, and other artificial lures. At least 150 yards of good trolling line is required for any part of Sebago Lake. A salmon that weighs 10 pounds or more (which are often hooked) will make long runs before being landed, and plenty of line is needed with which to handle him. A large landing net (usually furnished by the guides) is necessary, and gaffs are sometimes used."

RAYMOND, ME. STATE FISH HATCHERY.

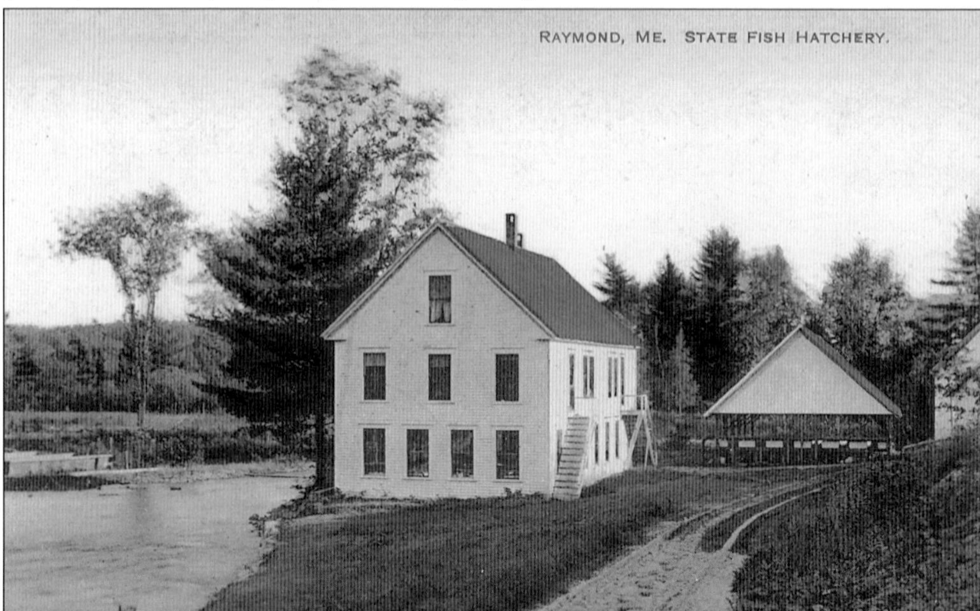

The salmon population in Sebago Lake was maintained by the local hatchery established in 1903.

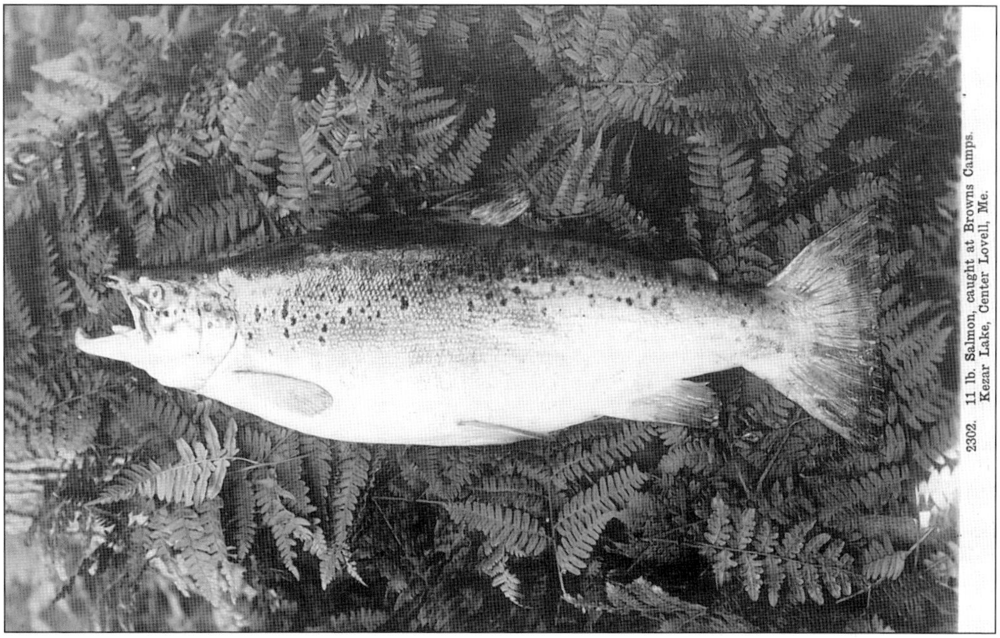

Kezar Lake came into popularity as an early fishing resort area, becoming a strong rival to Sebago. Around 1909, the average salmon was calculated to be 6 pounds, 14 ounces, while the largest on record was 13 pounds, 4 ounces. Benjamin E. Brown, who built at Kezar in 1897, owned the first cottage on the lake. He later expanded his building into a summer lodge, which burned in 1934 and later became Severance Lodge.

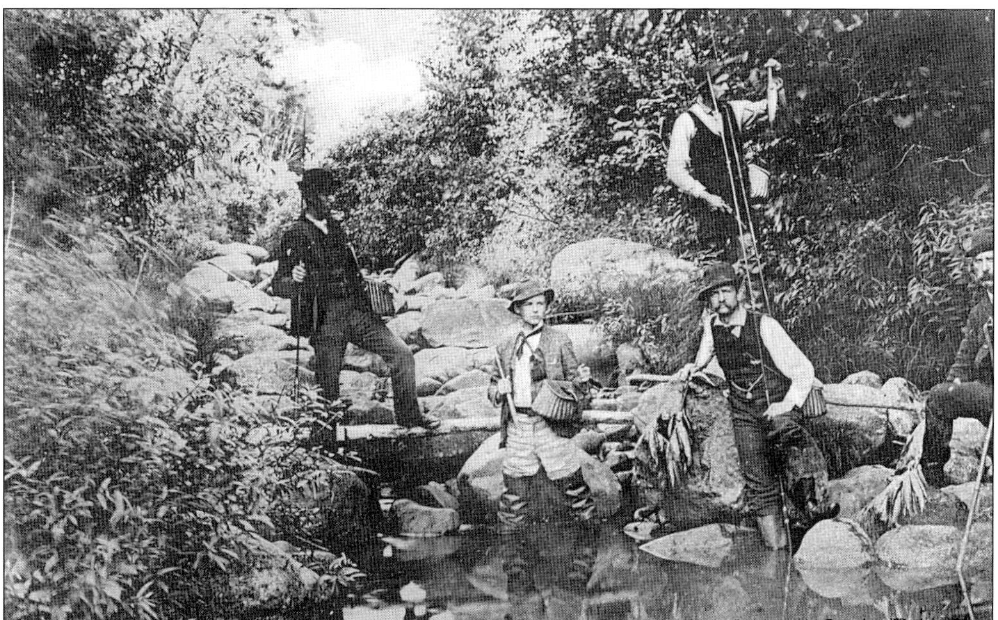

Near here is Lake Webb, which was famous as a fishing area. It was well stocked with bass, trout, and salmon and at one time, there was a hatchery there. Nearby is Swift River, known far and wide among those who favor brook fishing.

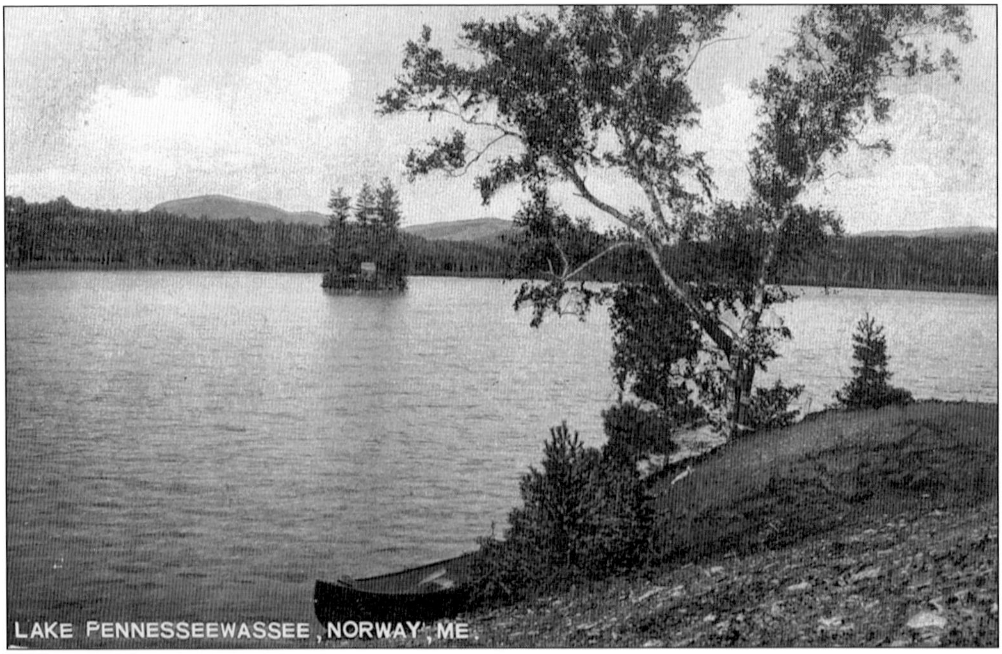

Although Lake Pennesseewassee is only 5 miles long and 10 miles around, it had a steamer on it until 1816. It was well known for its large bass.

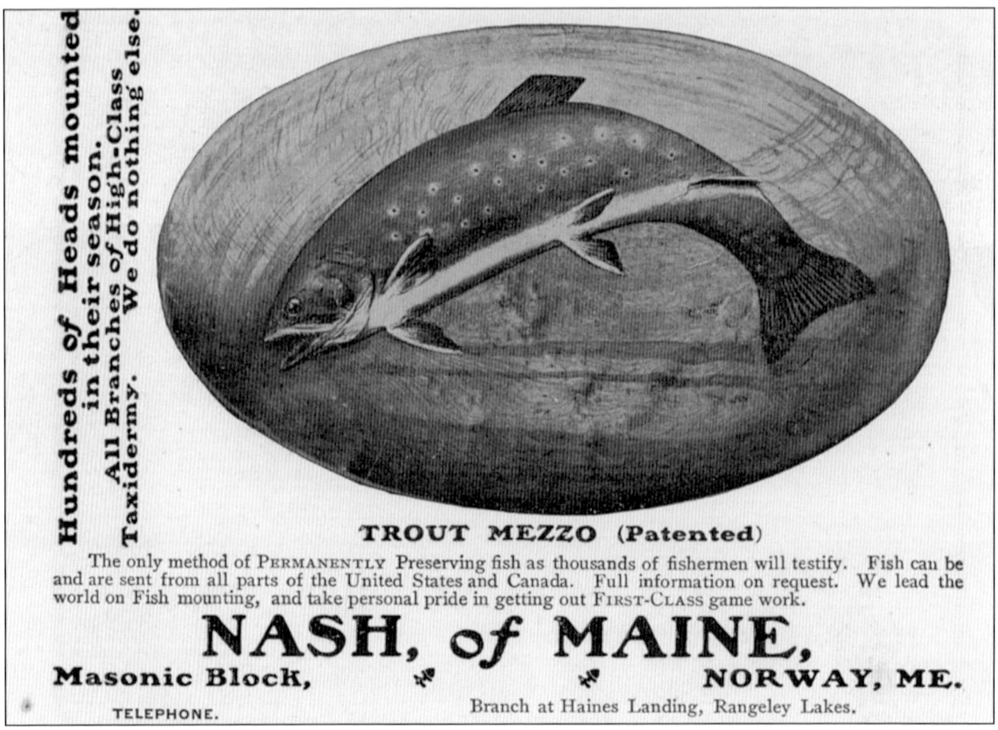

This is an advertisement for one of the most popular taxidermists in Maine. (From *In the Maine Woods*, 1904.)

Two

THE BELGRADE LAKES REGION

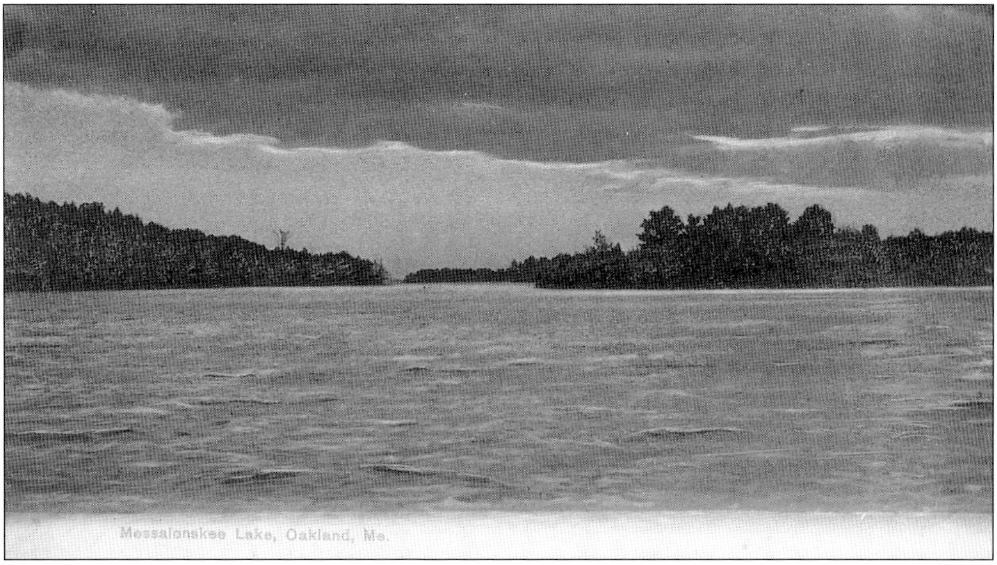

Messalonskee Lake was the favorite water of Dr. J. Herbert Sanborn, who carried out many experiments here with the aid of his good friend Emile Letourneau, brother of the famed newspaper outdoor columnist Gene Letourneau. Emile Letourneau developed the tandem streamer to eliminate "short strikes." Sanborn developed a green, black, and white fly, which within the first few minutes of its first trial caught a 4-pound brook trout, landed by Gene Letourneau. Not long afterwards, Sanborn was using the fly and hooked a salmon that gave him a long battle. It tipped the scales at 9 pounds, 3 ounces, and the fly was appropriately named the *Nine-three*. Messalonskee Lake also holds the state record for white perch: a 4-pound, 10-ounce fish taken in 1949 by Mrs. Earl Small of Waterville.

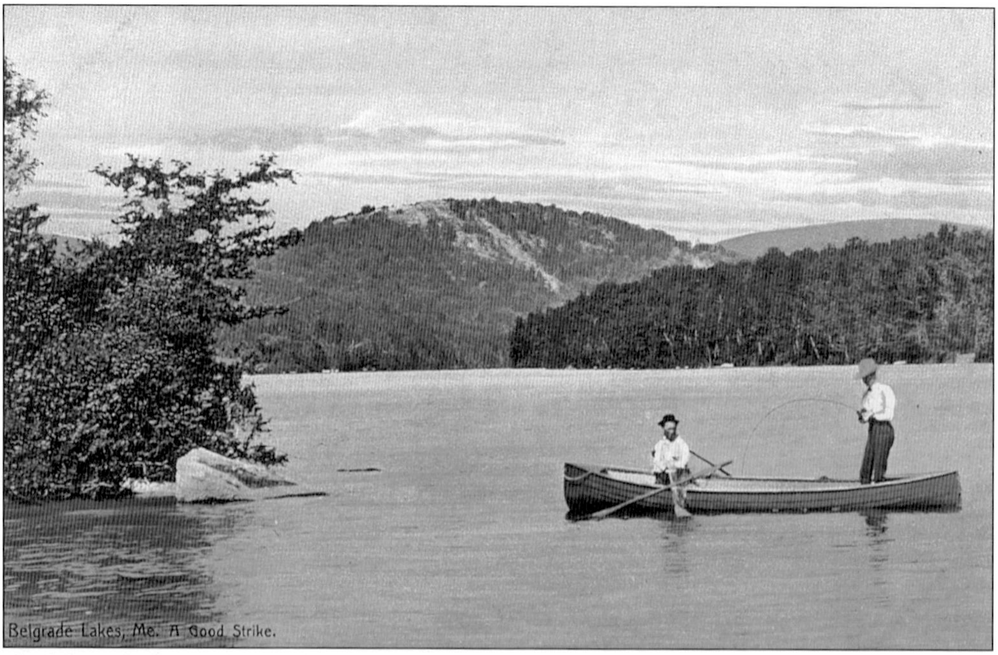

Fly-fishing for bass is the royal sport during the last of May and into June, 100 bass a day being a common record. As many bass may be caught in a day as can be landed, but the law allows only ten a day to be killed. That is ample for food purposes; the others must be returned to the water to thrive and furnish additional sport.

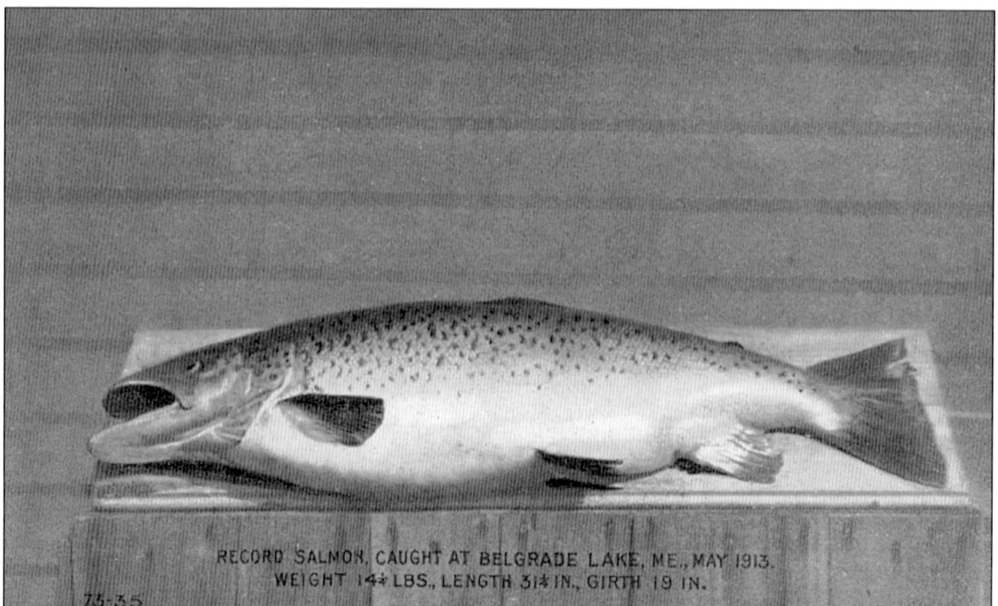

Salmon were introduced into the Belgrade Lakes in 1878. Fish of this size were once a common catch here.

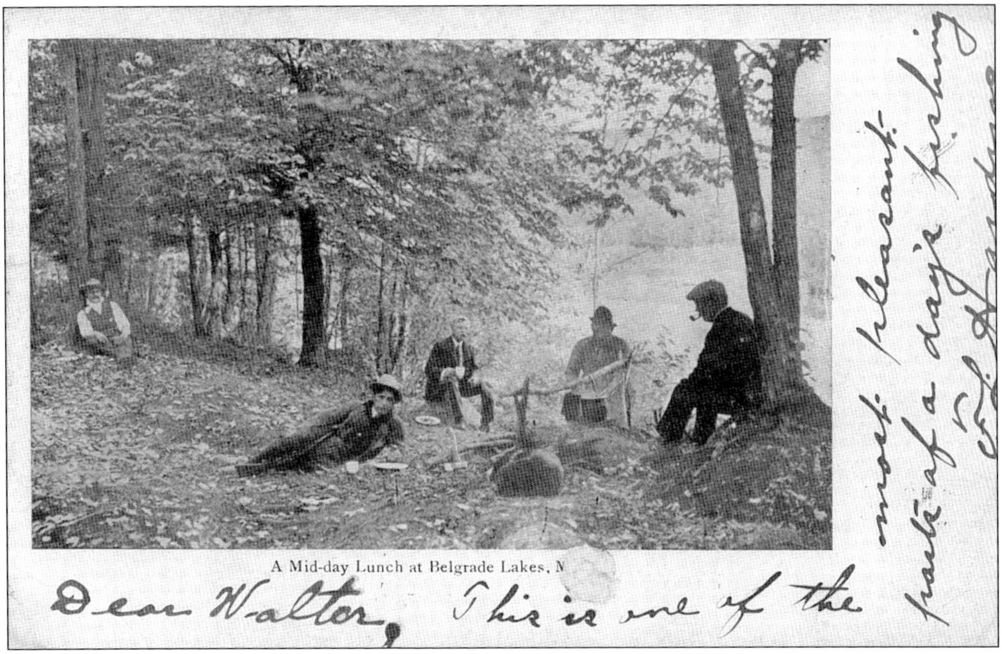

This card speaks for itself. During a day's fishing, noon meals were typically cooked on shore and sometimes were quite elaborate. When fishing was good, the catch often was the main course.

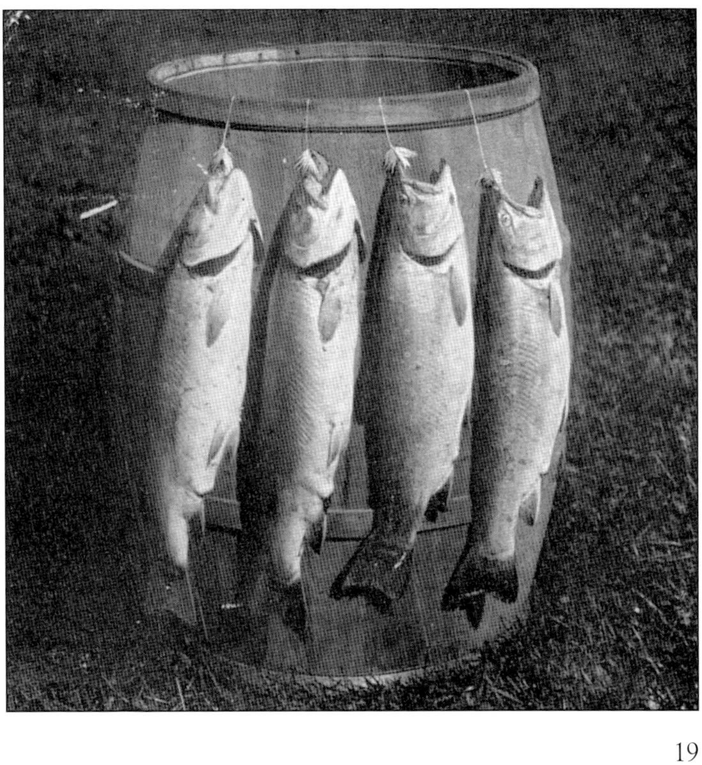

An early advertisement stated "the height of the early spring fishing season for square-tailed trout (*fontinalis*) is between the middle of May and the first week in June. Lures used were similar to those for Sebago Lake, with Rangeley spinners, which are gold or silver spoons on an artificial fly that is usually baited with worms."

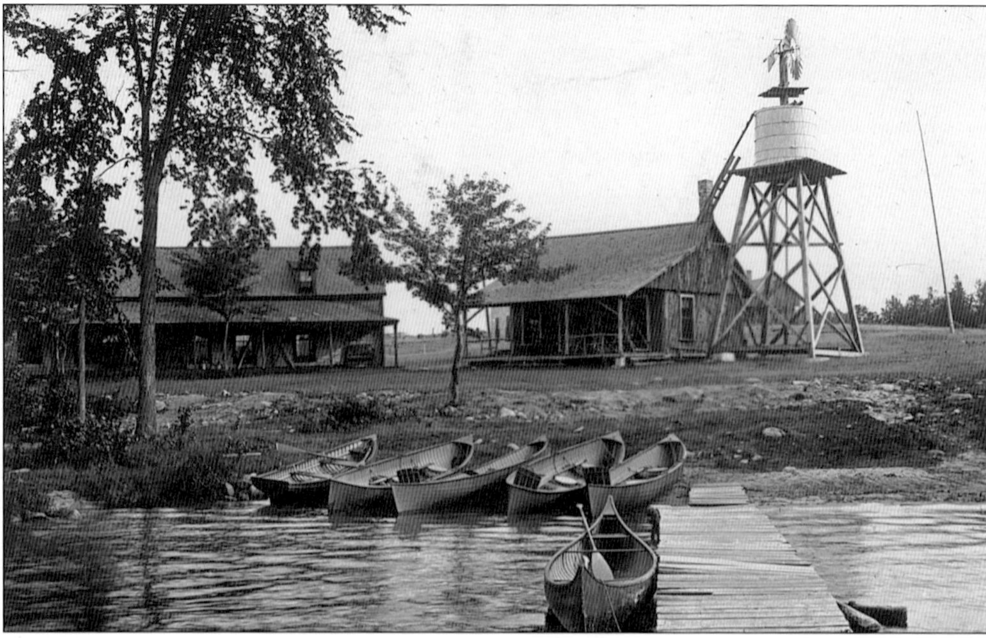

The boats shown here at Hillside Camps, Belgrade Lakes, were probably for rent by anglers staying at the camp. Much of the travel was by rowboat and, as demonstrated here, few boats accommodating outboard motors were available until much later.

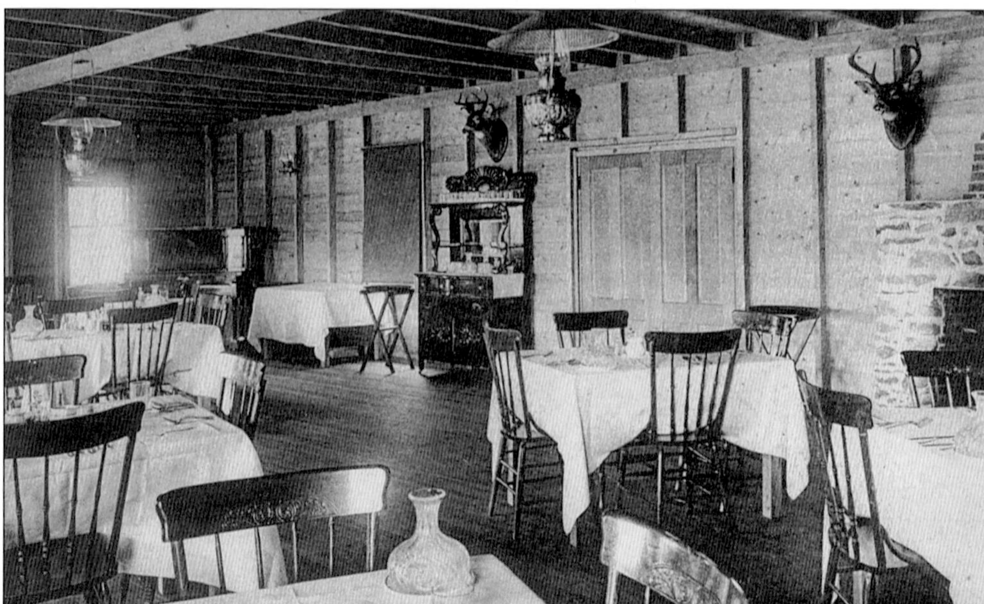

This image is of a typical dining room setting of camps of this era. Since there were few restaurants in most areas, resorts served elaborate meals as part of their package, called the American plan. Most dining rooms were semiformal and offered an extensive menu of mostly home-cooked dishes. Most people dressed for dinner.

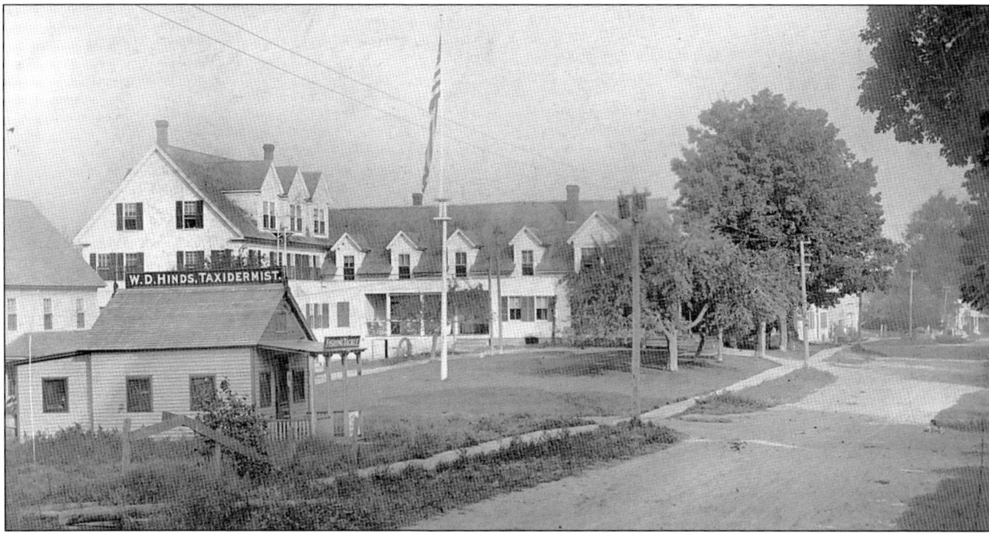

The Central House, located on the shore of Long Pond, could accommodate 100 people. Nearby was Hinds's taxidermy studio. The sign on the front reads "Fishing Tackle."

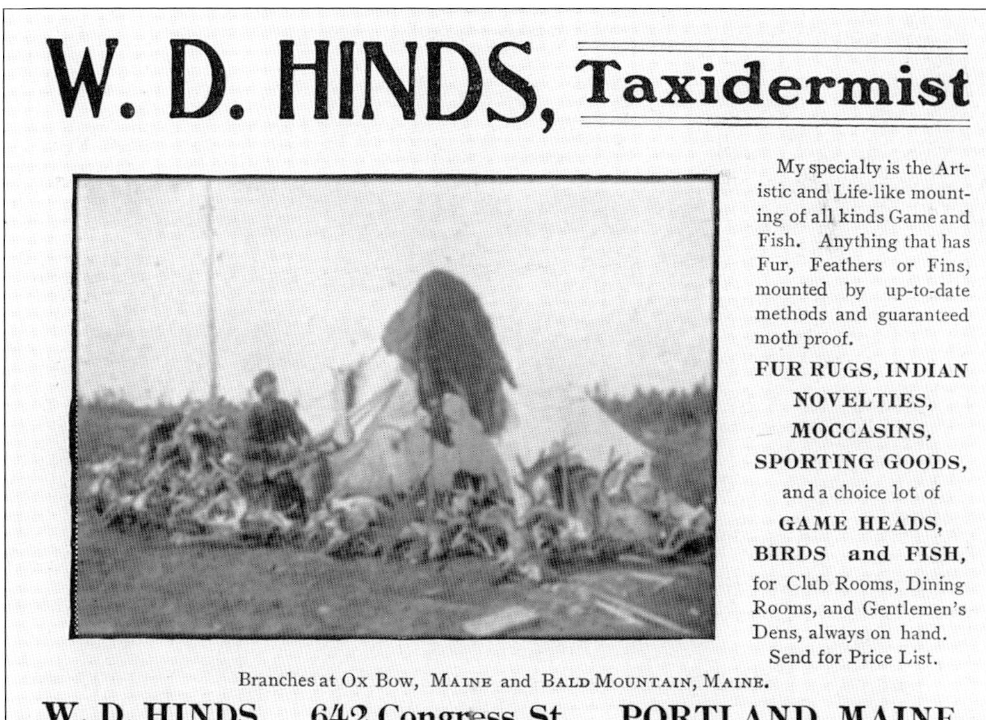

This is a copy of Hinds's advertisement from *In the Maine Woods*, 1904. Note that Hinds had studios in at least four locations.

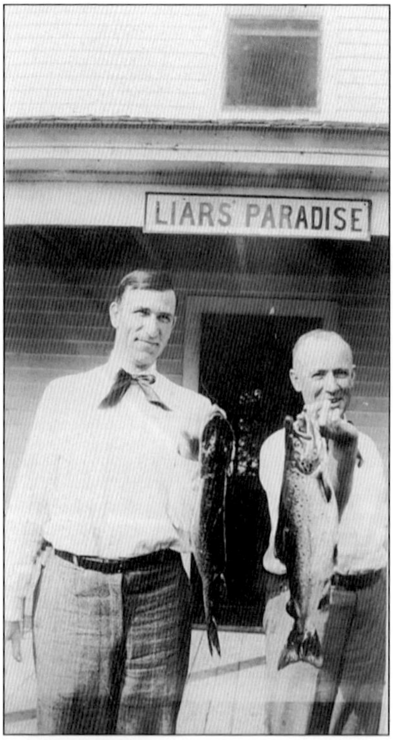

It seems that every book on Maine lakes or Maine fishing contains a photograph of Liars Paradise. The old saying goes, "Most fishermen are born honest, but they soon get over it." These two gentlemen do not have to lie; the truth is in the picture. The fish on the left is a pickerel; the salmon on the right weighed 6.5 pounds.

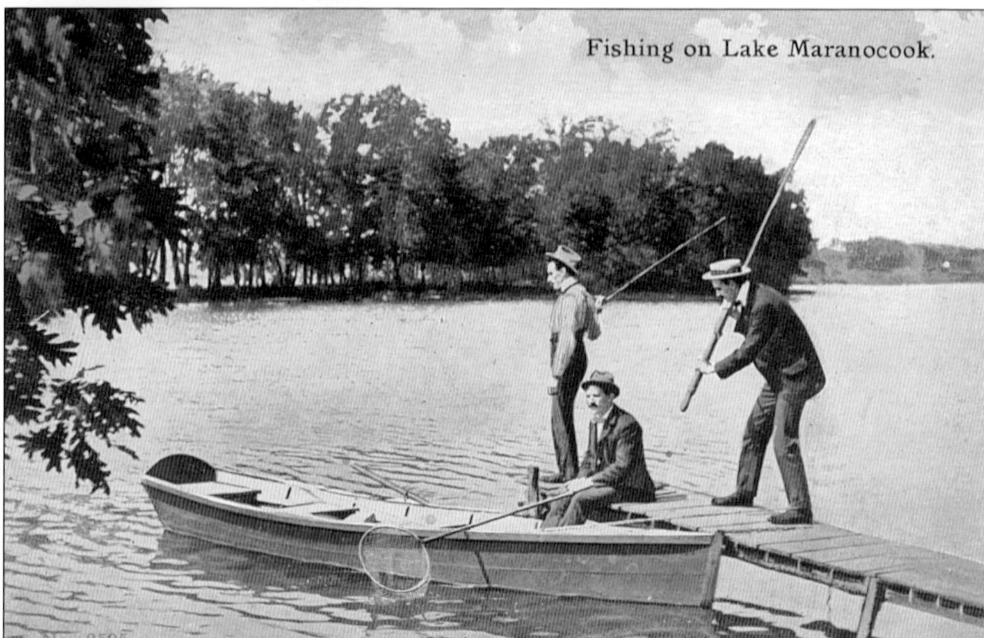

Three anglers get ready to go out on the water. Note the dress of the fishermen. Most early photographs of anglers show them in dressy attire, while the guides are clad in more practical working clothes. Teddy Roosevelt used to fish Lake Maranacook with his guide Bill Sewall. Camp Roosevelt for boys was originally established here, with Sewall conducting nature programs. In 1928, the camp was moved to Pleasant Lake.

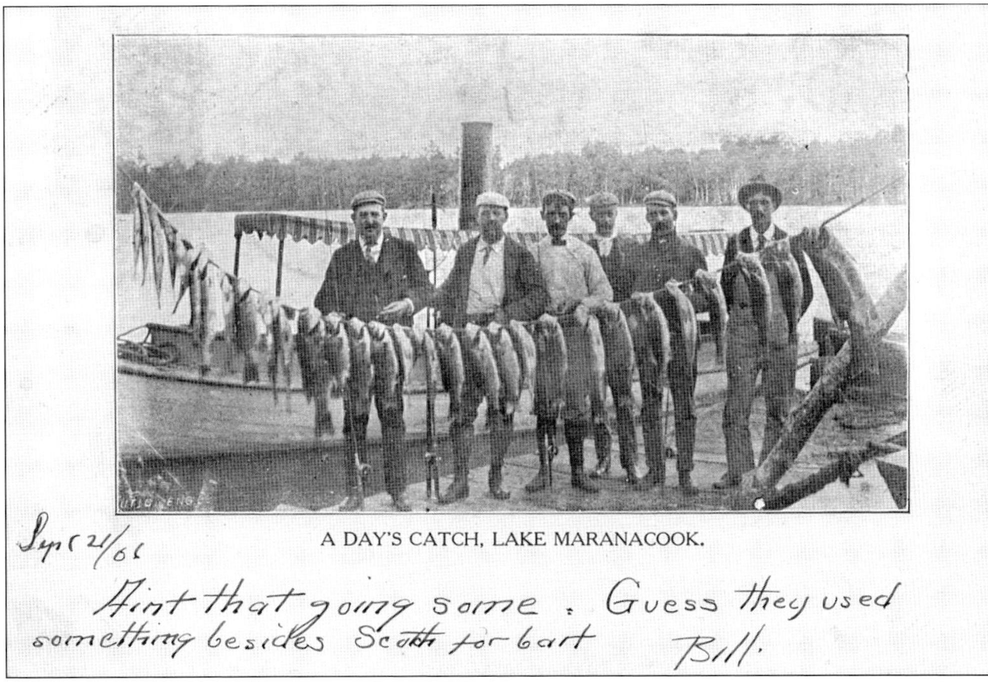

Lake Maranacook became popular during the 1800s when the Maine Central Railroad purchased the surrounding land and established a huge picnic area. At this site, the Maranacook Hotel was built. It was destroyed by fire in 1905. Several of the establishments on the lake provided steamer service to Winthrop and other locations.

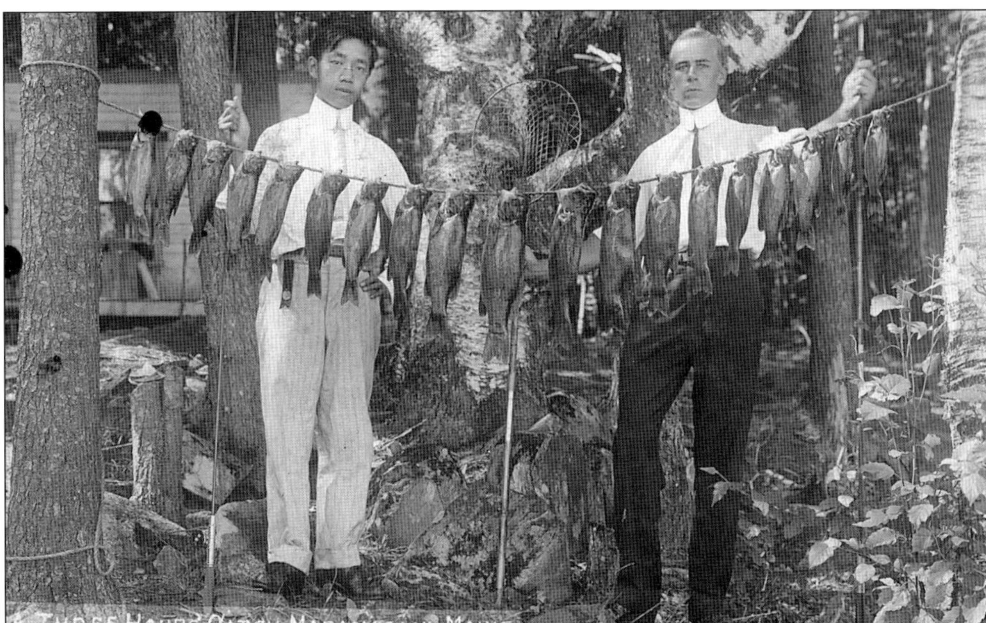

Maranacook has many bays and coves, mostly fed by springs. The lake has long been known for salmon, trout, bass, and white perch.

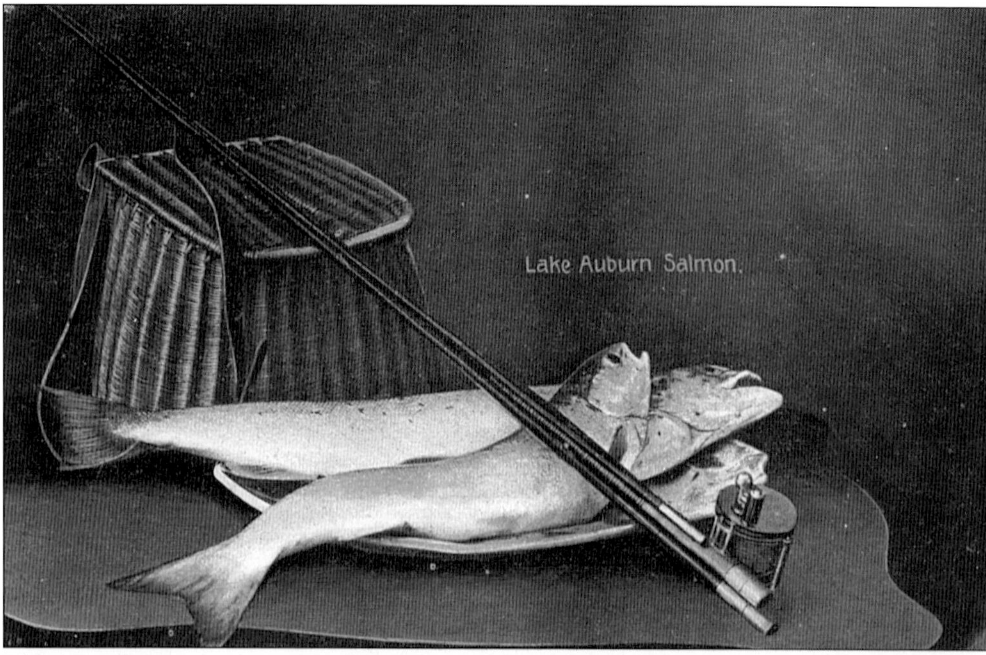

The first salmon were introduced in Lake Auburn in 1889. Note the style of tackle shown in this photograph.

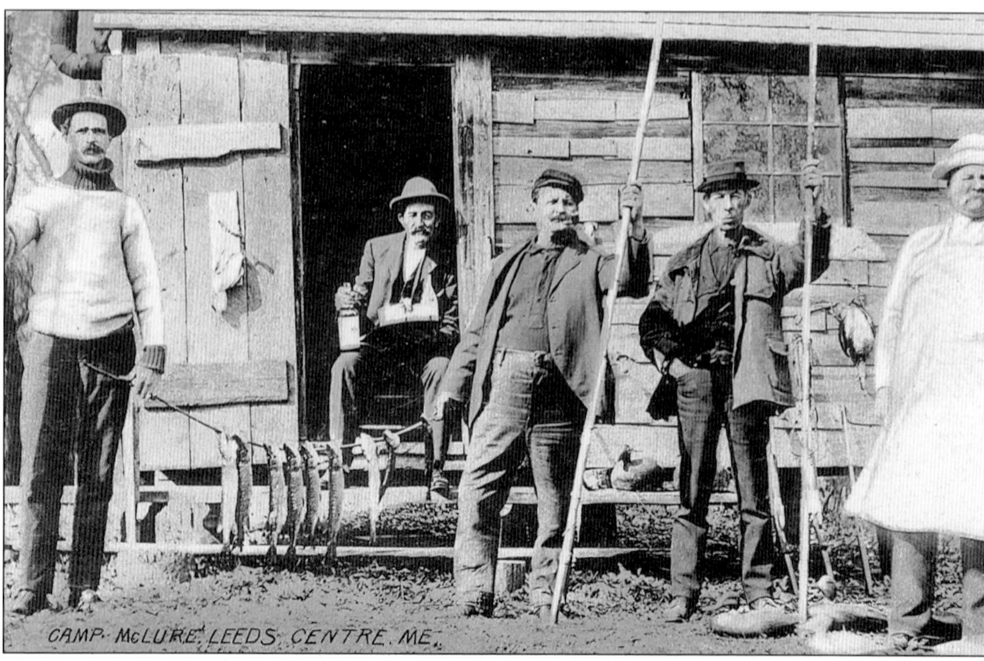

This gang appears to be celebrating the day's catch of a nice string of pickerel, no doubt taken in Androscoggin Lake.

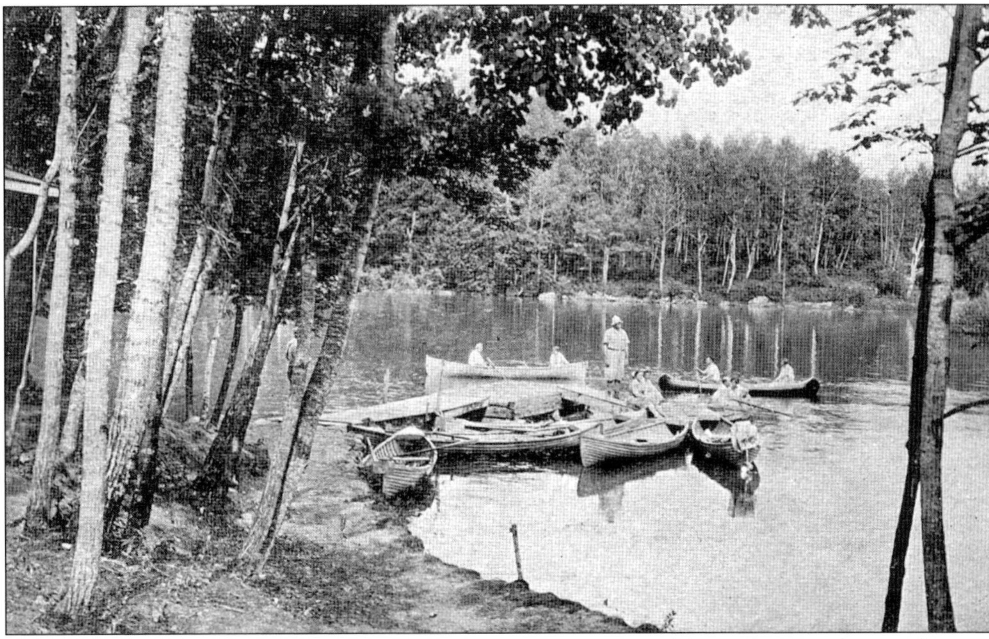

Shown here is the waterfront at Pleasant Point Cottages on Webber Lake in East Vassalboro.

GUIDE FOR NORTHERN MAINE particularly Fish River and Eagle lake section and the Allagash Trip. Tents and outfits furnished. Guides engaged. Supplies purchased, etc. Address Sam Dubay, Reg. Guide, Mishoe, Maine

Guide for Green River Lakes and Tributaries. Moose, Deer and Caribou hunting. Best trout and togue fishing in the Dominion. Address for terms and dates, **GIB FRANCIS, Reg. Guide, Edmundston, N. B.**

Guide FOR MIDDLE BRANCH SECTION CAMPING PARTIES, ETC. **H. E. SIMPSON, No. Vassalboro, Me.**

Many guides advertised their specialties for different areas. This advertisement appeared in 1907 as part of *In the Maine Woods*.

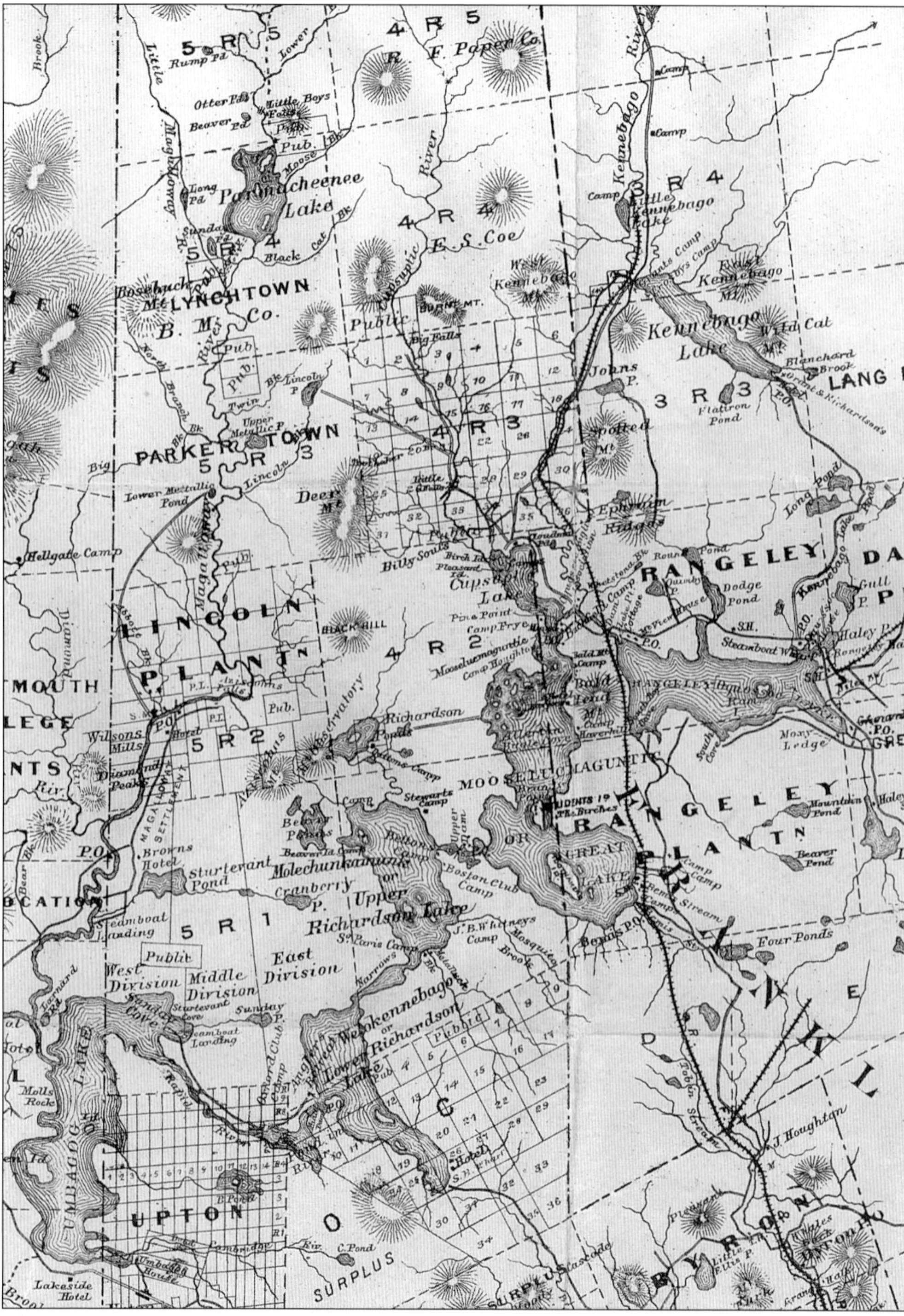

This is a portion of an early map of Oxford County showing the Rangeley Lakes region. Along with the railroad, the major roads and many of the popular resorts are depicted.

Three

The Rangeley Lakes Region

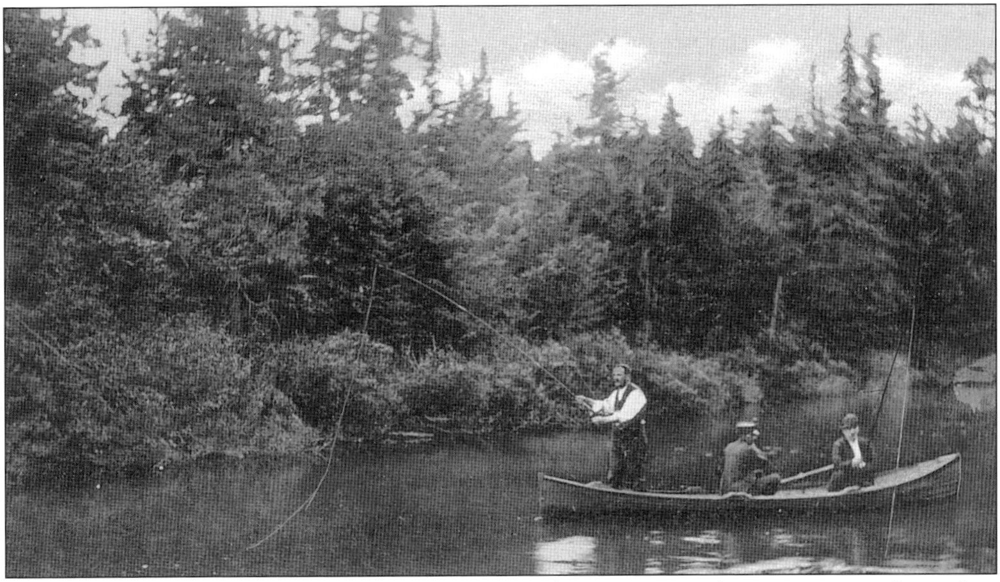

As soon as the ice leaves the lakes and ponds, the salmon, trout, and togue come to the surface and until late in June, fine sport is had either trolling or fly-fishing. When the water begins to get warm, the fish seek the cool depths. During the warm months, one has to locate them over the spring holes. In most of the lakes and ponds fed by cold springs, the water stays cool all summer and in these waters, the angler finds endless opportunity for the pursuit of that greatest of all piscatorial sport, fly-fishing. In September again, when the cold nights chill the water, the fish come to the surface and begin to gather on the spawning beds. Then fly-fishing is at its best. (From *In the Maine Woods*, 1909.)

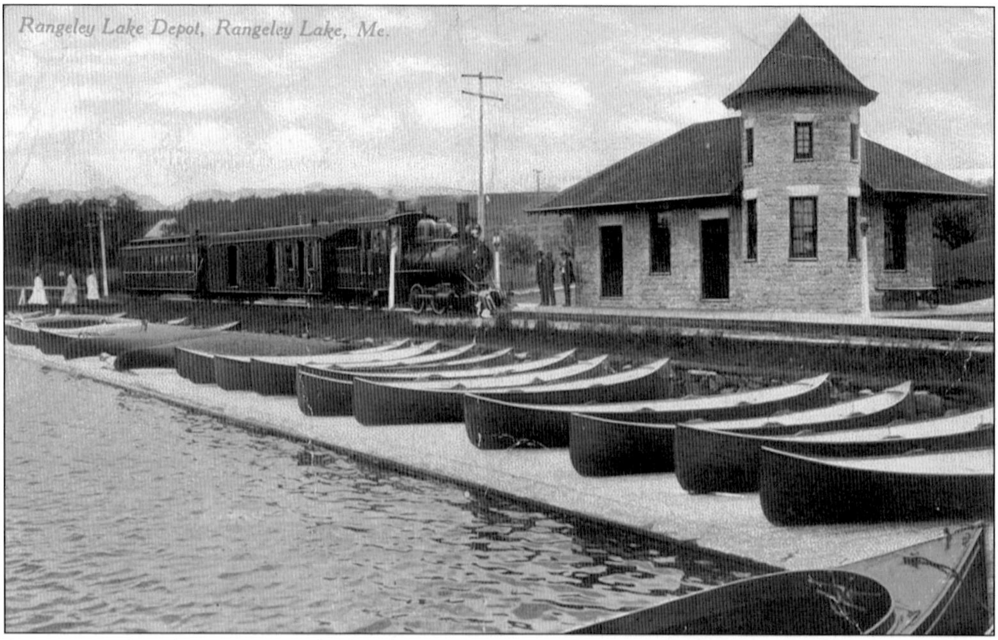

A stone railroad station was located near the Rangeley Lake House. For many years, travel to the Rangeley region was by Maine Central Railroad to Farmington and then by stage to Phillips and the lakes. In 1879, the Sandy River Railroad, Maine's first narrow-gauge line, began operation from Farmington to Phillips, cutting the stage journey by half, bringing a traveler 20 miles closer to the Rangeley Lakes. Both railroads were discontinued in 1936.

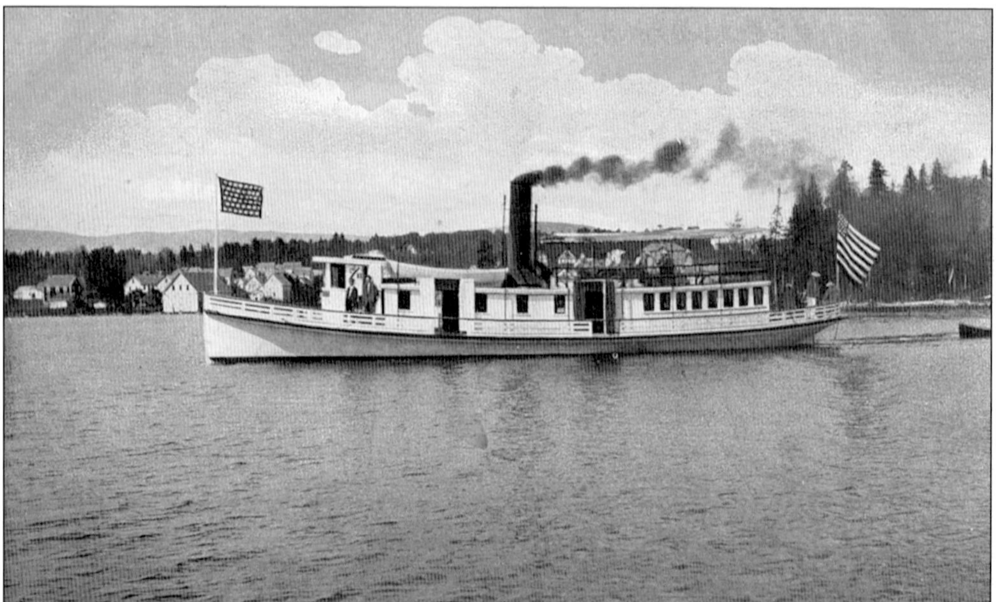

Several steamboats carried travelers around the lakes from one location to another. The *Rangeley* was owned and operated by the Rangeley Lake Steamboat Company, which was founded in 1901. There were actually two steamers named Rangeley, the latter remaining in service until it burned about 1940.

This is an advertisement for the stage line. (From *Guide to the Rangeley Lakes*, 1879.)

STAGE LINE

FROM

PHILLIPS TO RANGELEY,

SAMUEL FARMER, Proprietor.

HAVING purchased the entire Stage property and route from Phillips to Rangeley, we take pleasure in announcing to the travelling public that we have added to the route a

FINE COVERED MOUNTAIN WAGON,

with seating capacity for twelve grown people and have supplied for the same eight fine young horses, four for each end, changing alternately at Beach Hill; also *good and careful drivers*, who will look well after all the baggage and comfort of all who patronize the route.

Also the proprietor is supplied with fine private teams, both single and double, open and covered, and we hope and trust by

Moderate Charges and Square Dealing,

to merit as heretofore nearly the entire business on this Route.

Stages leave the Barden House, Phillips, daily, calling at the Elmwood for Madrid, Greenvale and Rangeley, arriving at Greenvale at 11 A. M., and Rangeley at 12 M. Returning, leave Rangeley, at 1 P. M.; Greenvale, 2.30 P. M., arriving at Phillips at 6.00 P. M. Fare from Phillips to Madrid, 75 cts.; Greenvale $1.50; Rangeley, $1.75.

Express taken at Moderate Rates.

SAMUEL FARMER.

angeley and Dead River Region

TEN HOURS RIDE FROM BOSTON . . .
ONLY ALL-RAIL AND QUICKEST ROUTE .
Finest and Grandest Scenery in the Country

NEW ENGLAND'S GREAT SUMMER RESORT.

HED VIA NARROW GAUGE SANDY RIVER AND PHILLIPS & RANGELEY RAILROAD

Commodious Steamers ply the **RANGELEY LAKES**, making close connections for Mooselookmeguntic, Cupsuptic, Mollechunkamunk, okennebacook, Umbagog and Parmachenee Lakes, and by buckboard with Kennebago and Seven Ponds.

☞ Remember to purchase through tickets for Eustis and Dead River Region via Phillips & Rangeley Railroad and Dead River on, and here a Stage connects with trains taking passengers to **Stratton** and **Eustis** the same day.

This is an advertisement for the Sandy River and Phillips & Rangeley Railroad, Maine's first narrow-gauge railroad. (From the *Maine Central*, 1895.)

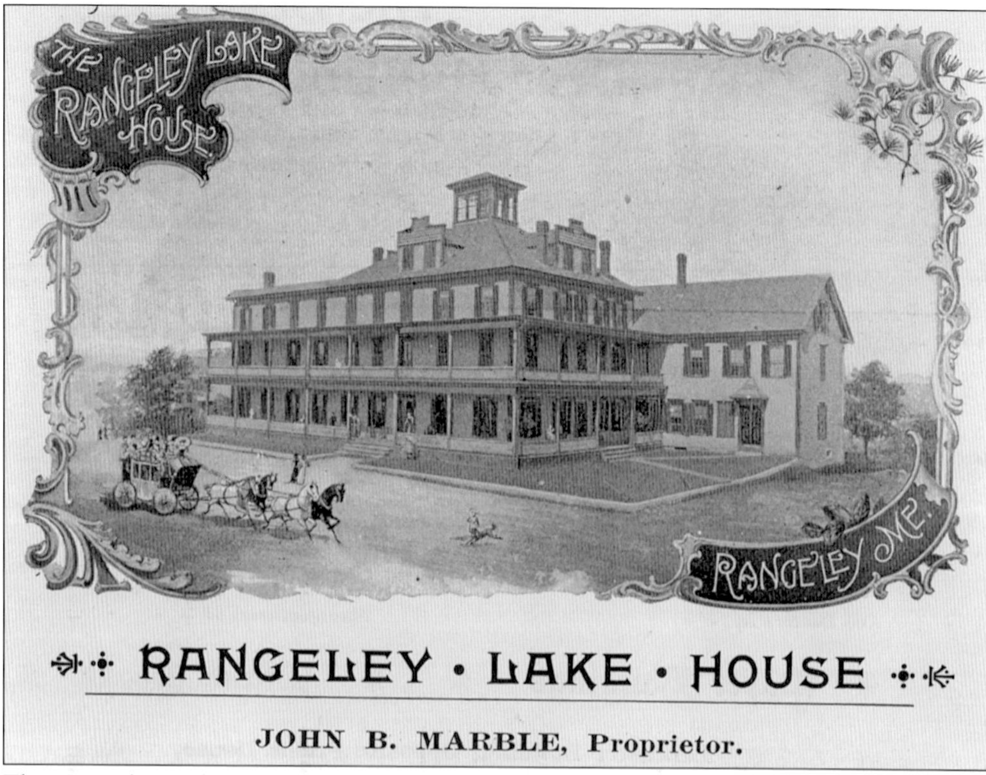

The Rangeley Lake House was a popular early establishment which, in 1895, could accommodate 250 guests. Exclusive in clientele, it charged a top price of $4.50 per day, while other establishments only charged $2 to $3. Its name was changed to Rangeley Lake Hotel in 1928. (From the *Maine Central*, April 1895.)

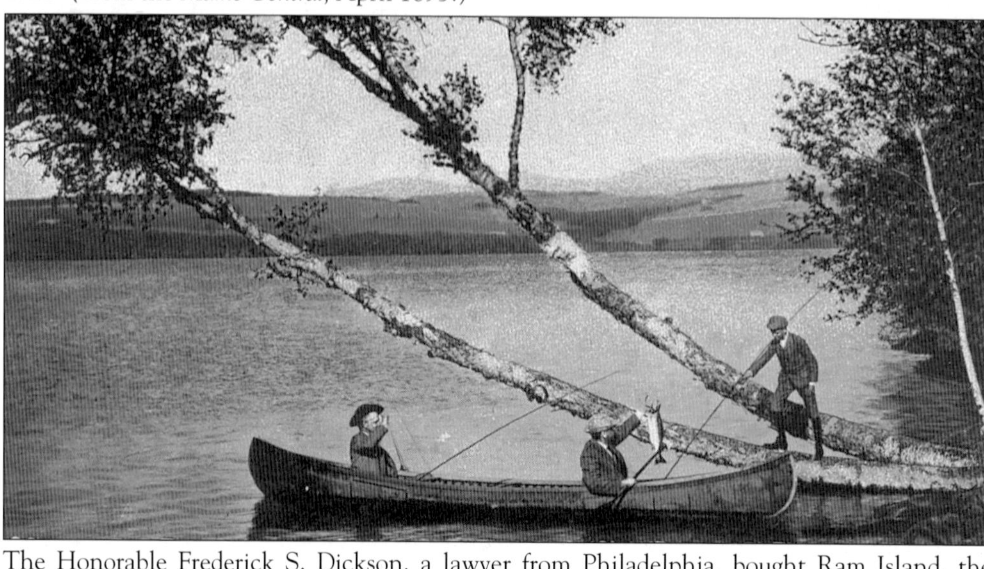

The Honorable Frederick S. Dickson, a lawyer from Philadelphia, bought Ram Island, the largest in Rangeley Lake. He established a large estate on the island and, here, steadies the birchbark canoe with his paddle, while his guest passes an 8-pound trout to the younger Fred Dickson. (From the *Maine Central*, May 1896.)

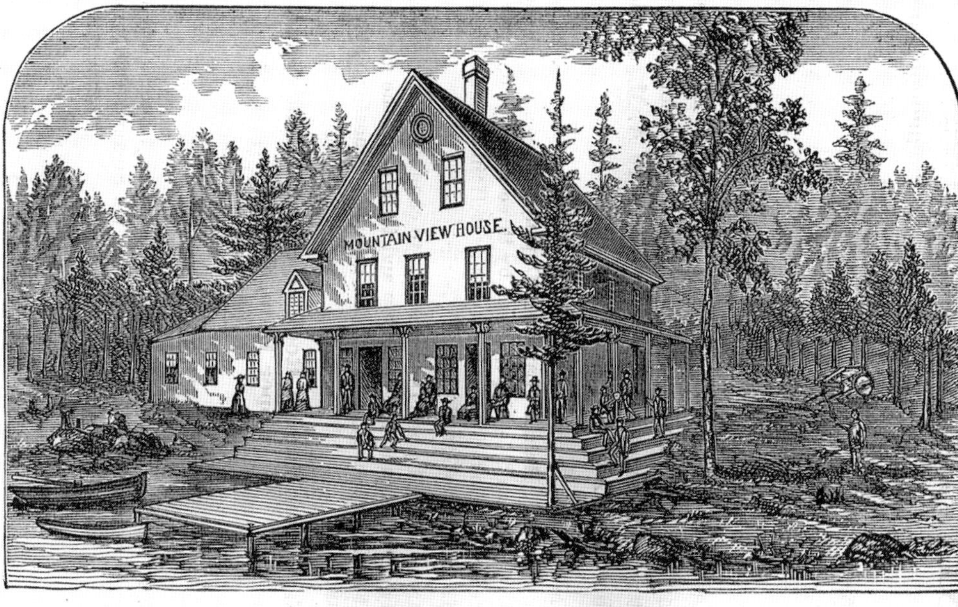

AS BEFORE ENLARGED.

Here is an advertisement for the Mountain View House before it was enlarged. It was located at the foot of the lake and contained about 50 rooms. (From *Guide to the Rangeley Lakes*, 1879.)

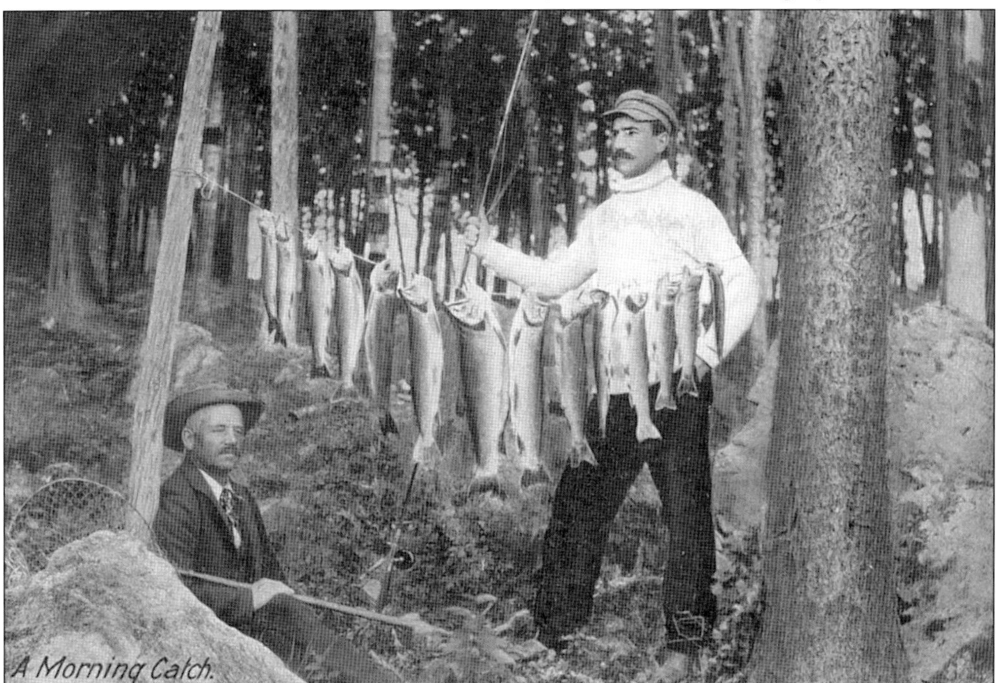

Shown are J.H. Henley of Brunswick and guide Freeman Tibbetts. During the week that Henley stayed at the Mountain View House in June 1895, he caught 64 trout weighing a total of 103 pounds. The middle trout in this photograph weighed 7 pounds. This was Henley's first trip to the Rangeleys.

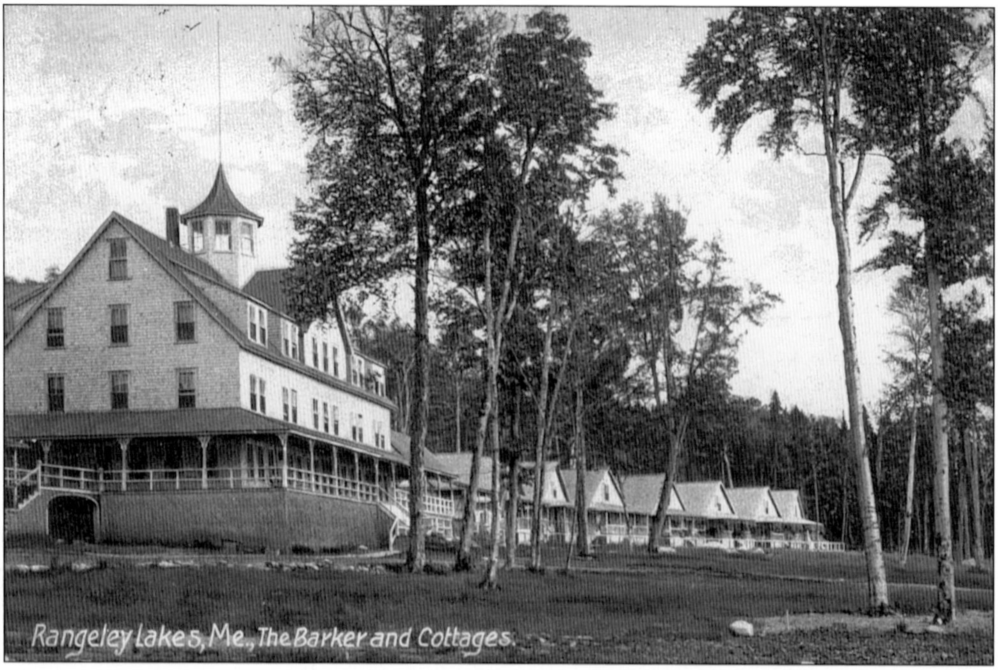

The first log cabin open to the public in Rangeley was built by Capt. Fred C. Barker at Bemis *c.* 1870. Barker began his career as a guide, established his own steamboat operation with seven boats, and was one of the first to use a Rangeley boat. His lodging enterprise expanded to a hotel and some 50 log cabins. He opened the Barker Hotel in 1902. With the close of the railroad, business dwindled. Barker died in 1937, and his descendants kept the hotel open with a small clientele until 1966.

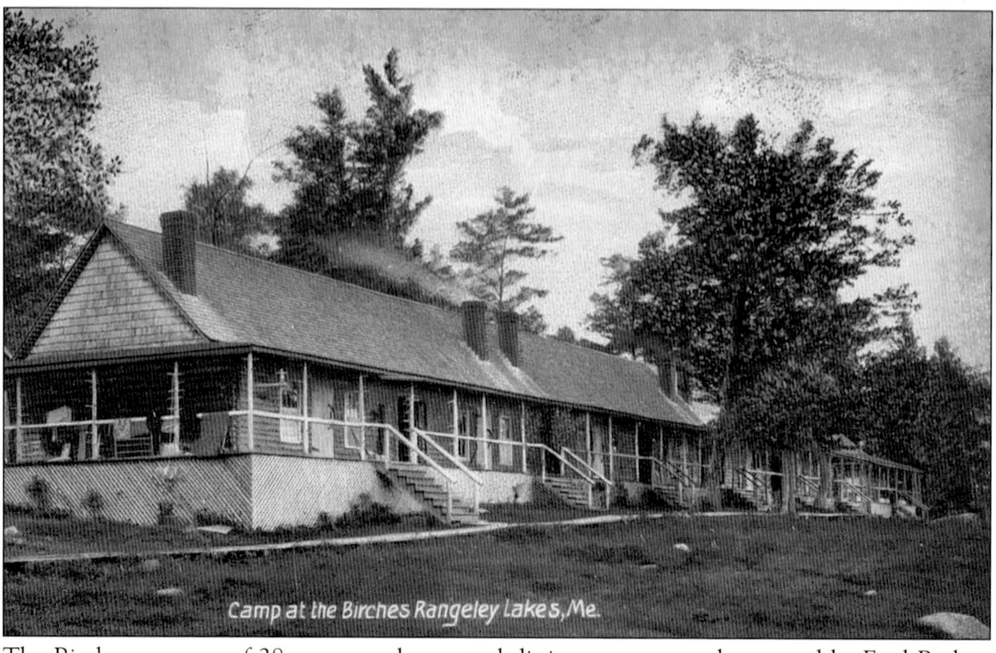

The Birches, a group of 28 camps and a central dining room, was also owned by Fred Barker. Located on Students Island in Lower Richardson, it was heavily damaged by fire in 1925.

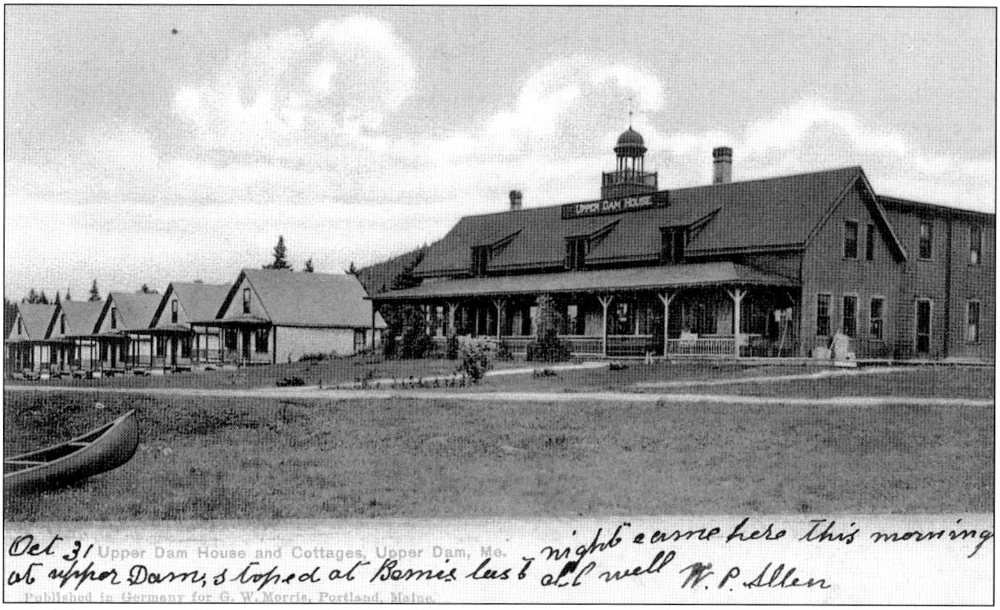

The Upper Dam House was built by the Union Water Power Company in 1882. It could accommodate 100 guests. The dam is 1,500 feet long and in addition to its usefulness for waterpower, was used for log driving for a number of years. There was once a mill at this site that produced lumber, shingles, and clapboards for the construction of camps and houses in the vicinity.

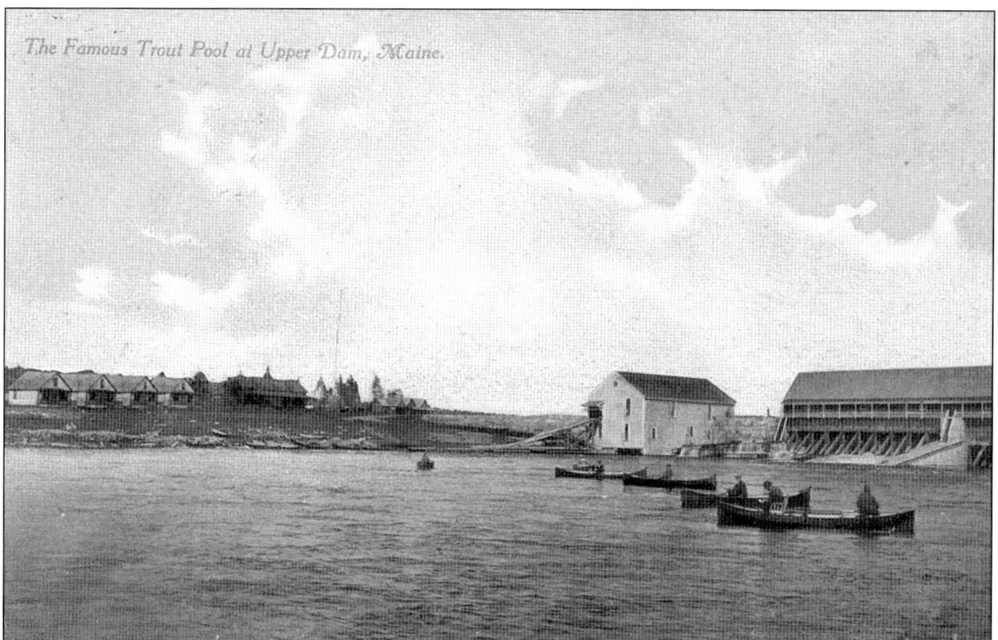

At one time, more trout weighing from 6 to 10 pounds were caught here in one season than from any other place.

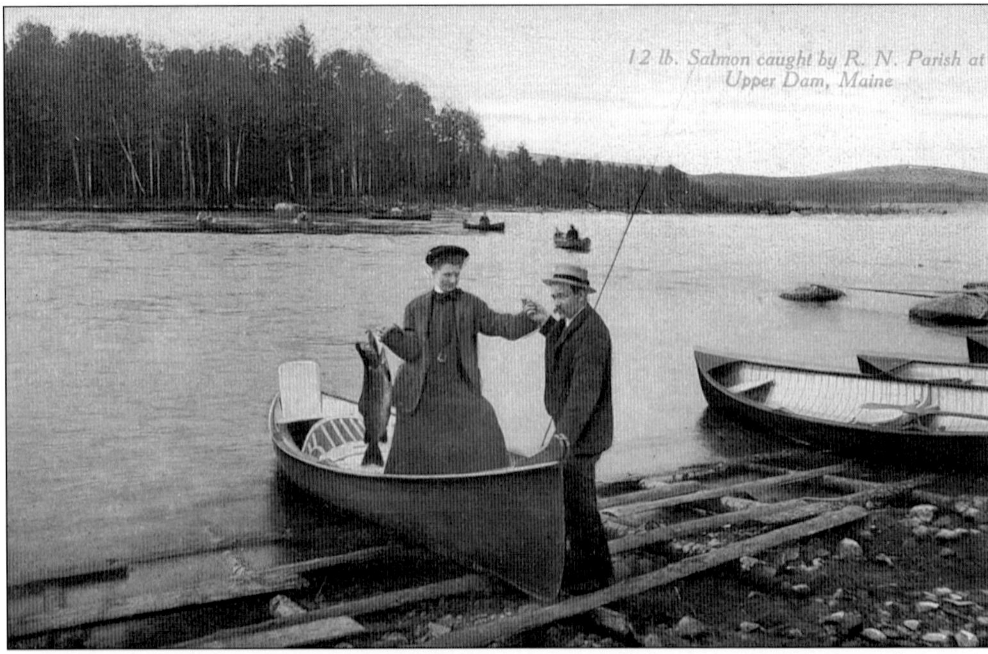

It was here on July 1, 1924, that Carrie Stevens first tested her new fly, the Grey Ghost. She used a 9-foot Thomas rod equipped with a Hardy reel and Ideal line. She landed two salmon and then a big brook trout weighing 6 pounds, 13 ounces, which took second place in the Field & Stream Fishing Contest for that year.

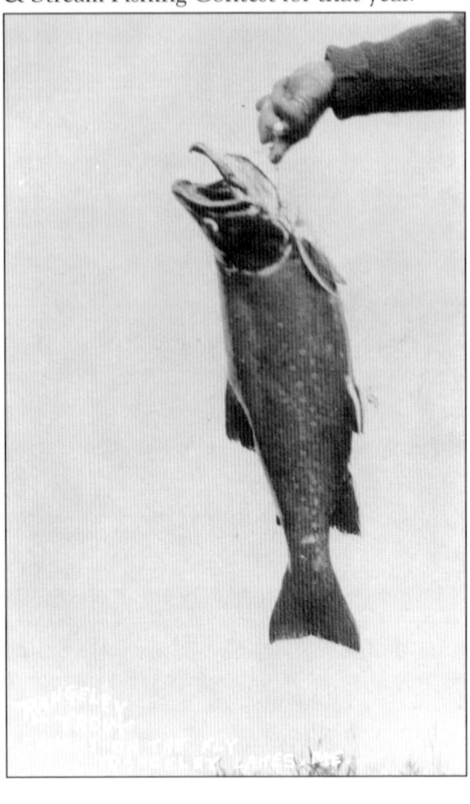

This was a typical brook trout from this pool years ago. Besides Carrie Stevens's second prize, the third prize in the contest was a 6-pound, 11-ounce trout taken at Upper Dam Pool, and fourth prize was a 6-pound, 10-ounce trout, also taken at Upper Dam.

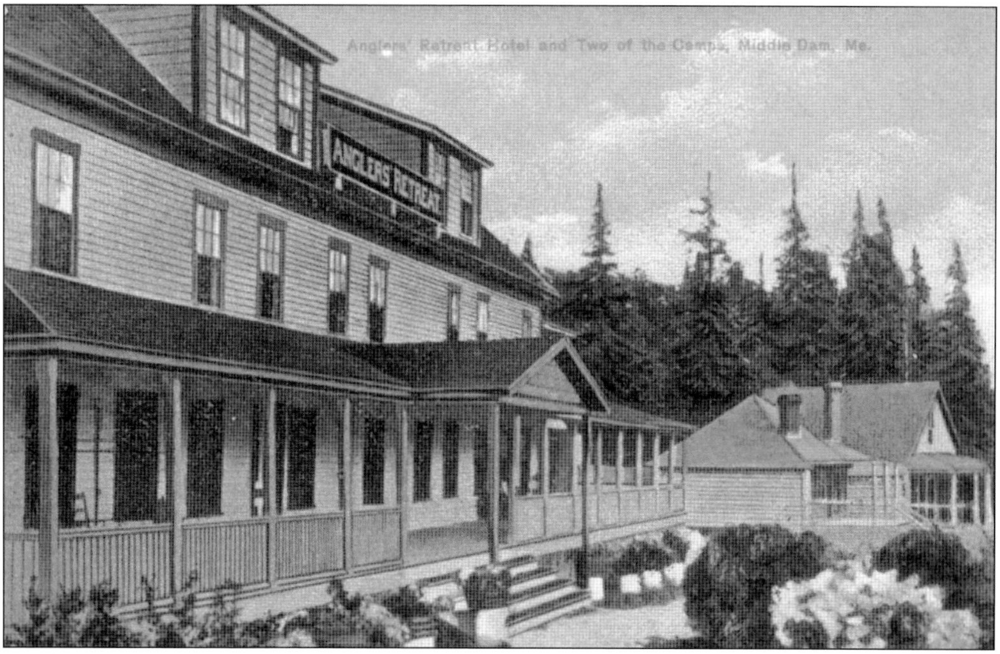

Angler's Retreat was located at the foot of Lower Richardson at Middle Dam. It advertised "handsome bedsteads, woven wire springs, and 40-pound hair mattresses."

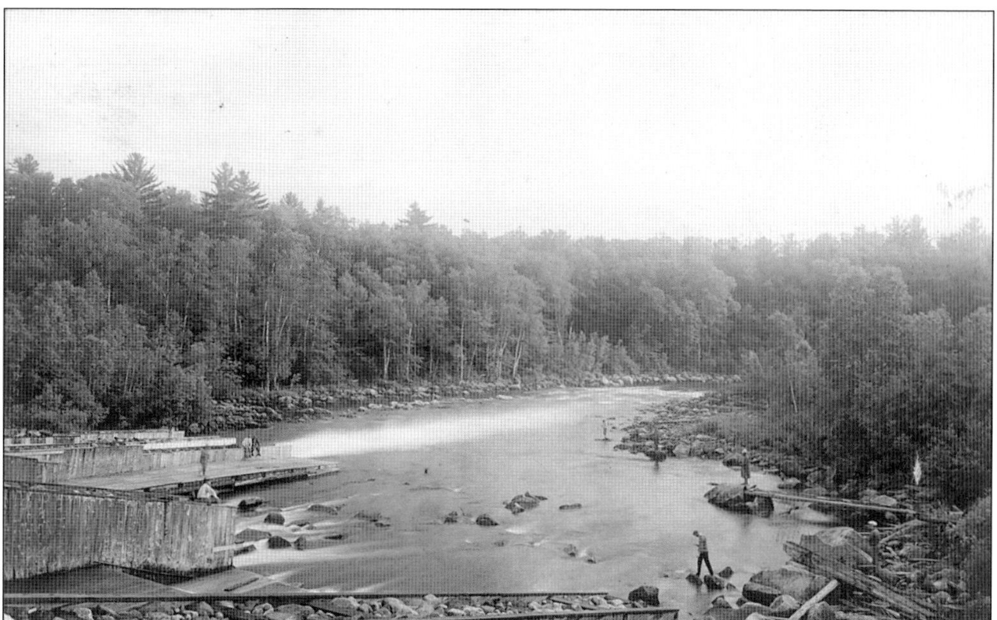

Several anglers fish the pool below Middle Dam while the water is low. Below here is the Rapid River, said to be the most picturesque stream in Maine.

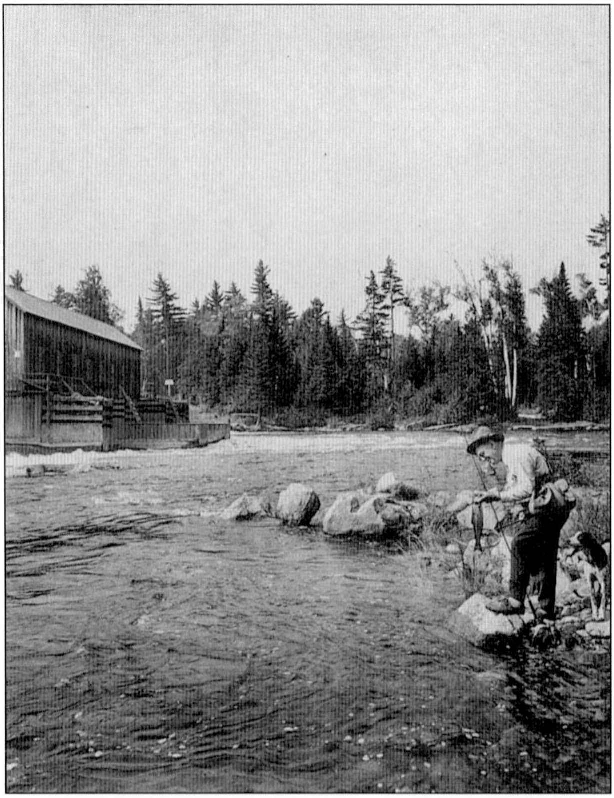

An angler inspects his latest catch at Lower Dam, located farther down the river.

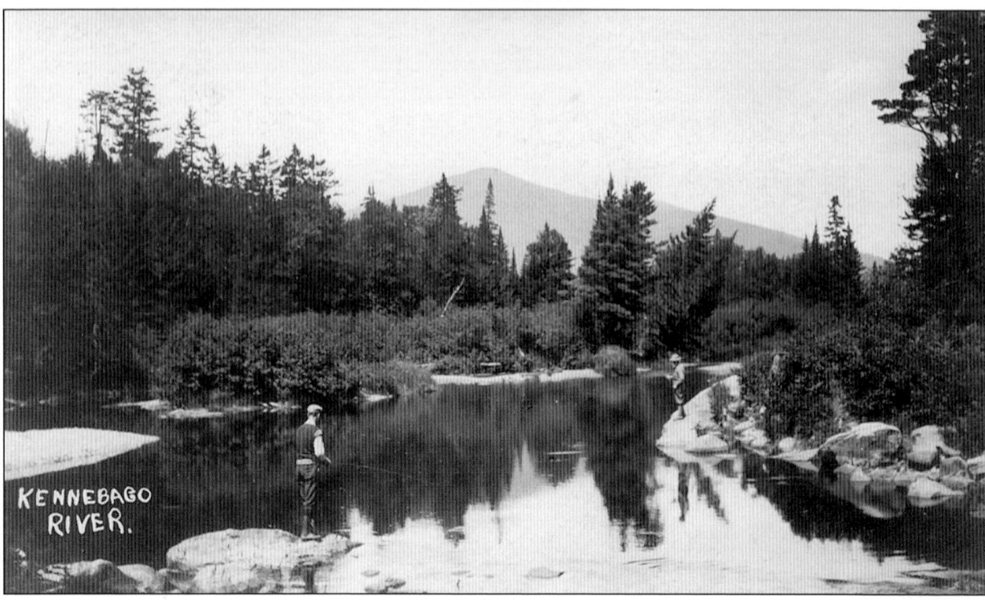

These anglers are on the Kennebago River, a favorite stretch of water between Kennebago Lake and Cupsuptic Lake. At the junction of the Kennebago River and Rangeley Stream was a favorite fishing site known as Indian Rock. Sixteen trout with a total weight of 100 pounds were once taken here by two fishermen in less than one hour. A group of six fishermen claims to have taken 200 trout from that area at one time.

Four

Down East

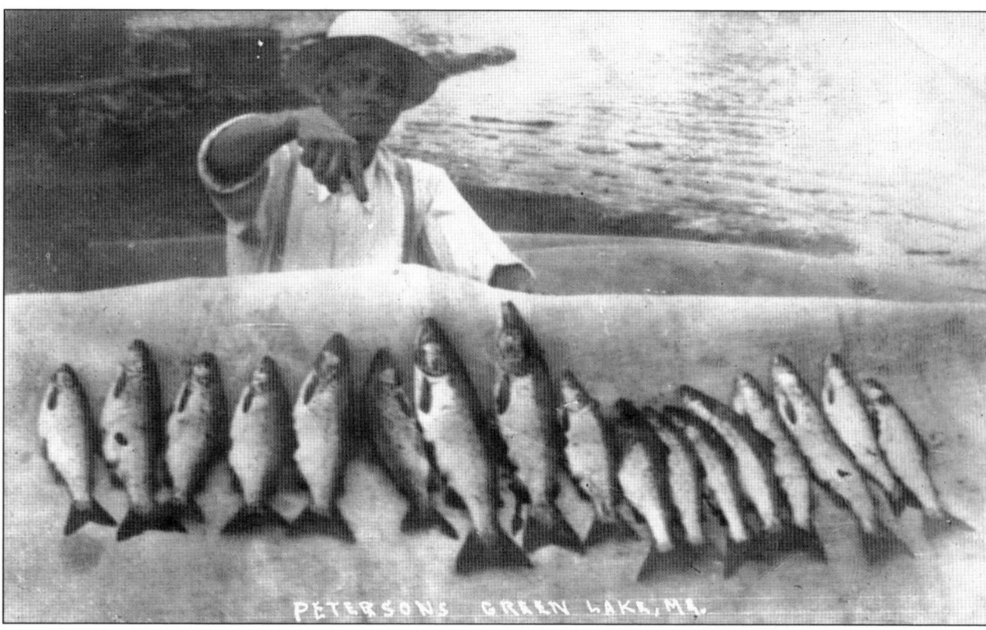

Green Lake, located in Hancock County, is one of the four original landlocked salmon lakes.

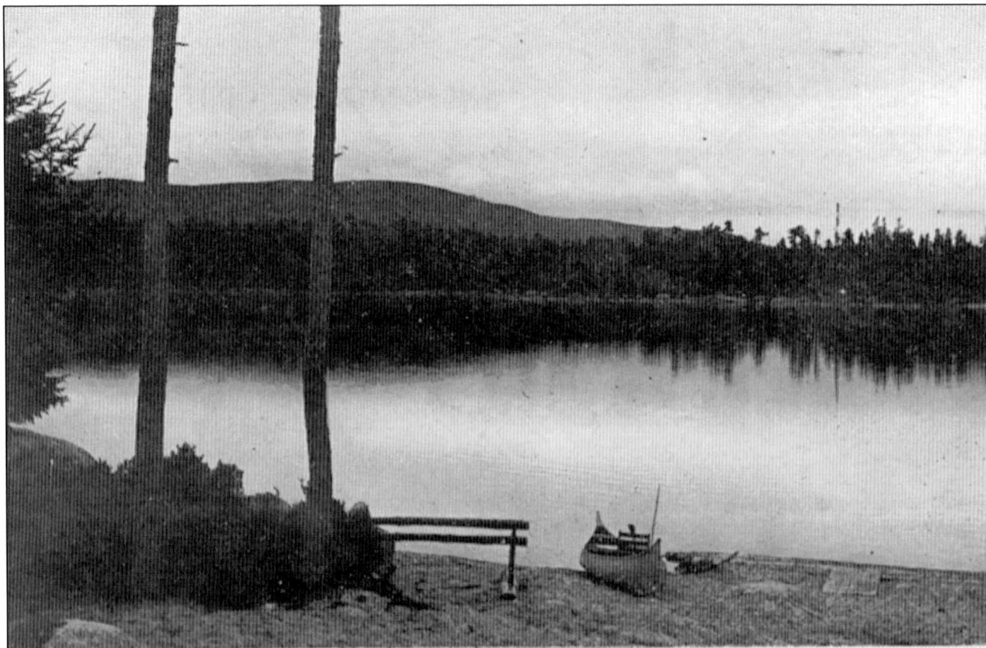

Mopang Lake, from Corliss Camp. S. S. Hutchinson, Pub

Somewhat remote from other lakes in Washington County and north of the Machias chain is Mopang Lake. It is accessible from Route 9, the "Airline."

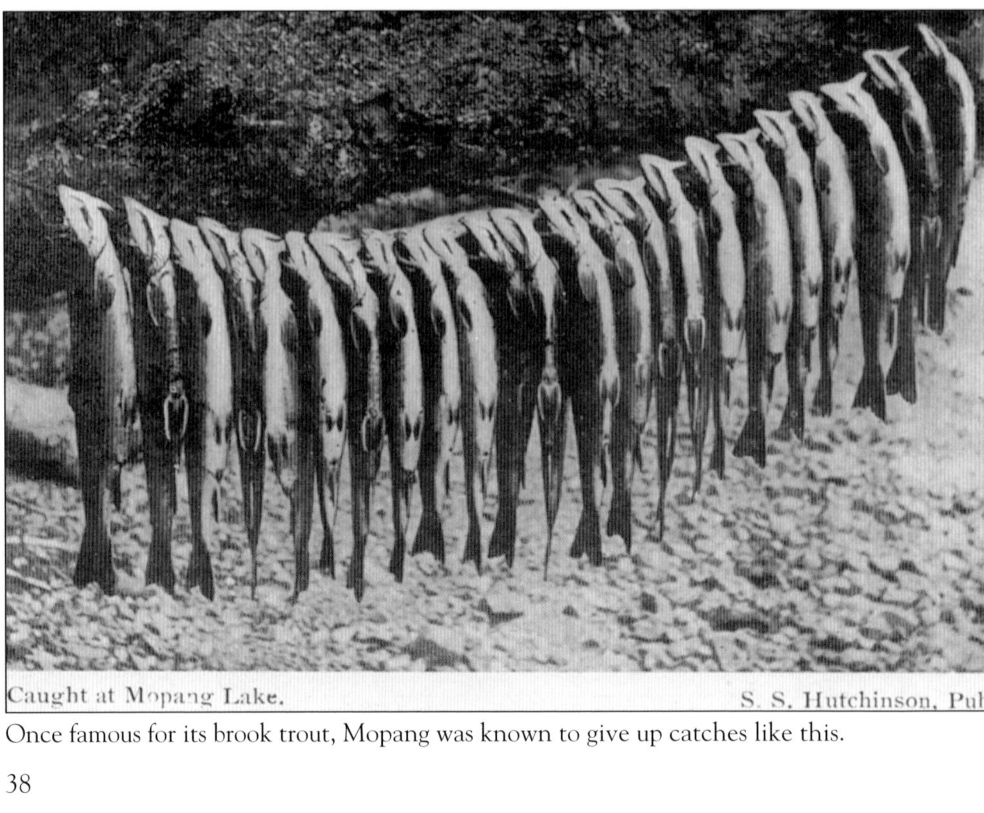

Caught at Mopang Lake. S. S. Hutchinson, Pub

Once famous for its brook trout, Mopang was known to give up catches like this.

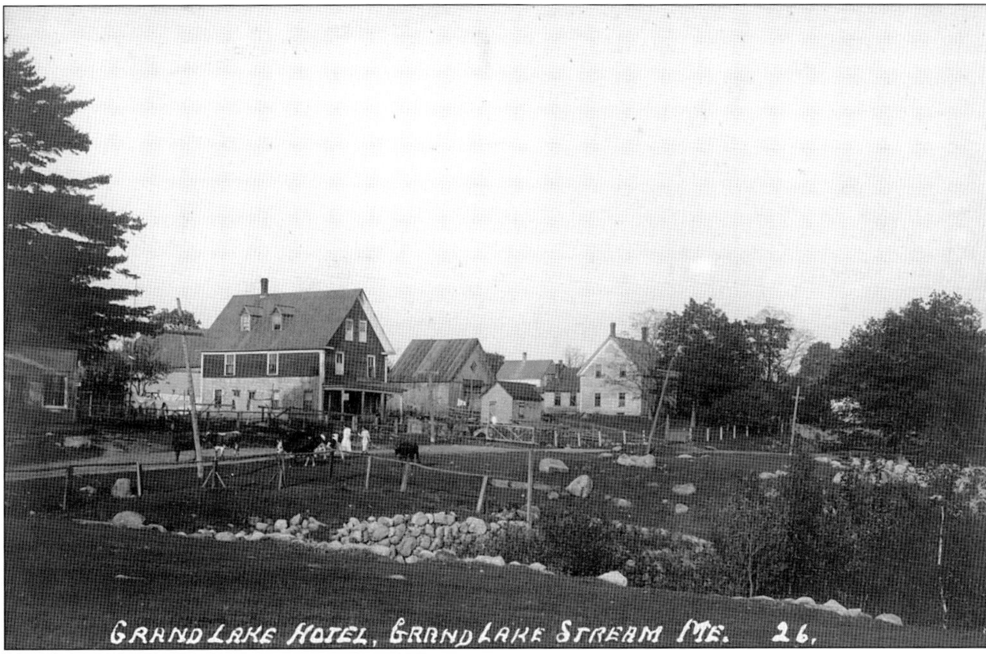

Until roads reached the town, Grand Lake Stream was reached by rail to Princeton and then by team around or steamer across Big Lake to the carry and then by team again. There were good accommodations in the village, with several establishments centered around the salmon fishery.

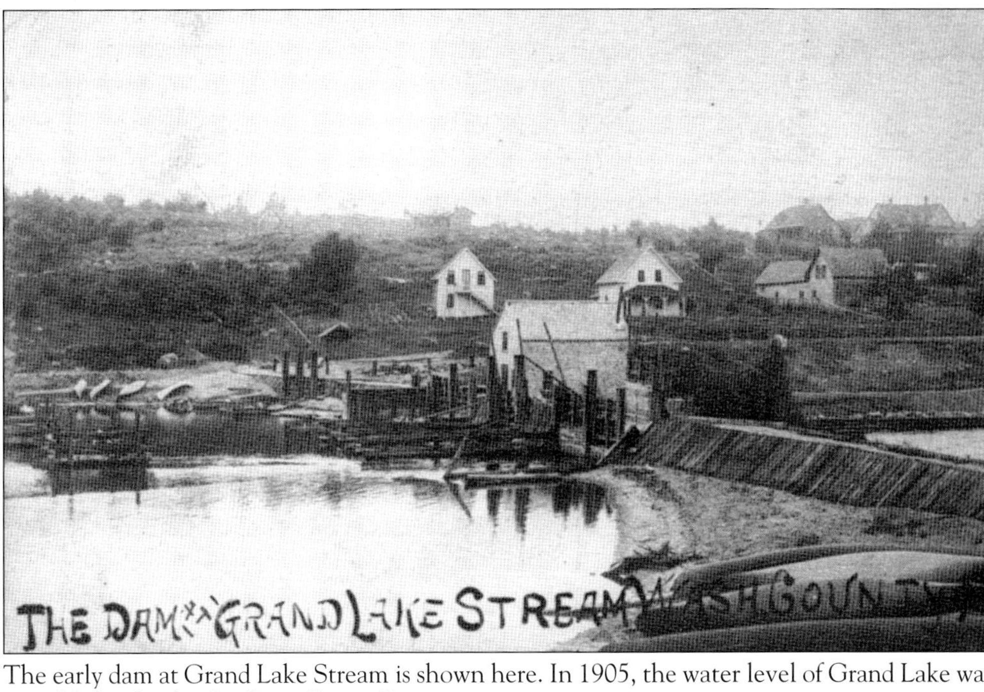

The early dam at Grand Lake Stream is shown here. In 1905, the water level of Grand Lake was raised 7 feet by the St. Croix Paper Company.

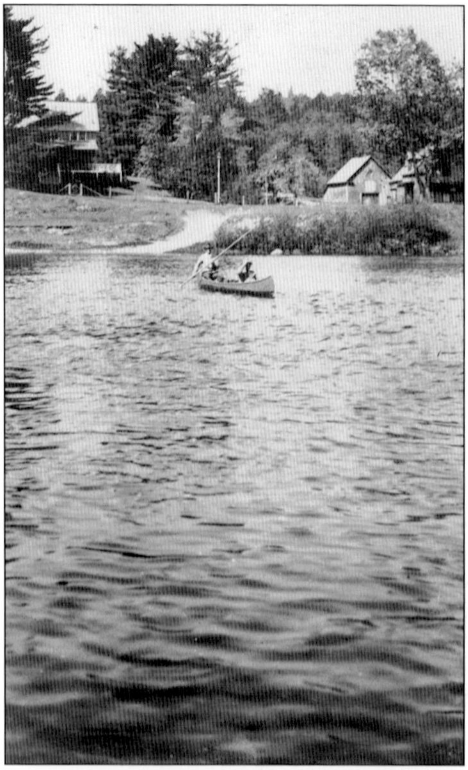

Grand Lake for some time has been famous for its fabulous salmon fishing, being one of the original landlocked salmon waters. An early advertisement stated "from the first of June to the first of July is the royal sport with the rod, particularly fly-fishing for salmon in Grand Lake Stream, the outlet of the lake. If one is to do much fly-fishing, it is advisable to bring a good variety of flies to be prepared for all the salmon's eccentricities in taking a fly. Size of hooks 8 to 12 are the best."

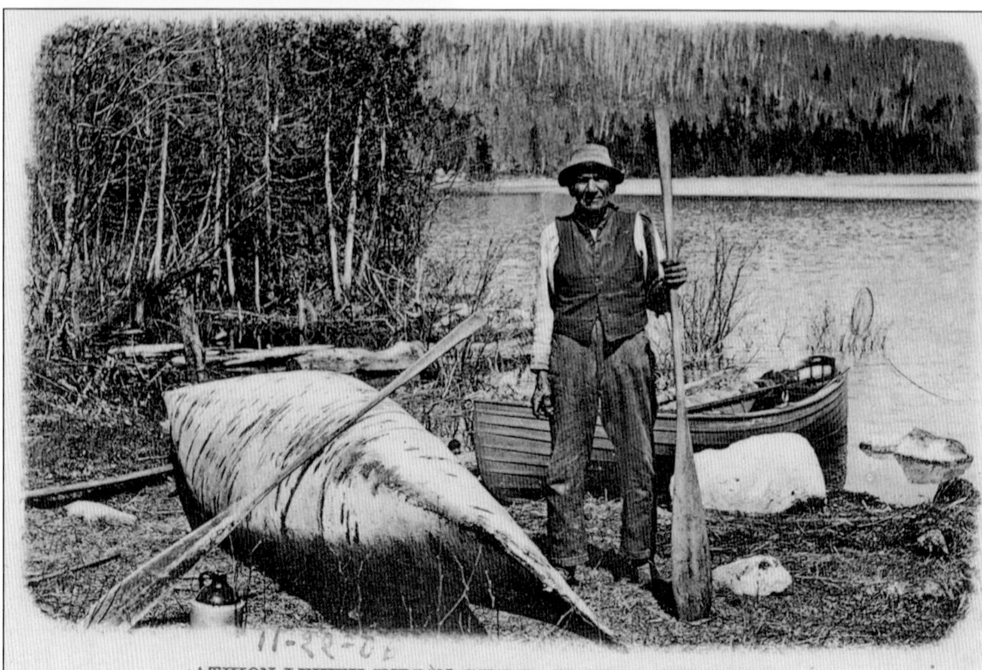

There were many Native American guides in Maine during the early part of the century, particularly here next to the Passamaquoddy Reservation. Relatively few remained by the 1950s. Two types of craft are pictured here, a rowboat and a birchbark canoe.

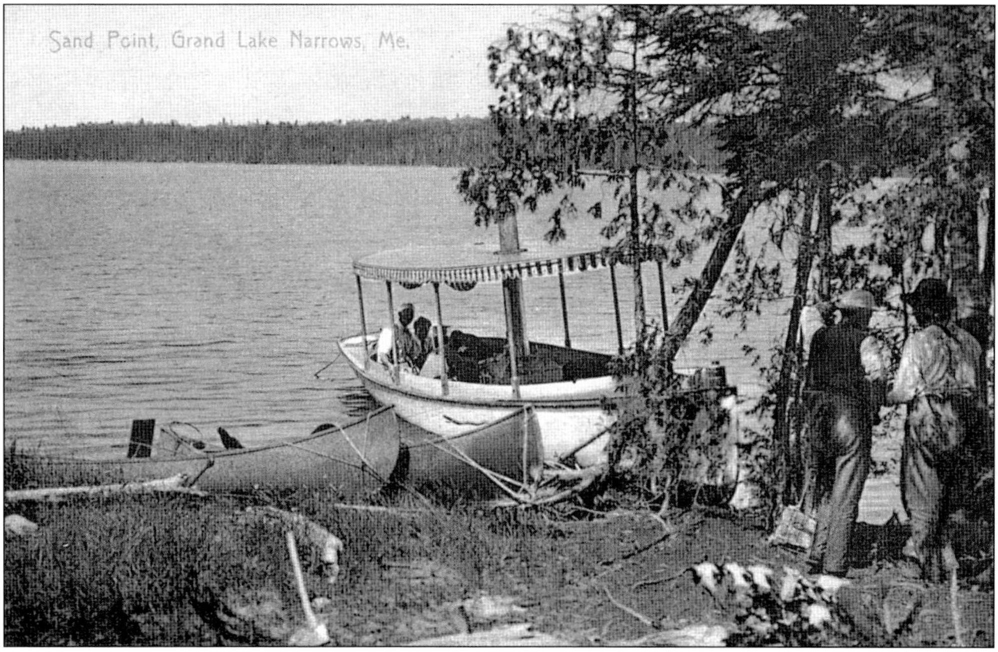

A group of anglers takes a break from fishing to have a shore cookout. With canoes in tow, the steamer has taken the party to a distant location on the lake. The launch is parked or anchored while the fishing is done from the canoes.

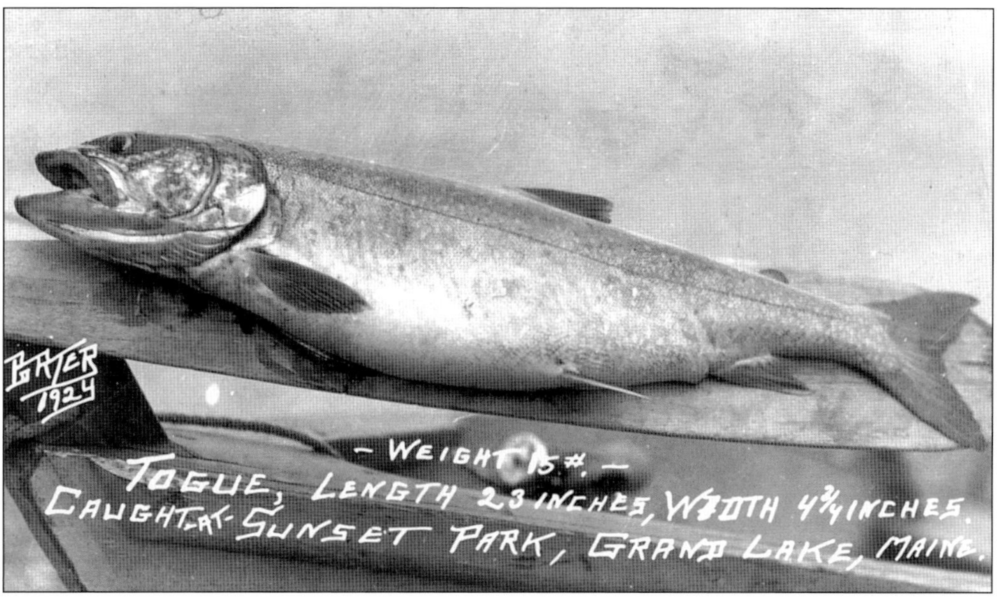

The ice leaves the southeastern lakes of Washington County nearly three weeks earlier than the lakes in the Moosehead and Rangeley regions. Ice-out is a favorite time for many, as salmon and togue may be taken by trolling flies at or near the surface of the cold water. Larger fish are more likely to be taken at this time than after they seek the cooler depths in midsummer.

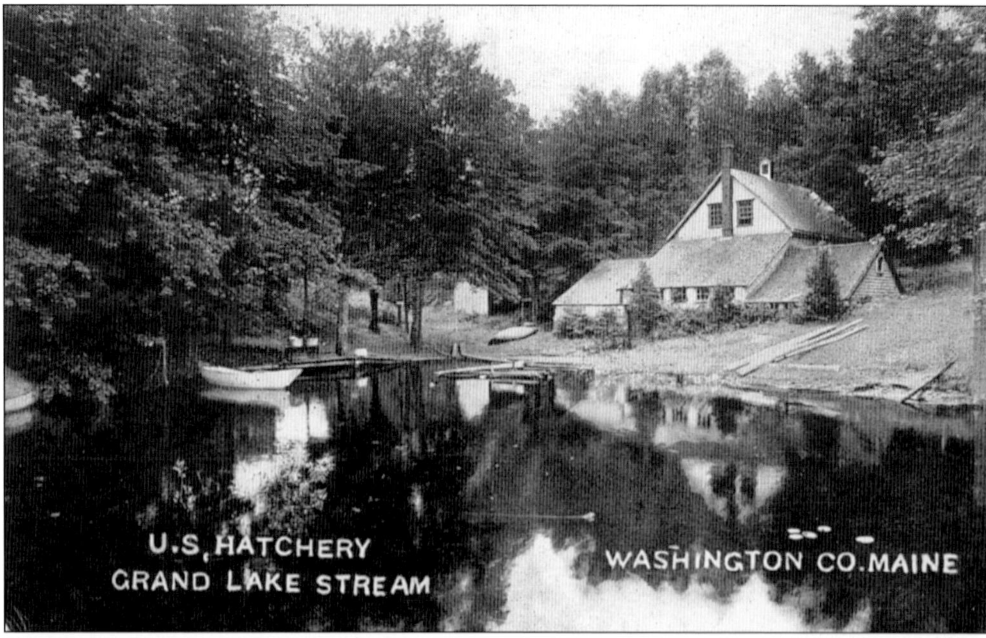

This hatchery was established in 1868 as a joint effort between the Maine and Massachusetts departments of fisheries and was taken over by the U.S. Fisheries Commission in 1872. Salmon and togue here have been weighed up to 32 pounds. One net haul of white perch is reported to have been 700 fish.

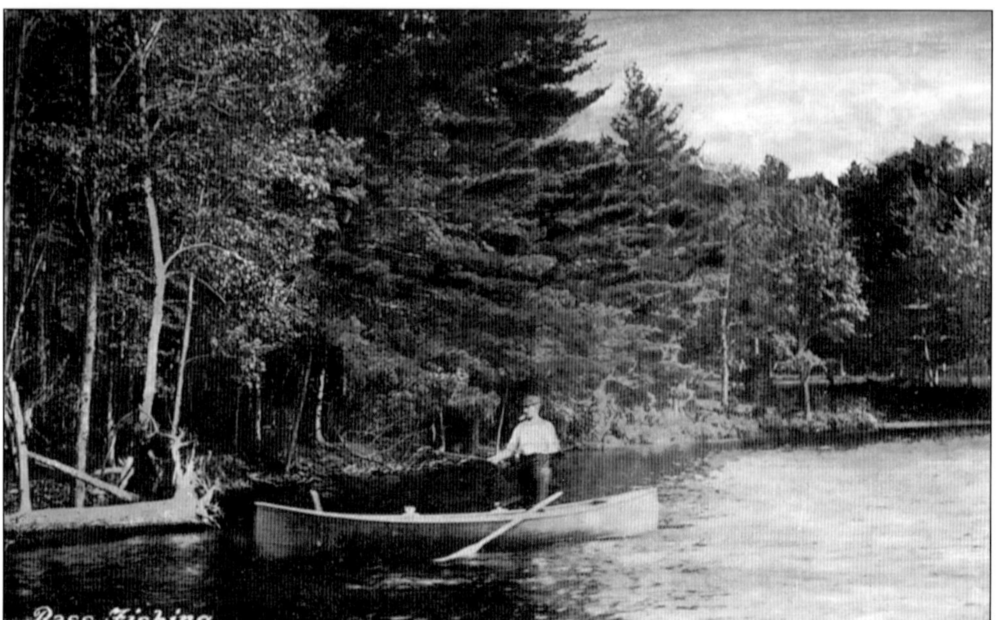

The lakes and ponds Down East, particularly those of Washington County, have long been known for great bass fishing. In fact, this area has some of the best smallmouth bass fishing to be found anywhere.

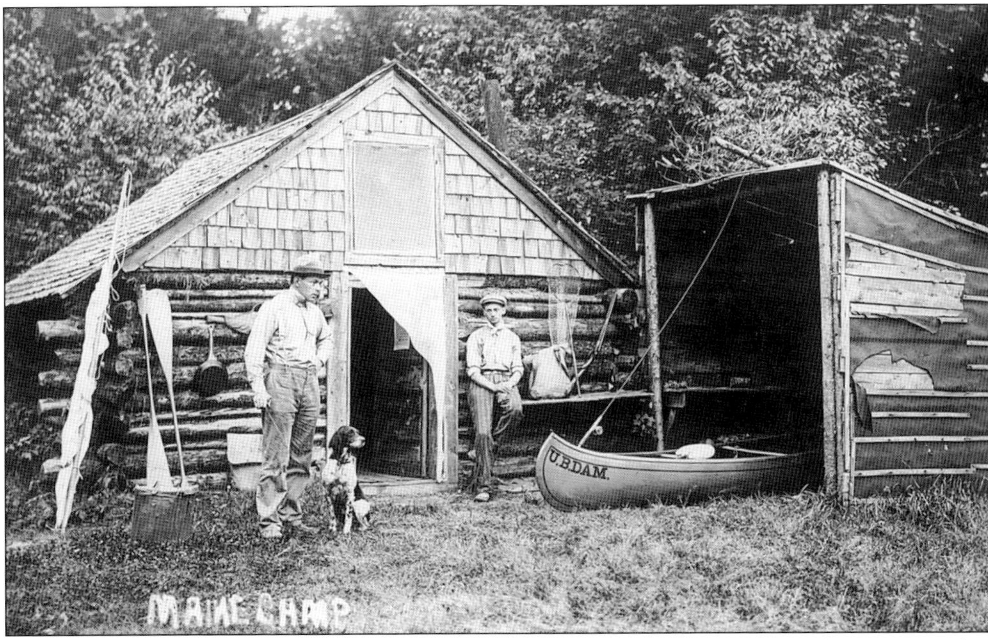

This Maine camp appears to be well equipped. The back of the card is postmarked "Cherryfield, 1915."

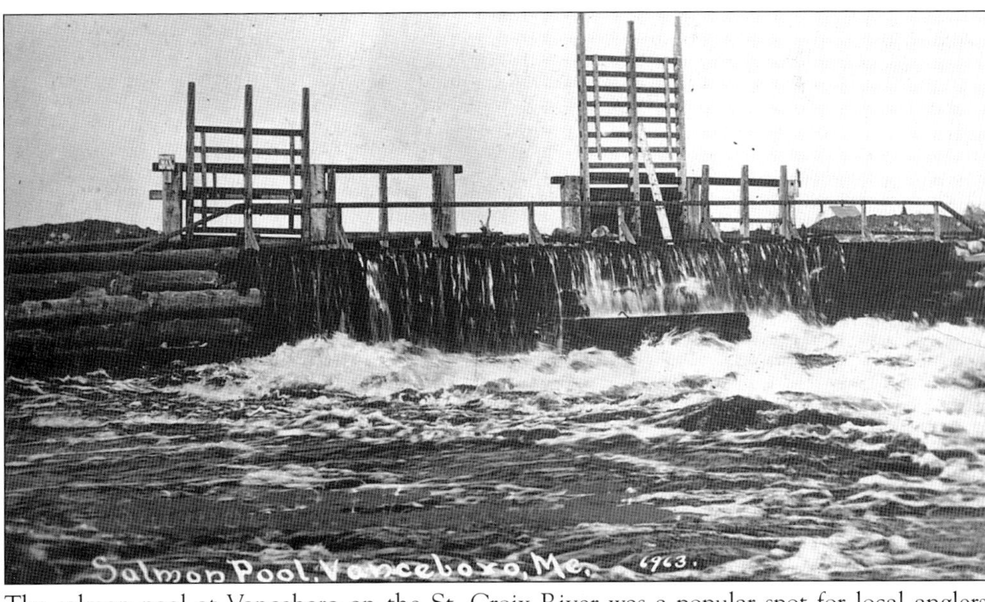

The salmon pool at Vanceboro on the St. Croix River was a popular spot for local anglers. Dams such as this one created the best of both worlds: control of high water and retention in times of low water, preserving habitat for fish.

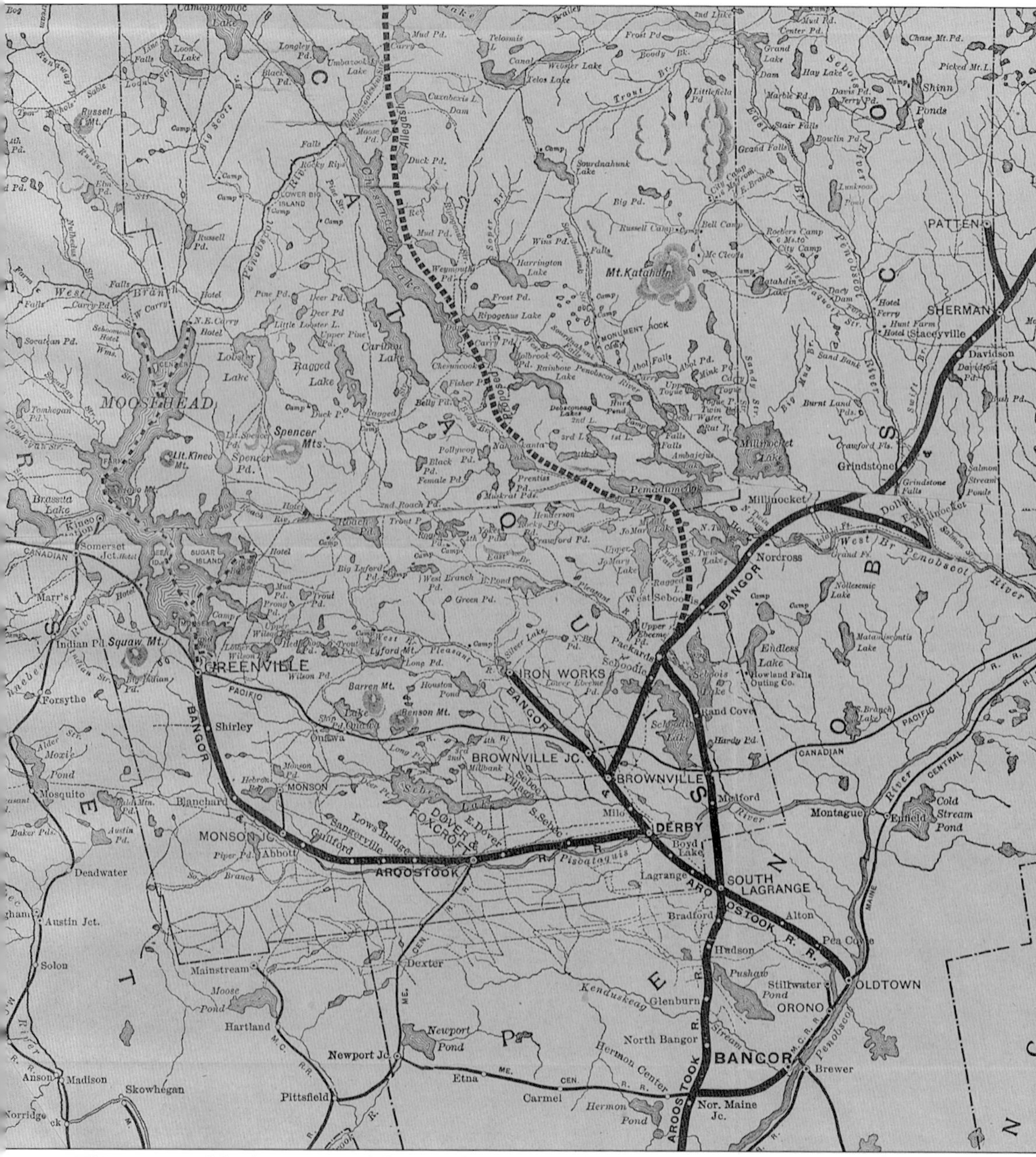

This map is of the lower part of the Penobscot River system. (From *In the Maine Woods*, 1915.)

Five

The Penobscot River Valley

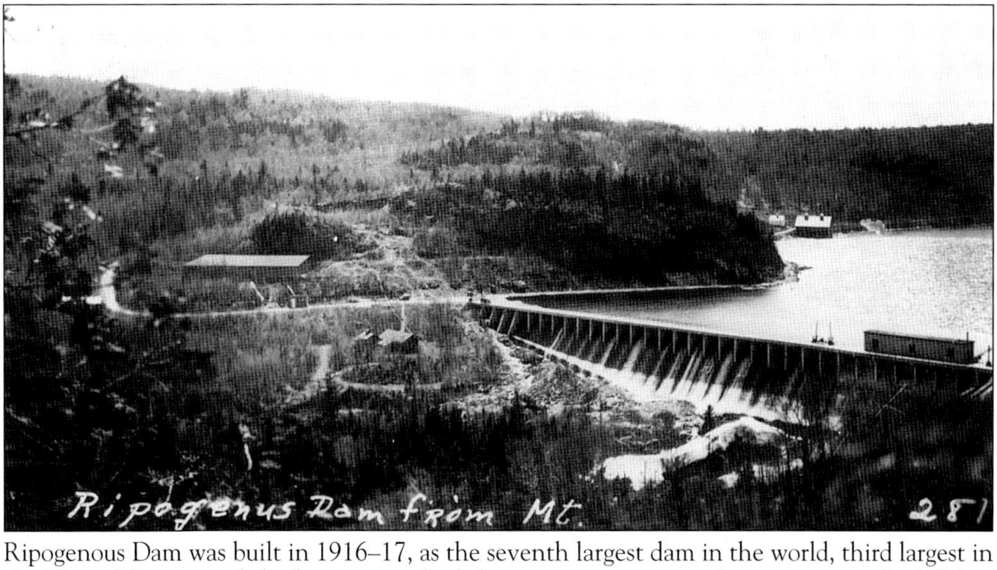

Ripogenous Dam was built in 1916–17, as the seventh largest dam in the world, third largest in the United States, and the largest ever built by a private company for its own use. In 1936, it was reported that the paddle down from the carry was attractive, but not as attractive as it was in former years before the dam was built. The report went on to state that the West Branch trip had been "dammed out of popularity by the concrete ridge thrown across the river at the outlet of Ripogenous Lake." The river below the dam is the famous West Branch, which is so popular today. While the West Branch of the Penobscot technically begins near the Canadian Border north of Jackman, most people refer to this section near Millinocket. It has long been known for its large fish, particularly salmon.

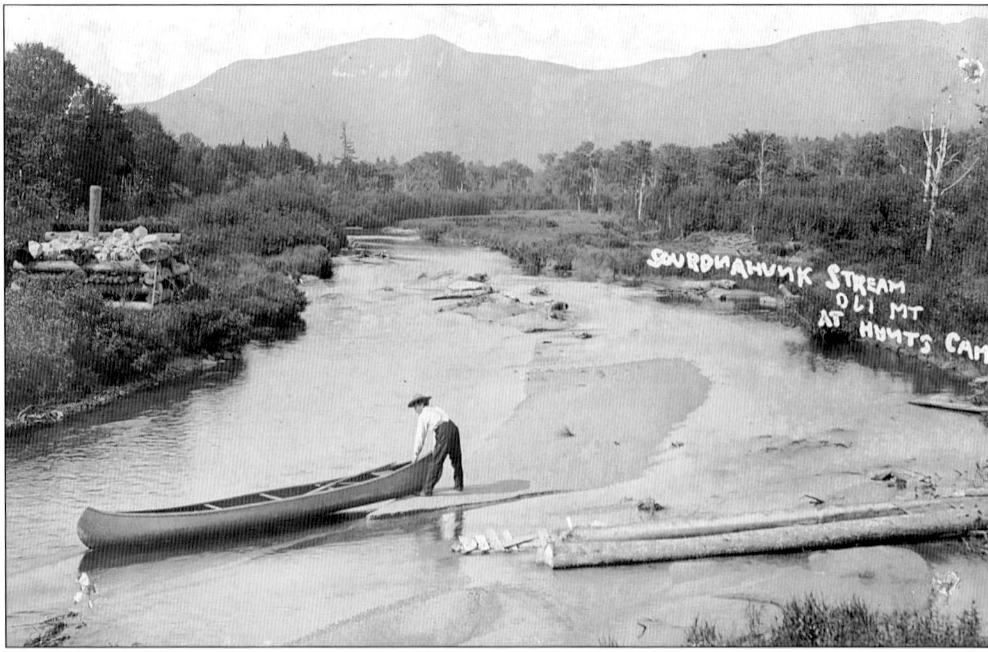

The lake and stream known as "Sourdyhunk" have long been known for their fabulous trout fishing throughout the season. In 1917, Frederick B. Hyde landed a 4-pound, 3-ounce trout after a terrific struggle lasting one hour and 12 minutes, using a No. 12 fly of his own design and tying with a 2-ounce rod and a tapered G line. Proven dry flies here are the various Halford's, March Brown, Pale Evening Dun, Ginger and Red Quill, White Miller, Royal Coachman, Greenwell's Glory, Black Gnat, and Ants.

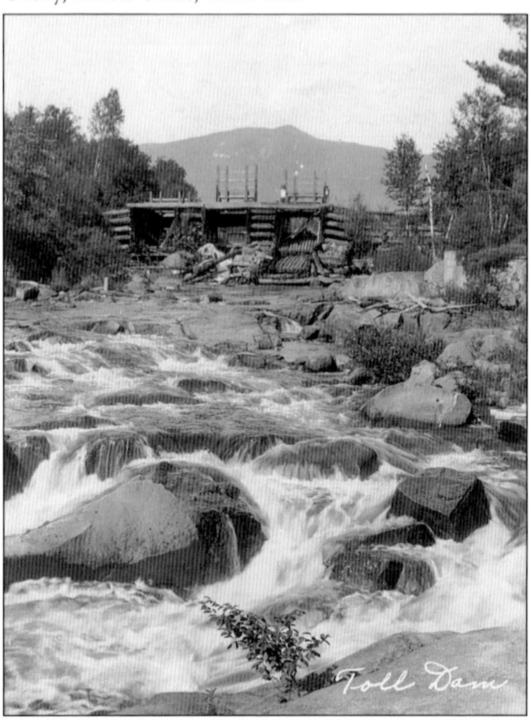

Located 12 miles below the pond and 3 miles above the West Branch, this pool was a favored fishing spot. In the early morning of September 16, 1932, a hurricane hit the region, in some areas changing the face of the landscape, as evidenced by rocky slides on Mount Katahdin and surrounding peaks. It rained 12 inches in less than 24 hours, causing the Sourdnahunk to rise over 12 feet and wash away the Toll Dam.

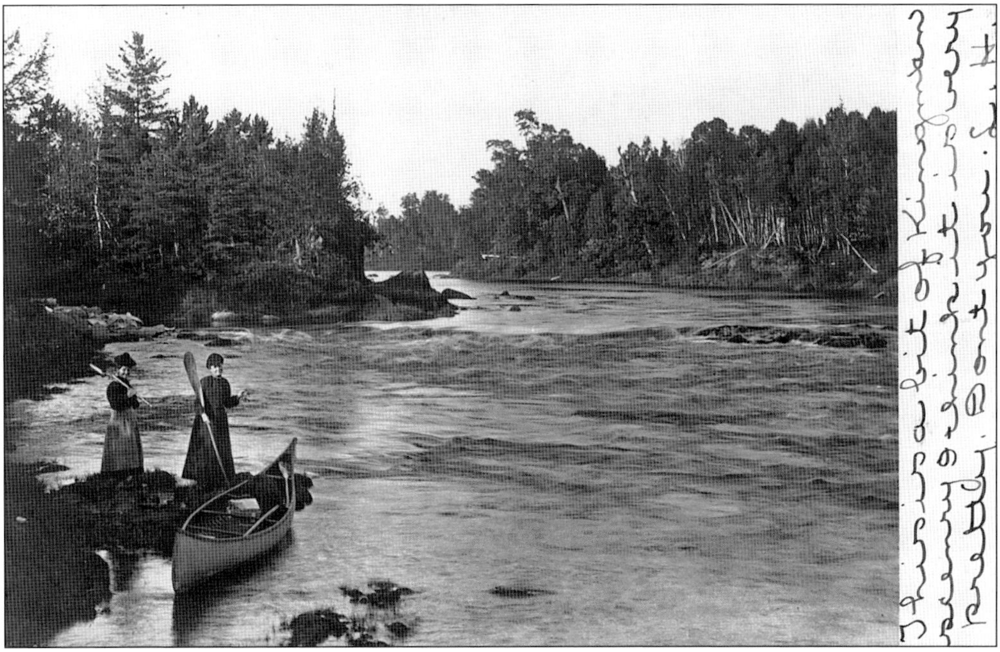

The Mattawamkeag River is a major tributary to the Penobscot, with its source at Mattawamkeag Lake near Island Falls. Theodore Roosevelt visited here in the early 1880s, introduced to the Maine woods by guide Bill Sewall. William Wingate Sewall was the first white child born in Island Falls and first met Roosevelt when the future president was "a frail youth of 18." The two eventually became close friends and in later years, Sewall visited Roosevelt at the White House. (From *In the Maine Woods*, 1923.)

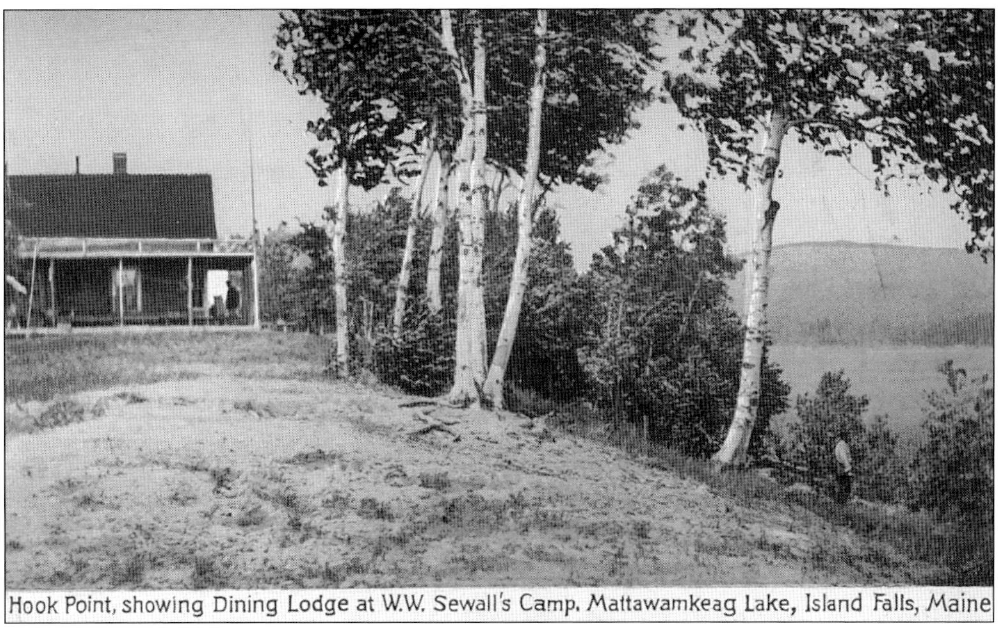

Bill Sewall was known as a guide full of woods lore and eager to introduce a visitor to the pleasures of the out-of-doors. He was characterized as a born raconteur, typical of so many Maine guides.

THE LEADING TAXIDERMISTS OF AMERICA

The Most Complete Sportsmen's Supply Store in Maine

The S. L. Crosby Co.

186 Exchange Street, Bangor, Maine

Agencies at All Important Game Centers in Maine, New Brunswick and Newfoundland

Every workman in our employ has been here from 5 to 25 years—is experienced and thoroughly skilled—is a real artist in his line. This feature, together with the fact that we have commodious quarters and the most modern facilities, insures absolutely perfect results on any and all orders entrusted to us. We guarantee complete satisfaction, whether it is game or fish that we mount; AND WE DELIVER THE MOUNT WHEN PROMISED. All work warranted moth proof.

Hundreds of Moose, Deer, Caribou, Mountain Sheep, Antelope and Elk Heads are mounted by us every year. We make a specialty of handsome game heads for hotels, club rooms, etc. Send for price list.

Any Maine express office can furnish our shipping tags.

Directions how to prepare big game heads for mounting

We especially invite visitors to inspect the immense array of Sportsmen's Supplies, Woods and Taxidermy Specialties which we have on hand at all times. Our line includes a complete and wonderfully varied assortment of mounted Game Heads, Fish, etc., and Guns, Rifles, Ammunition, Fishing Tackle, and Hunters' Complete Equipments, Tents, Sleeping Bags, Knapsacks, Leggins, Moccasins, Hunting and Wading Boots, Knives, Axes, Pedometers, Flashlights, Gold Medal Camp Furniture, Canoes, Canoe Seats, Chairs, Snowshoes, Rugs, Deerfoot Novelties, Indian Baskets, Indian Novelties, etc., etc.

Hunter's Licenses for sale. Rifles and Shotguns for rent.

Our representatives meet all trains at Bangor during the

This is an advertisement for one of the most popular and well-known taxidermists in Maine. Located in Bangor, the S.L. Crosby Company was readily available to sportsmen throughout the state, whether for outfitting their trips or preserving their trophies. (From *In the Maine Woods*, 1906.)

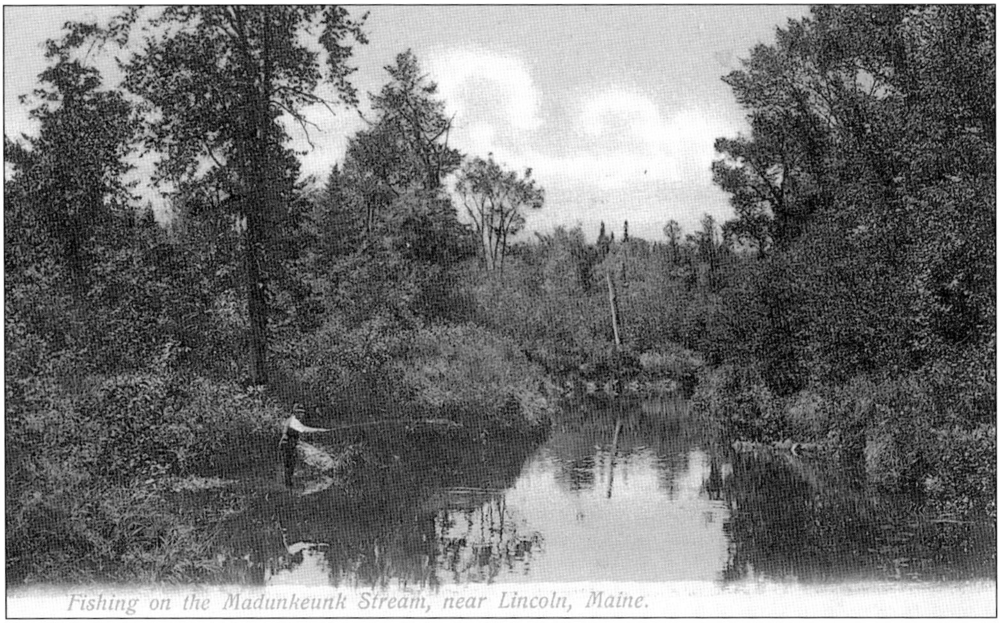

Shown is one of hundreds of trout streams found north of Bangor throughout the Penobscot drainage basin.

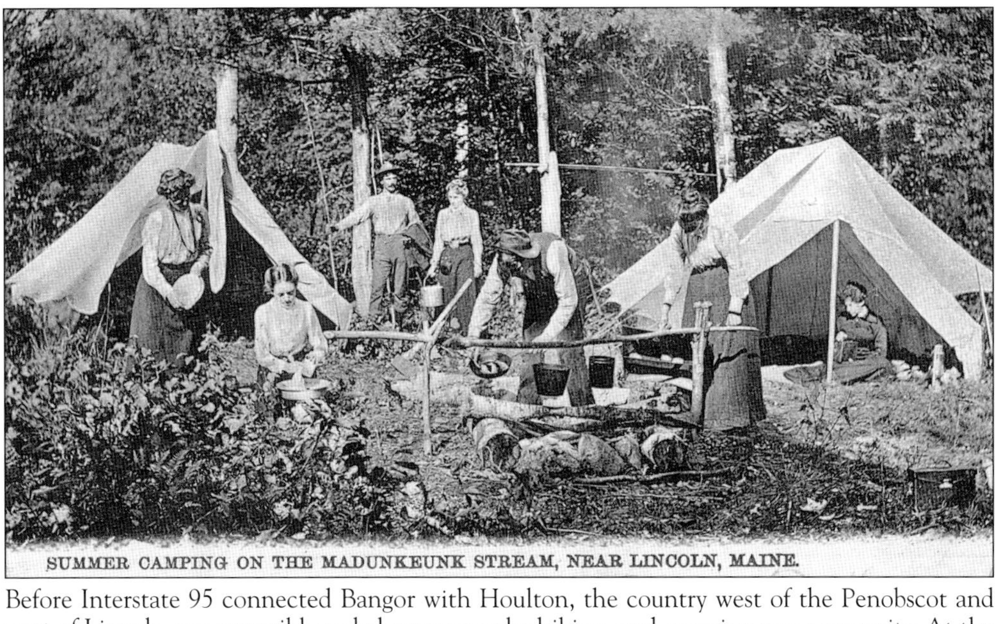

Before Interstate 95 connected Bangor with Houlton, the country west of the Penobscot and west of Lincoln was accessible only by canoe or by hiking, and camping was a necessity. At the beginning of the 20th century, this area was at the edge of wilderness.

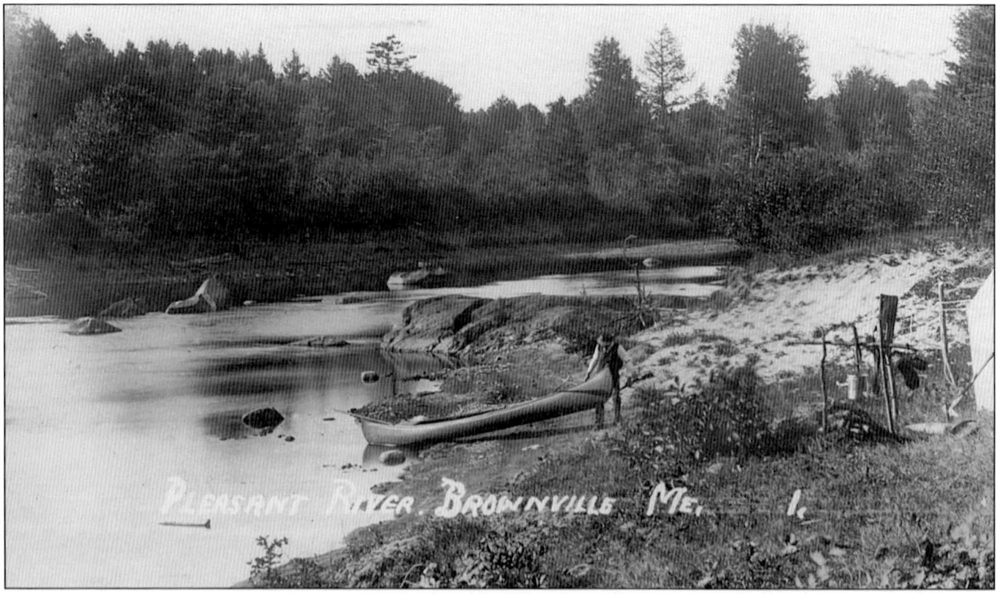

The Pleasant River (both east and west branches) is a tributary of the Penobscot, originating in the Roach Pond drainage just east of Moosehead. Easily accessed from the railhead at Brownville Junction and Katahdin Iron Works, it was a favorite of hundreds of trout fishermen over many decades.

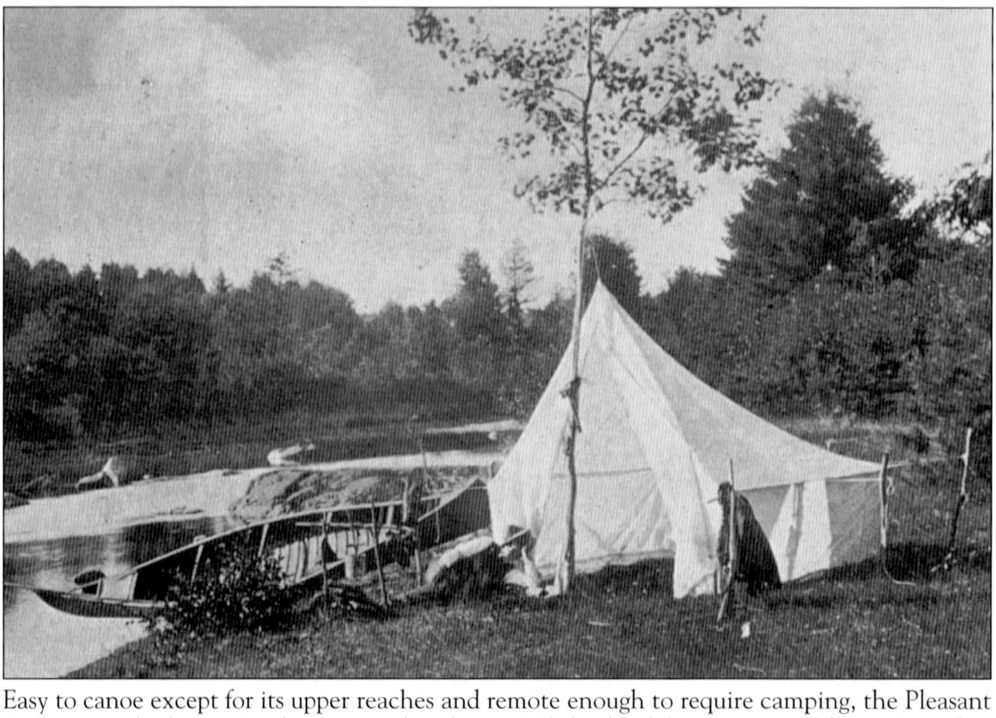

Easy to canoe except for its upper reaches and remote enough to require camping, the Pleasant River watershed contained trout in abundance. While the fish were not of large size, what they lacked in size they made up for in number; it was written that "the angler may be sure of securing all the fish from 9 to 12 inches in length [that] any decent sportsman can desire." (From *In the Maine Woods*, 1909.)

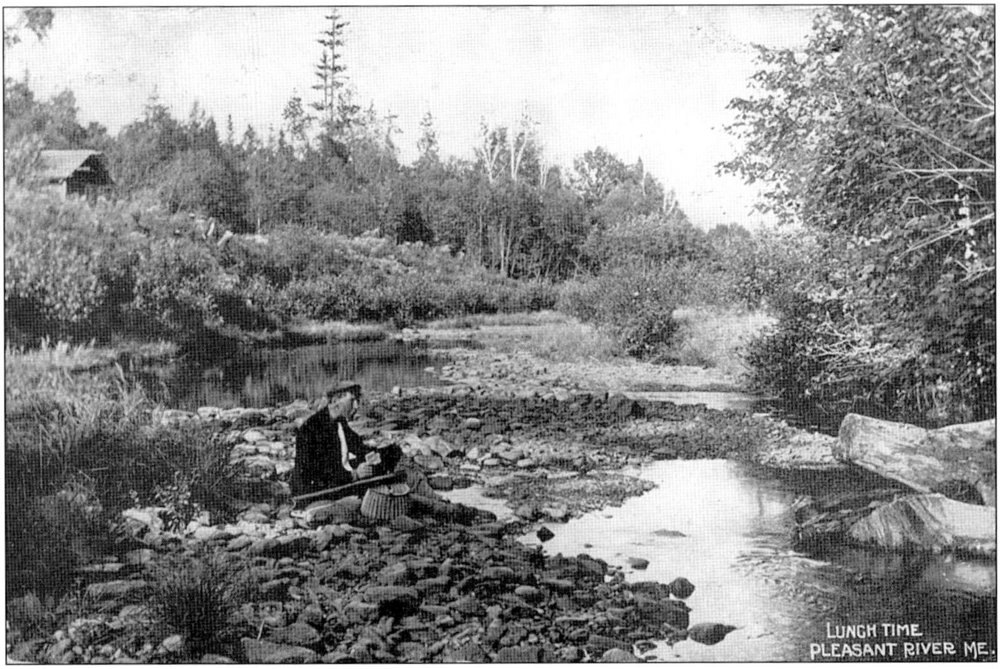

An angler takes time from fishing to enjoy his lunch. Popular flies for the Pleasant River and surrounding waters have been reported to be the old standards: Scarlet Ibis, Parmachenee Belle, Montreal, Preston, and Jenny Lind.

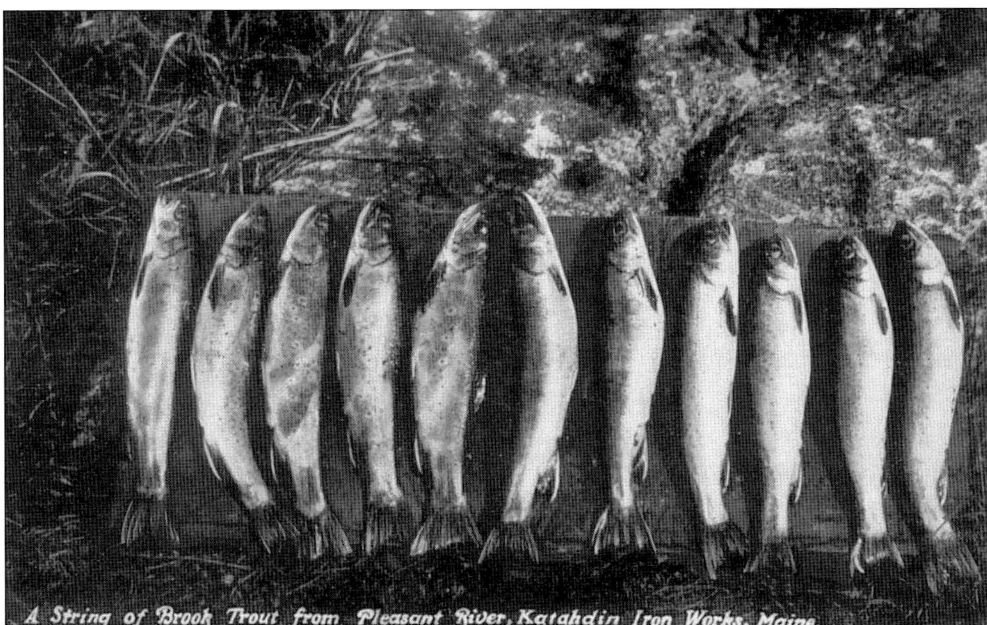

One of the popular establishments on the Pleasant River near Katahdin Iron Works was Brown's Camps. M.H. Yale of Jamaica, New York, wrote in 1906 that he and his son caught 672 trout in seven hours' fly-casting. They returned the greater part of them uninjured as they "used small fly hooks." (From *In the Maine Woods*, 1906.)

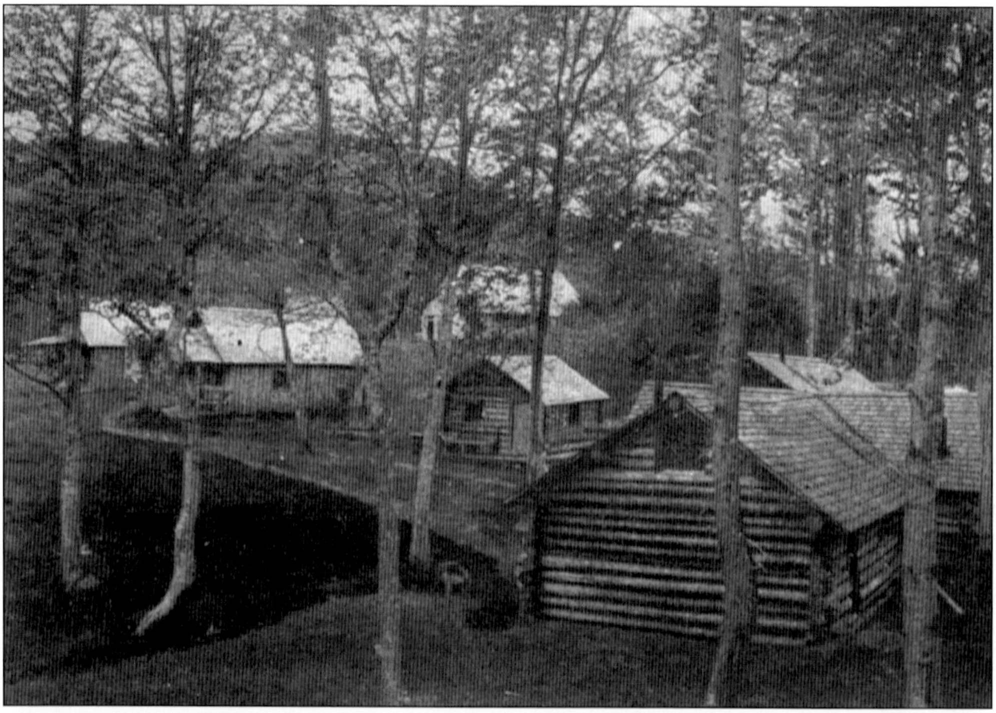

Freese's Camps could be reached by taking a buckboard from Katahdin Iron Works up the Pleasant River Valley past Silver Lake. The first 7 miles of the ride was smooth, after which large boulders and stumps were encountered; then the trip continued over the summit and down the other side to the destination. (From *In the Maine Woods*, 1909.)

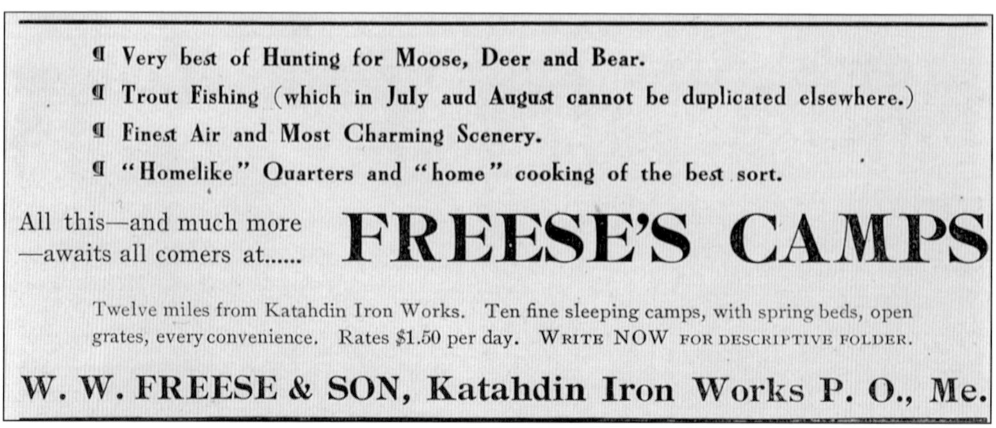

Having arrived at Freese's, the traveler was "assured of a hearty welcome, most comfortable quarters, and excellent fishing." Reports were that if the day was good and the season right, "the angler would find a fisherman's paradise, with fish rising freely to a fly and the only difficulty being to keep the catch down to proper proportions." (From *In the Maine Woods*, 1907.)

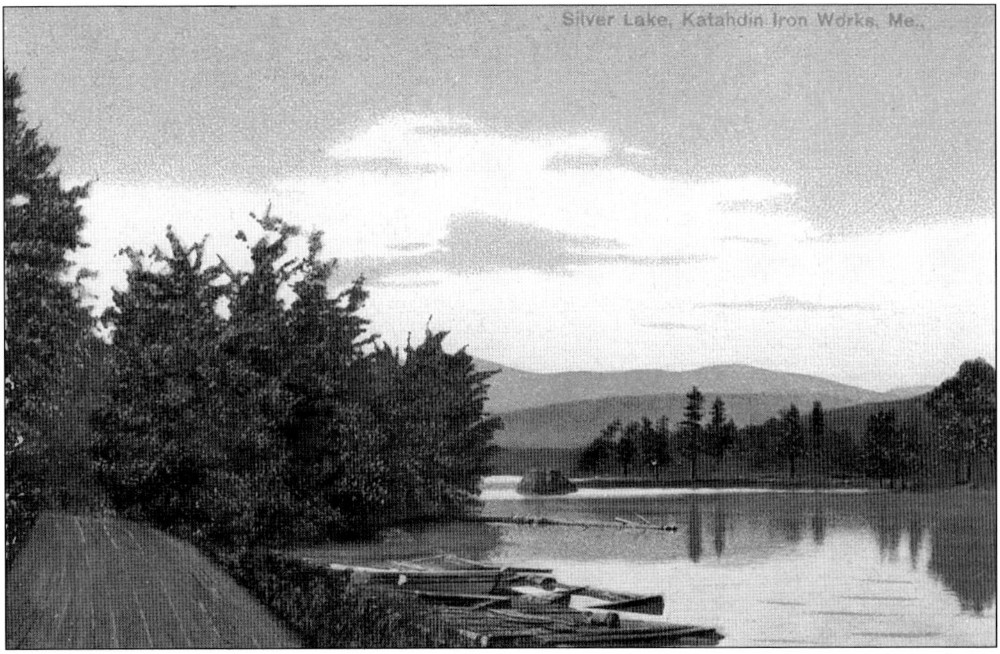

From Brownville, the Katahdin Iron Works Branch of the Bangor & Aroostook Railroad ran through the valley of the Pleasant River to the little village of Katahdin Iron Works on the shore of Silver Lake. "Monster pickerel were found in Silver Lake, and within a radius of 20 miles from the hotel are 27 different lakes and ponds from which the fisherman could make a choice and be assured of getting fine trout fishing." (From *In the Maine Woods*, 1909.)

Silver Lake Hotel, KATAHDIN IRON WORKS, MAINE.

F. H. EDDY, Prop.

Situated in the heart of the big game region, and near numerous trout ponds and good camps.

The famous MINERAL SPRING is close by the Hotel. Invalids and people seeking rest find the mountain air very beneficial, and hay fever is unknown here.

House has been recently put in good repair. All rooms with good view. Bath rooms with hot and cold water. First-class table.

The Silver Lake Hotel was a popular stop for not only fishermen but also vacationers and "summer colonists." The lake afforded pickerel and perch fishing way above the ordinary and an occasional salmon, as well as being a charmingly picturesque body of water. Everywhere in the region are springs of the purest water, famed for their medicinal value. (From *In the Maine Woods*, 1900.)

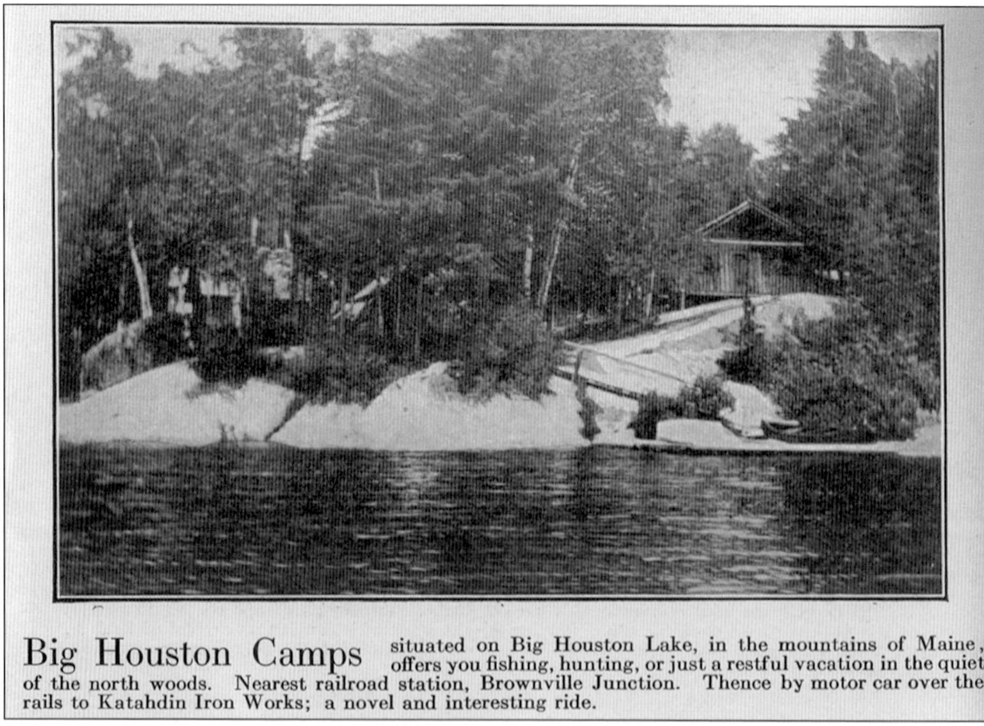

By leaving Boston at 9 p.m., one could reach the Iron Works by noon the next day and Big Houston Camps by 1:30 p.m. At the upper end of the 3-mile-long lake, the hills give way briefly to a gently rolling strip of woodland where the main camp, with its dozen or so log cabins, is located. (From *In the Maine Woods*, 1924.)

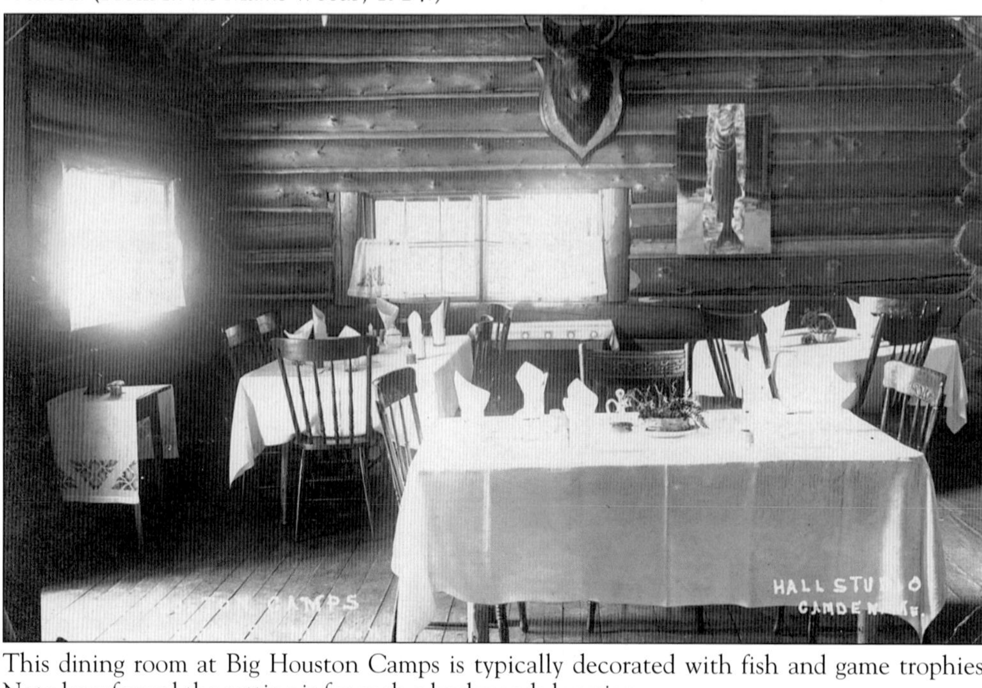

This dining room at Big Houston Camps is typically decorated with fish and game trophies. Note how formal the setting is for such a backwoods location.

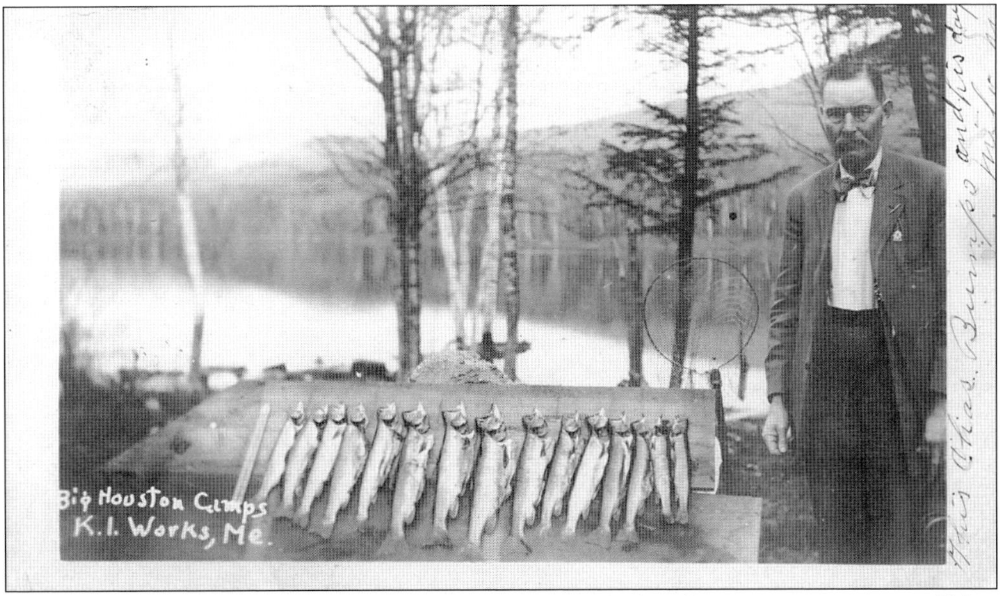

Except in the early spring or through the ice, there is very little fishing in Big Houston itself, but in the area there are dozens of ponds and streams. Some of these are artificially stocked; others have maintained themselves for years as natural breeding grounds for trout. Little Houston lies about one mile from camp. There, one may catch trout weighing up to 2 pounds and an occasional salmon. The water is deep but so clear that one may see the fish below the boat. (From *In the Maine Woods*, 1925.)

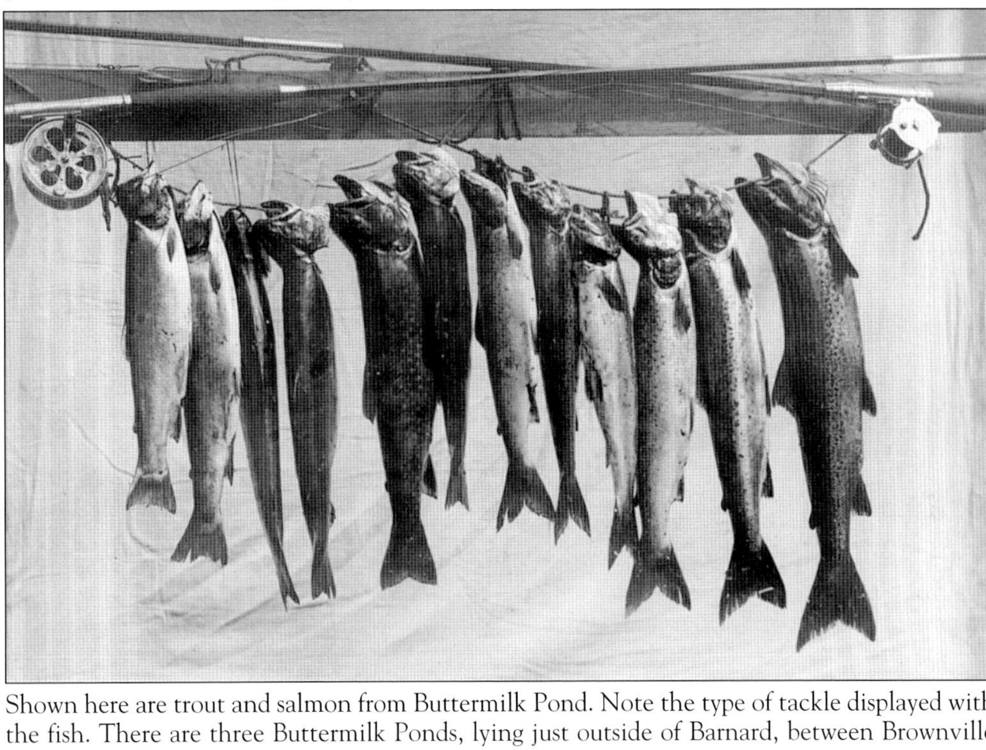

Shown here are trout and salmon from Buttermilk Pond. Note the type of tackle displayed with the fish. There are three Buttermilk Ponds, lying just outside of Barnard, between Brownville Junction and Dover-Foxcroft.

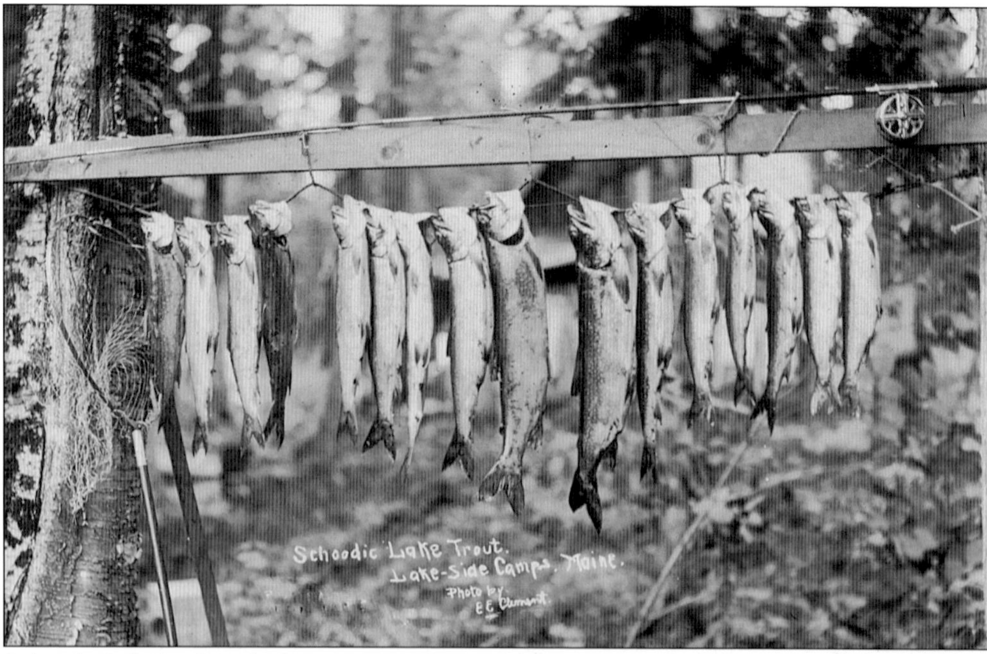

Schoodic Lake has long had a reputation for good fishing, particularly for togue. It was advertised as being close to Schoodic Station, and as having splendid trout, salmon, pickerel, perch, and bass fishing, with togue attaining 15 to 20 pounds in weight.

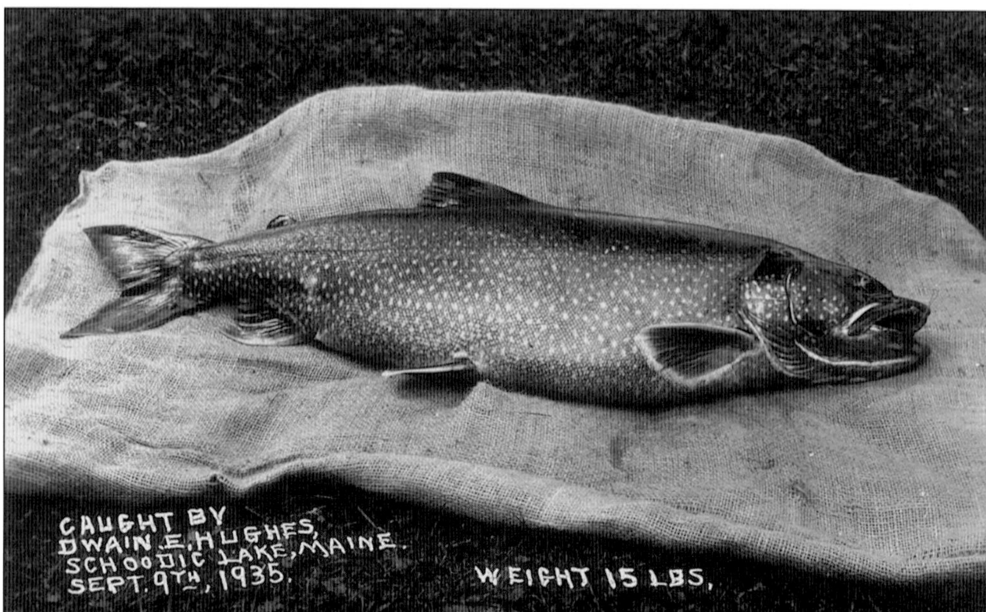

This is an example of a large togue from Schoodic Lake. Such catches were common up through at least the 1930s or 1940s.

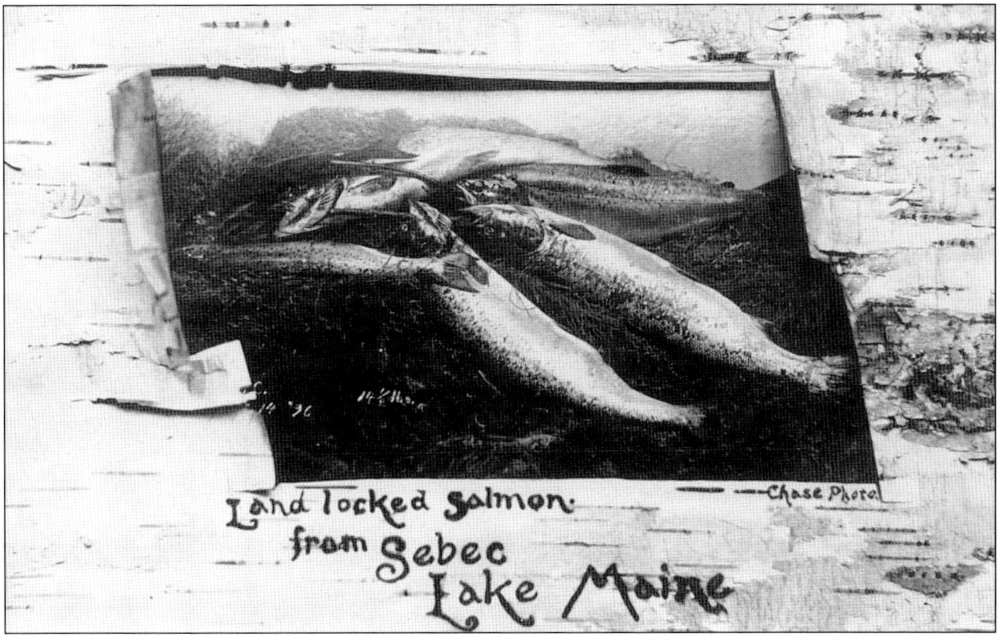

Sebec Lake is one of the four original landlocked salmon waters and has long enjoyed a tremendous reputation for its salmon fishery. Salmon here have been known to attain 10 and 11 pounds.

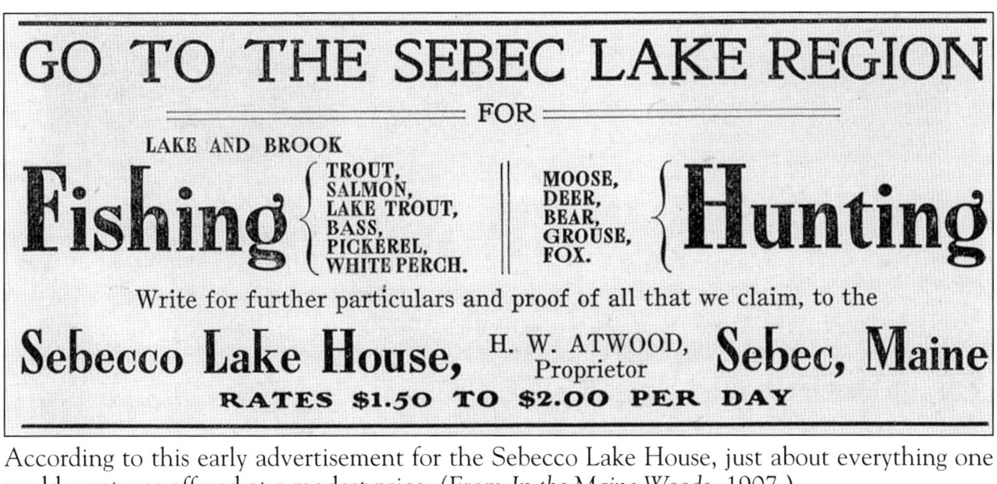

According to this early advertisement for the Sebecco Lake House, just about everything one could want was offered at a modest price. (From *In the Maine Woods*, 1907.)

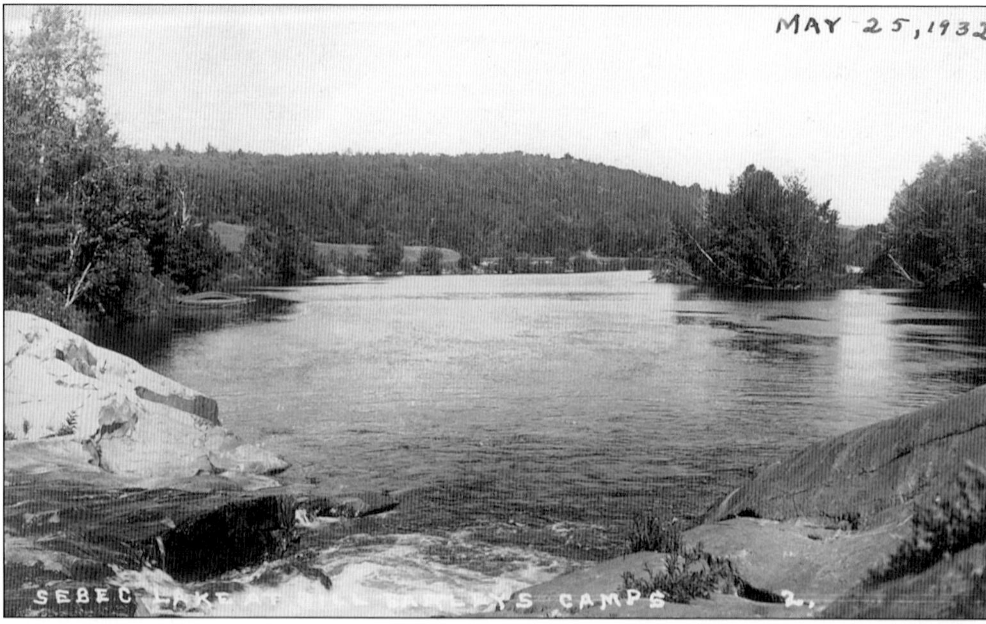

This is the famous salmon pool at Earley's Landing. Once the site of a substantial mill on Wilson Stream in Willimantic, Greeley's Falls has always been a favorite fishing spot. After the mill moved in 1902, Bill Earley purchased the boardinghouse and ran it as a hotel, eventually buying and erecting additional buildings and operating a resort for more than 50 years.

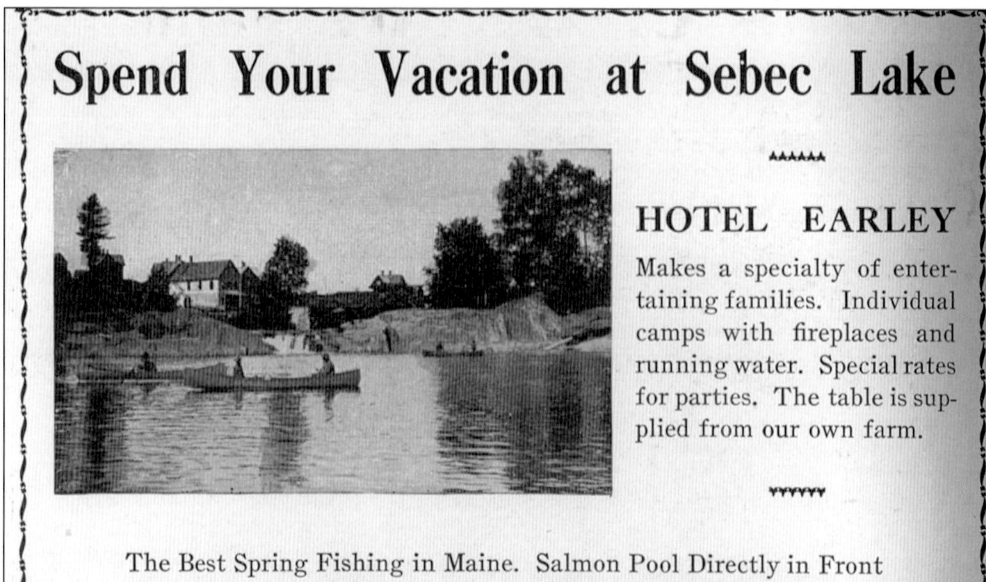

Earley's advertisement, as it appeared in *In the Maine Woods*, 1915, shows the falls from a different point of view.

Lake Hotel and Cottages

Here throughout the season the Landlocked Salmon and Black Bass fishing is unequalled in the State of Maine, as the house is at the head of the lake where the best fishing grounds are located. The house has modern plumbing and sanitary arrangements. Clustered near and in connection with the House are a number of cottages containing from three to five sleeping rooms and a sitting room with open fireplaces in each cottage, also one log cabin. They are entirely furnished and well cared for. Each cottage has a piazza overlook-

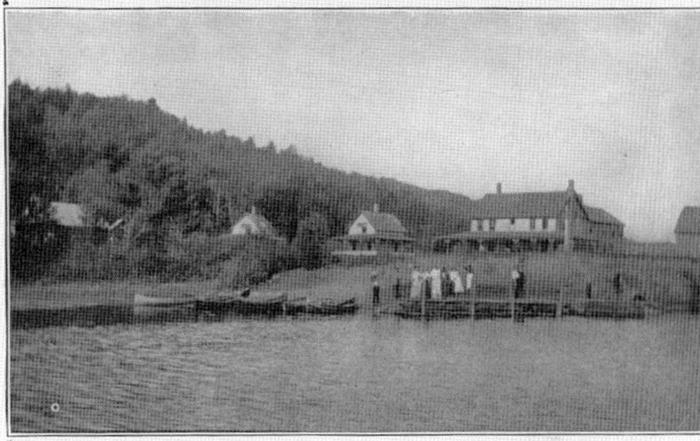

ing the lake, making an ideal place for parties or families to spend the summer. There is a tennis court well cared for, for the use of the guests. Steaks, Chops and Fish are broiled over a charcoal broiler. Postoffice and telephone in the house. Bath room in Cottages. Booklet and rates sent on request. Address

B. M. PACKARD, Proprietor

Piscataquis County — Sebec Lake, Maine

Located at the mouth of Wilson Stream, the Lake House, like many establishments of this type, attracted loggers, spruce gum collectors, anglers, hunters, and trappers, as well as those who came to board for the summer. The Lake House, built in 1866, was purchased by Burton Packard in 1894, operated as a family business, and developed into a fishing resort, which remains today. (From *In the Maine Woods*, 1912.)

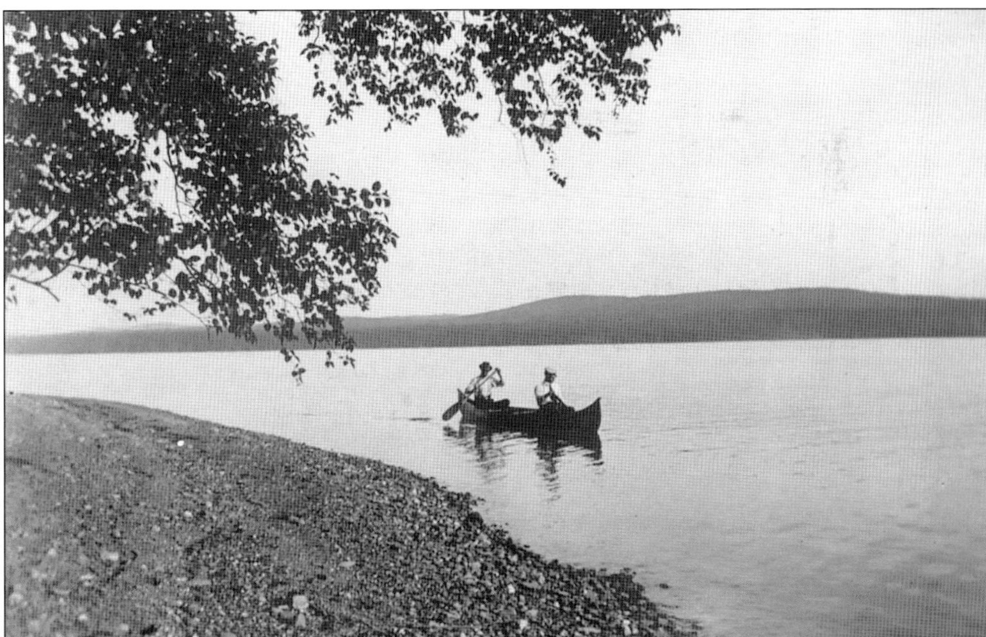

Sebec at 12 miles long and 4 miles wide contains not only an abundance of salmon but also trout, bass, pickerel, and white perch. Excellent trout fishing has been known in its tributary waters.

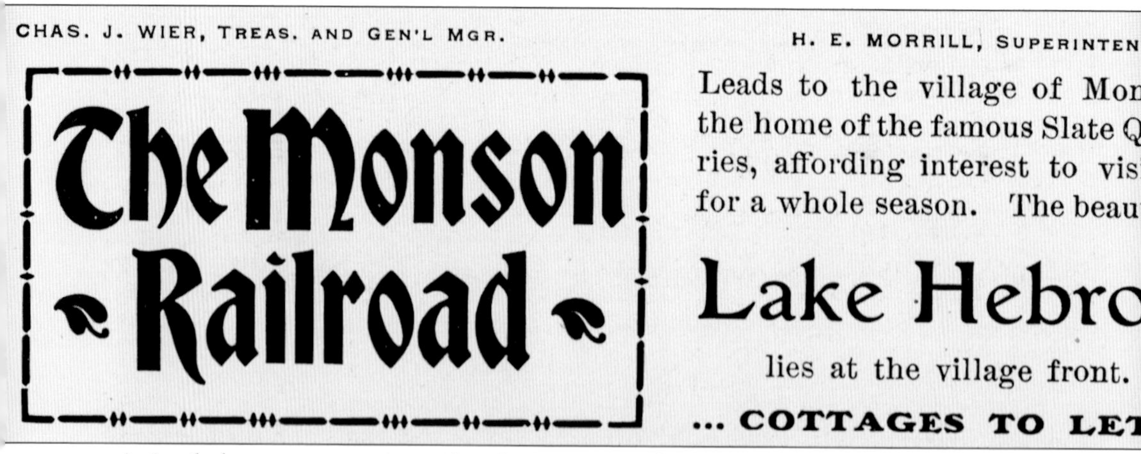

A 6-mile-long narrow-gauge railroad in operation from 1883 to 1943, the Monson was built to move slate from the quarries in Monson to the main line. It has since found usefulness in moving tourists, and anglers have used it to reach the desirable fishing sites near Monson. In 1916, it carried 7,589 passengers. (From *In the Maine Woods*, 1906.)

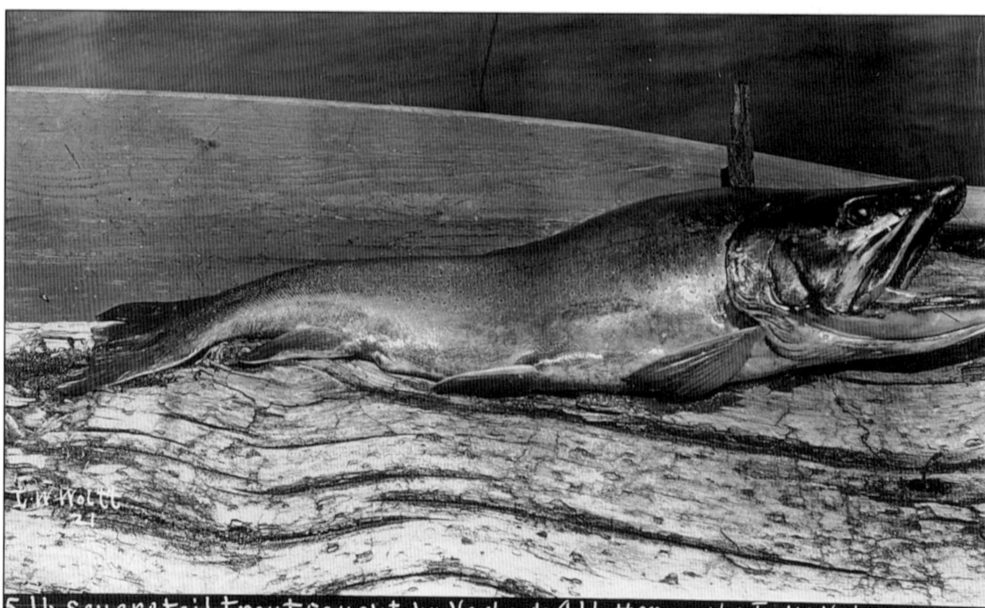

Shown here is an example of a fine trout taken from Lake Hebron, well known for its salmon and trout fishery.

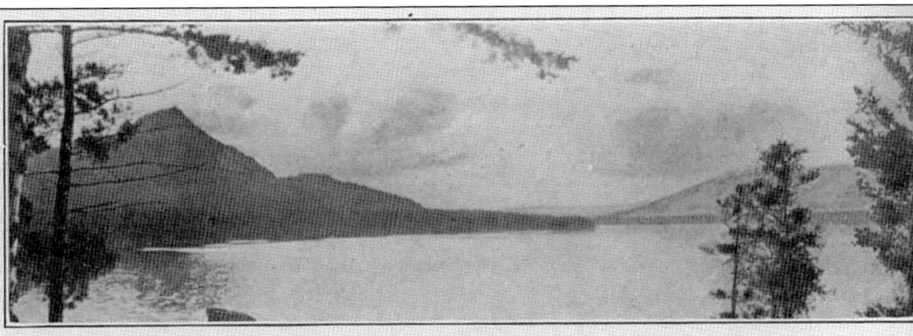

LAKE ONAWA

On Lake Onawa, called by many the most beautiful lake in Maine, are situated **ONAWA LAKE CAMPS**, formerly Young & Buxtons but now under new management. Onawa, one of the original Landlocked Salmon lakes of the State, is entirely surrounded by mountains and was screened a year ago and is now showing wonderful fishing. The camps have been completely refurnished with new beds and running water and new boats provided. A fine sand beach for bathing. A beautiful place to spend your summer vacation and the hunter will here find large game in abundance. Terms and descriptive circulars sent on request.

ADDRESS

FROM Nov. 1 to June 1	FROM June 1 to Nov. 1
C. P. CLOUGH 123 Georgia, Ave., PROVIDENCE, R. I.	ONAWA LAKE CAMPS ONAWA, MAINE

Several establishments were located either on Lake Onawa or in the immediate vicinity. This is an advertisement from one of them, showing a beautiful view of the lake. Onawa is 4 miles long and 2 miles wide and is encircled by bluffs. It is a reliable trout and salmon lake. (From *In the Maine Woods*, 1927.)

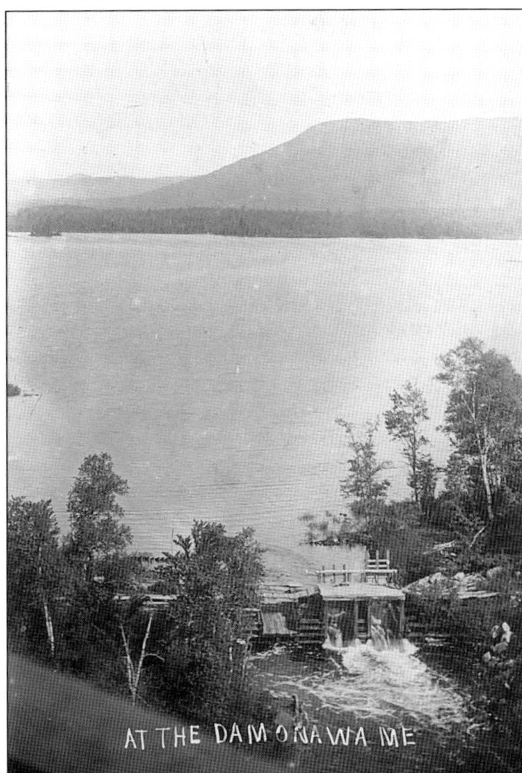

The dam shown here once existed at the outlet of Lake Onawa and the beginning of Ship Pond Stream, which flows from here into Sebec Lake. This photograph was taken from the Canadian Pacific Railroad trestle, which is 1,017 feet long and stands 138 feet above the stream.

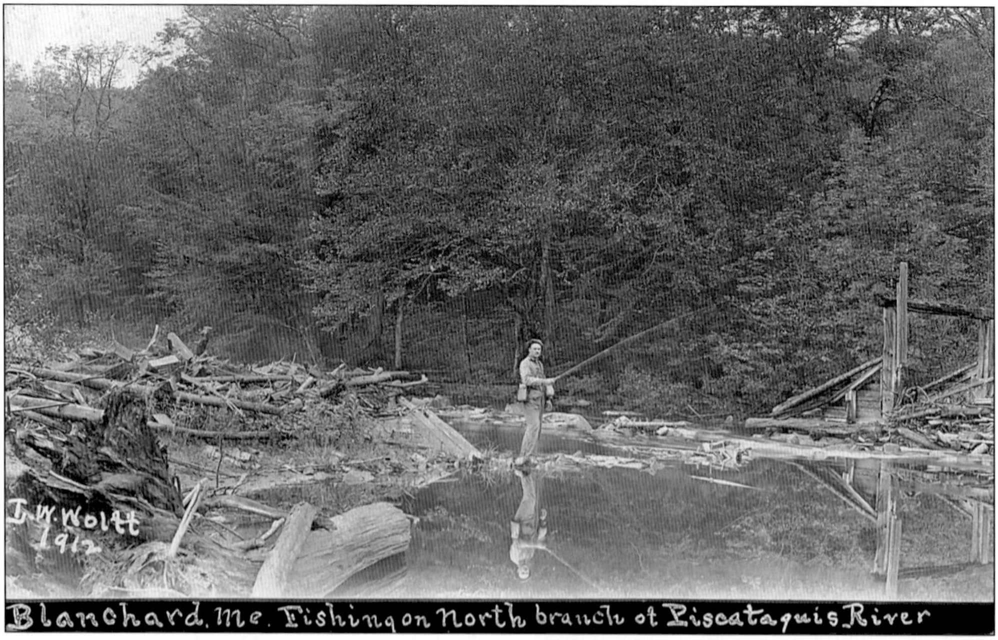

There are a number of small streams and rivers in the Monson region. The Piscataquis flows out of Shirley to the north and southeasterly into the Penobscot. There are many trout pools in these waters.

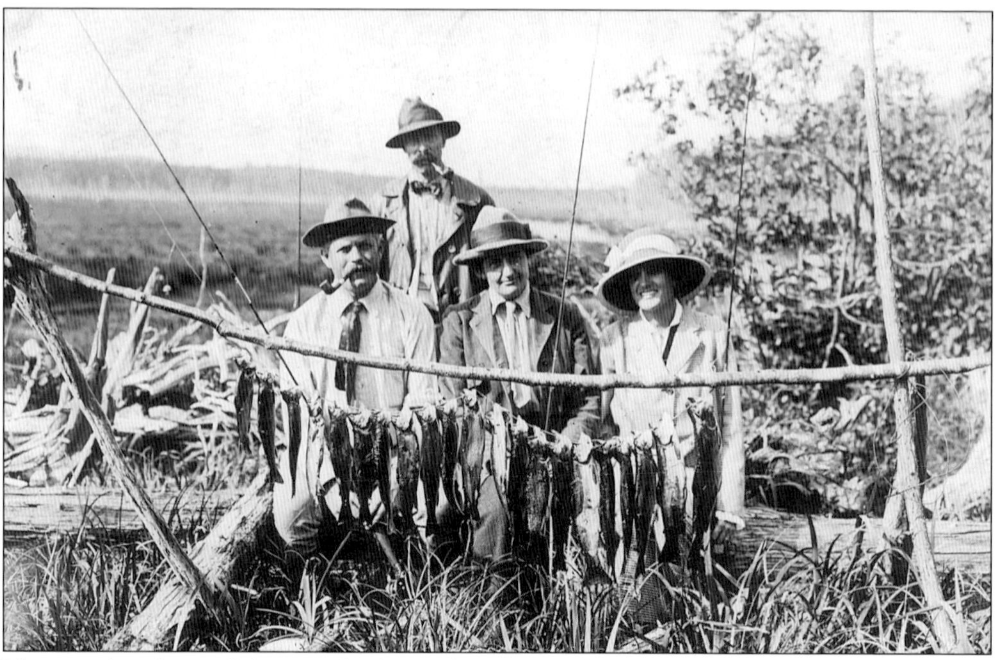

These anglers show off their catch of trout from one of the areas in the Monson region.

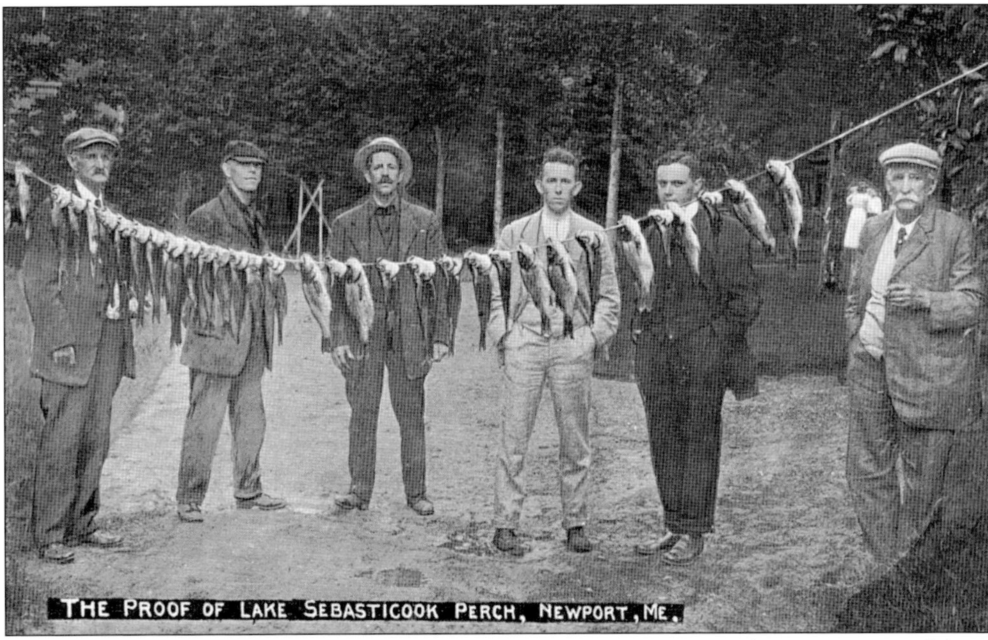

Before extensive pollution, Lake Sebasticook in Newport was a tremendous warm-water fishery, as these two photographs attest. Sporting camps provided accommodations, and access by rail was easy. Anglers were generally very successful.

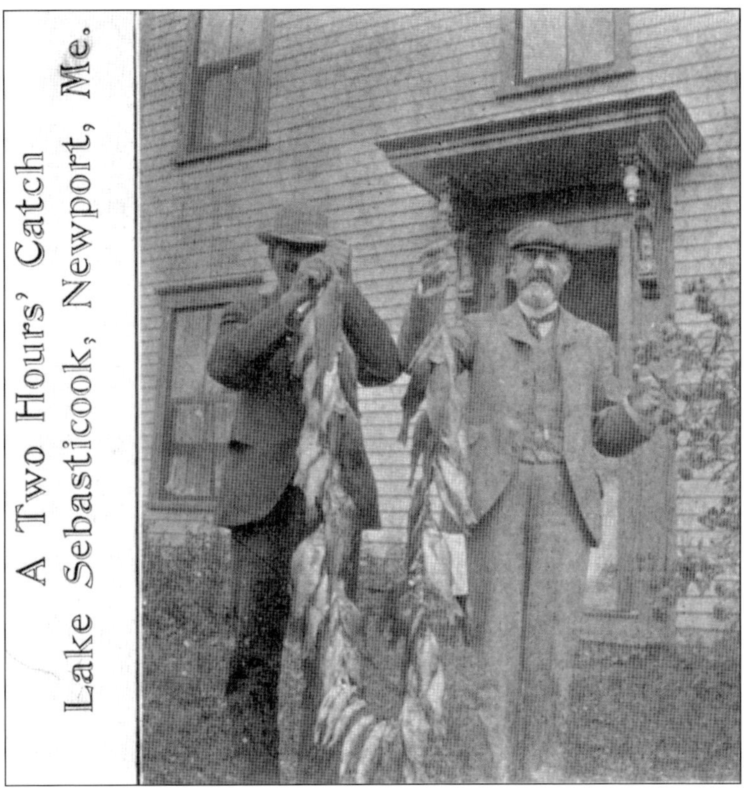

Two happy anglers pose in front of one of the establishments with their string of perch.

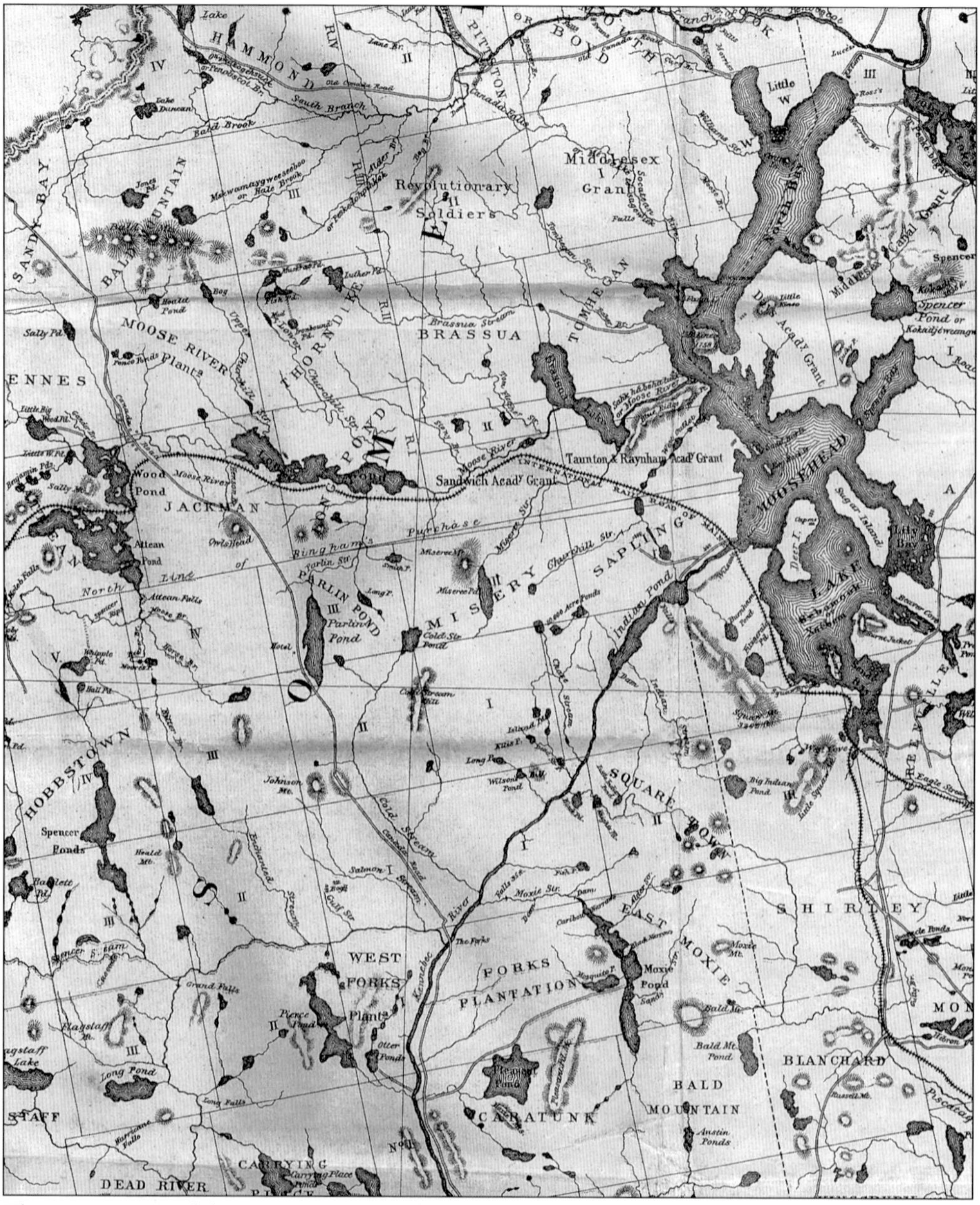

This is a section of the 1900 Lucius Hubbard map of northern Maine, depicting the upper end of the Kennebec River Valley.

Six

The Kennebec River Valley

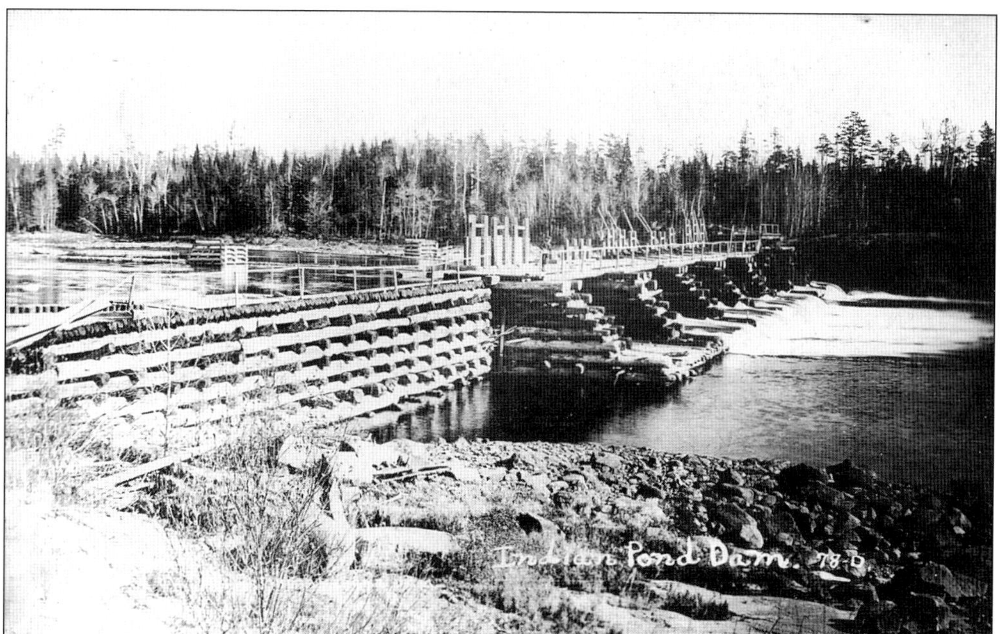

This image features the dam at Indian Pond, which was considerably upriver from where Harris Station, built in the early 1950s, is located today. Indian Pond was well known for togue as well as large and vigorous trout. Later, the Somerset Branch, or Kineo Branch, of the Maine Central Railroad passed not too far to the west.

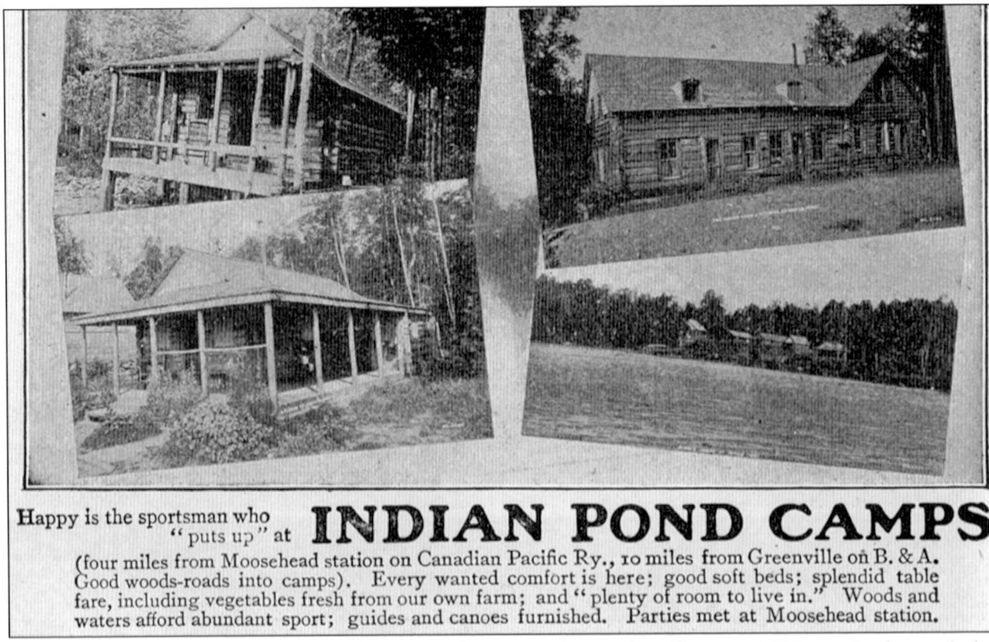

Located at the head end of Indian Pond, near where the East and West Outlets of the Kennebec River entered, Marr's Camps was a well-known and successful establishment until the mid-1950s, when the completion of Harris Station flooded the site. (From *In the Maine Woods*, 1907.)

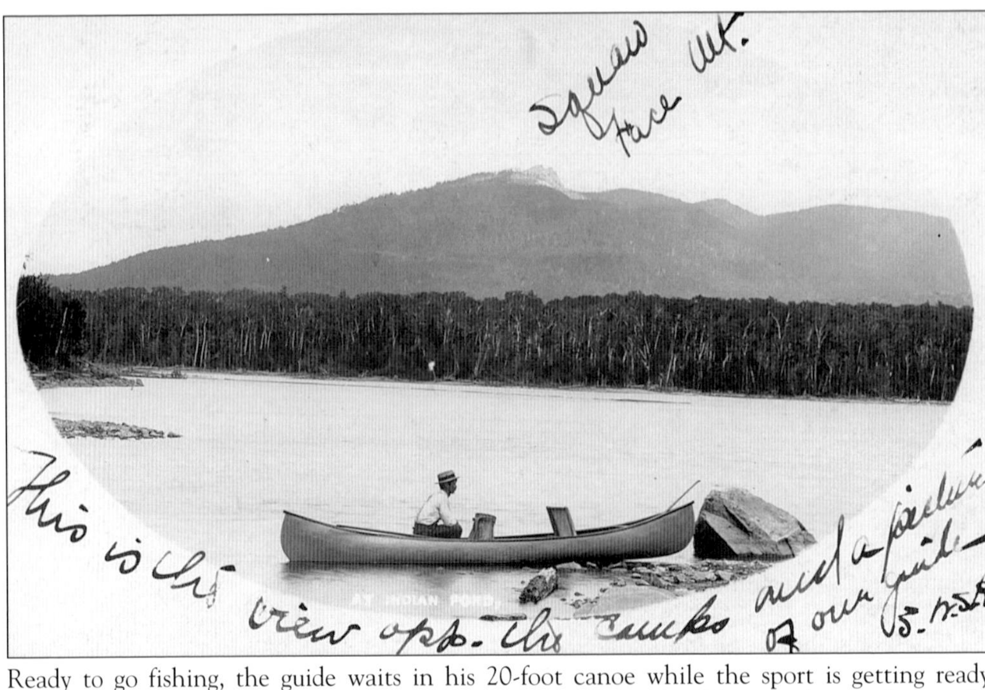

Ready to go fishing, the guide waits in his 20-foot canoe while the sport is getting ready, presumably having breakfast or lunch in Marr's dining room. The pond or either outlet could easily be fished from a canoe, and sometimes anglers poled the several miles upriver to Moosehead Lake for a day's fishing.

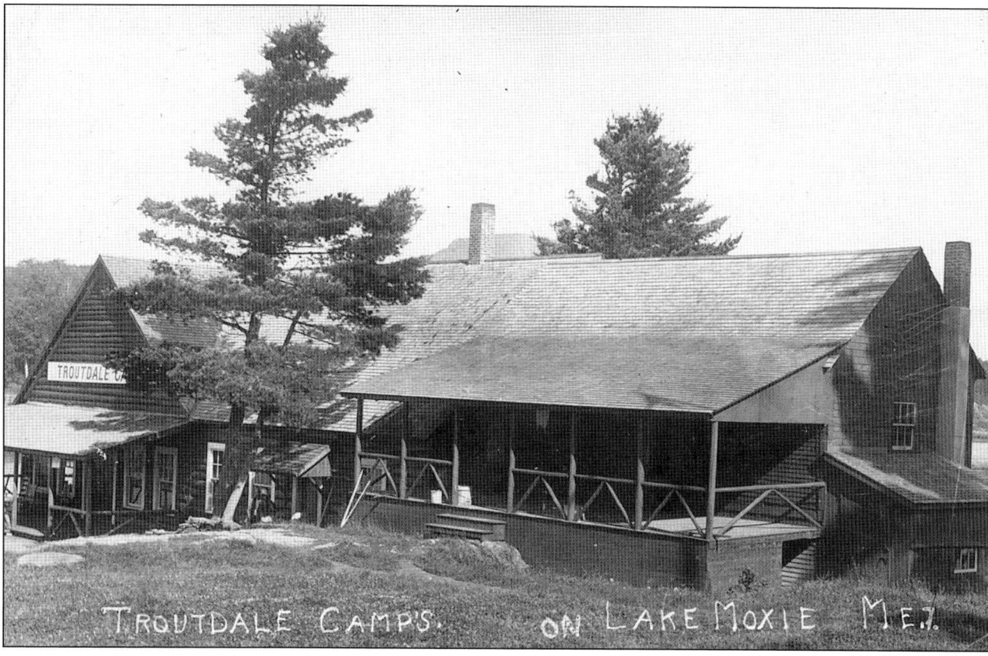

Farther down the line was Troutdale, a famous establishment on Lake Moxie. At that time, this area was serviced by the Maine Central Railroad line from Bingham or by a tote road running from Shirley Mills west to the Forks, crossing the dam at the outlet of Lake Moxie.

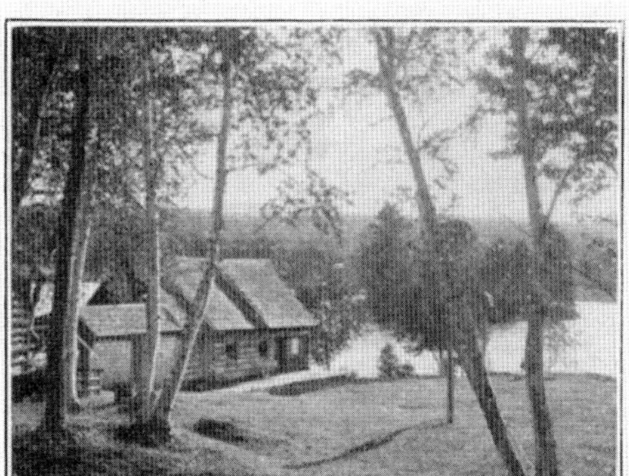

The Lodge at Troutdale Camps

TROUTDALE CAMPS

In the heart of the Kennebec Valley. Situated five miles from the end of the new road at Lake Moxie, but quickly reached in our own 'rail bus'. 1935 fishing the best in 10 years.

LOG CAMPS WITH BATH, HEAT AND ELECTRICITY

Away from the crowd.

Our cuisine is famous. Our own fresh milk, cream and vegetables. Fresh meats.

DEER, BEAR, PARTRIDGE

Hunting parties get their quota here. Ideal vacation facilities at moderate rates. Telephone and telegraph connection. Daily mail service. Free brooklet on request.

"IT'S DIFFERENT AT TROUTDALE"

Address Troutdale Camps

J. M. HARRIS, Prop. Troutdale, Maine

This advertisement for Troutdale Camps is from *In the Maine Woods*, 1936. Troutdale had its own railroad station, and the area was also known as Mosquito.

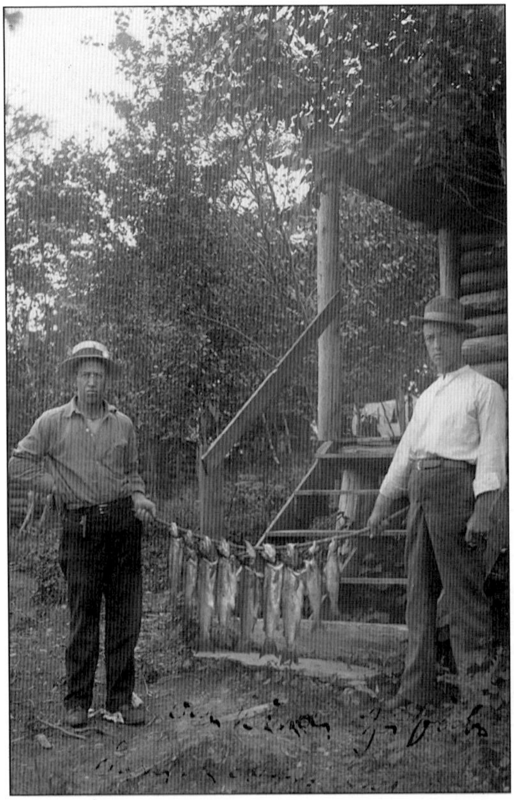

These anglers pose with a nice catch of trout from the Lake Moxie area. Moxie itself and its tributaries and outlying ponds and streams were well known for their abundance of decent-sized trout.

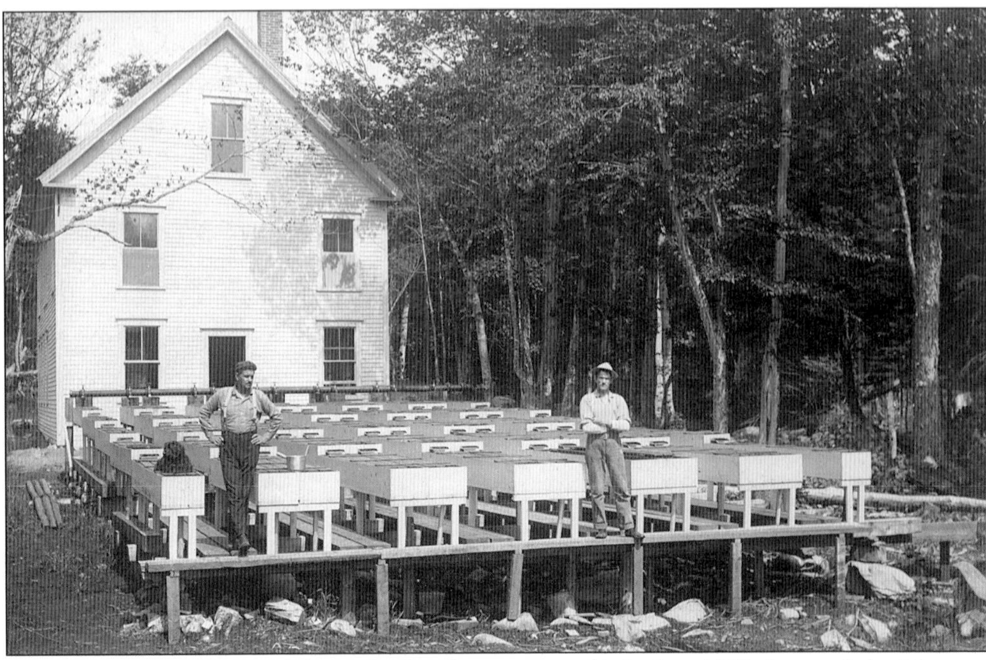

To support this wilderness fishery, this hatchery was established in 1907 close to Lake Moxie.

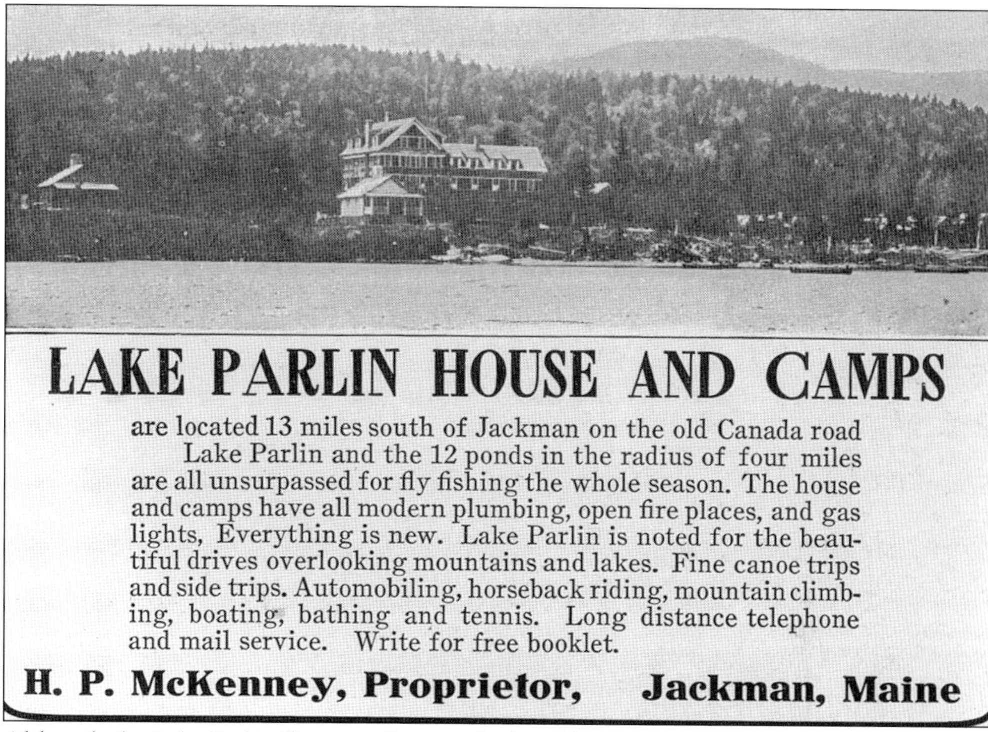

Although the Lake Parlin Camps still exist, the hotel has been taken down. New in 1909, the resort is situated approximately halfway between the Forks and Jackman, right on the Canada Road (now Route 201). This establishment was a central location to a great number of trout waters. Sizable trout were taken in this area on a regular basis for many years. (From *In the Maine Woods*, 1911.)

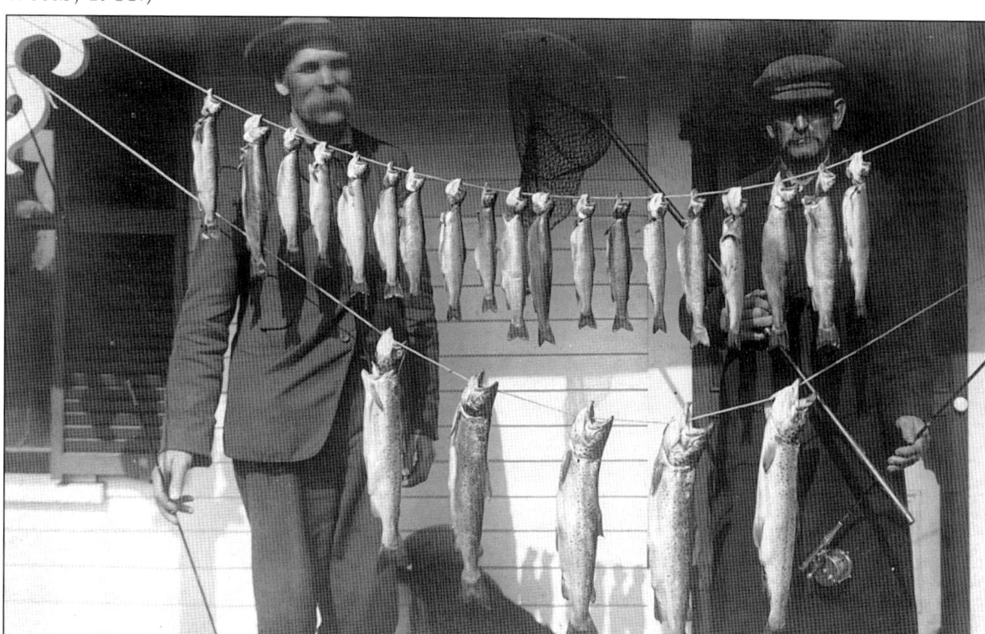

Two very successful anglers display their catch of brook trout and landlocked salmon.

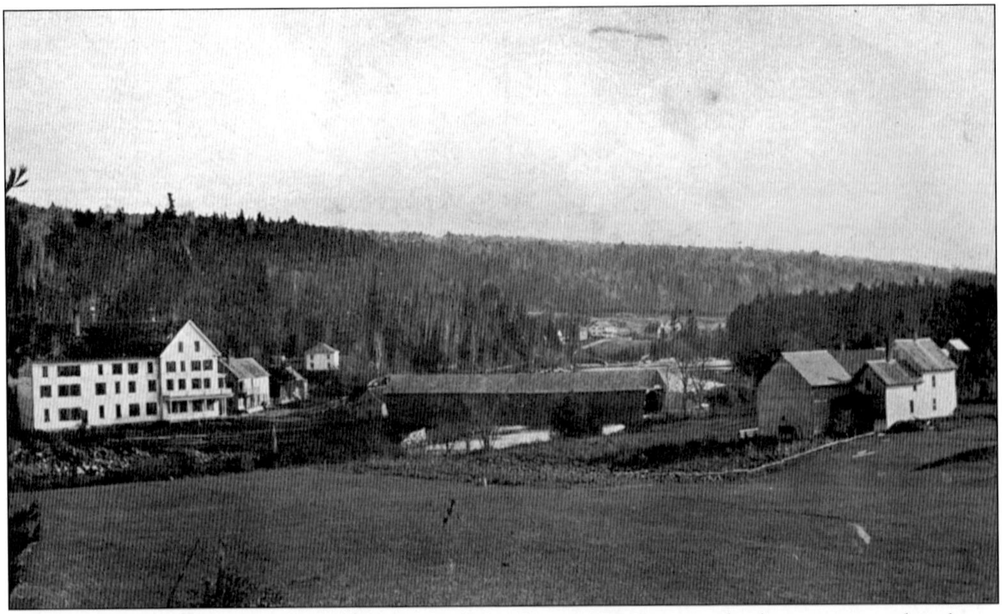

The Forks, named for the Dead River and the Kennebec River, which come together here, was a crossroads for travelers heading north. From here, there were two options to travel to Moosehead country, Flagstaff, Jackman, or Moxie. Literally hundreds of opportunities were available to the visitor here, and on almost any kind of water imaginable.

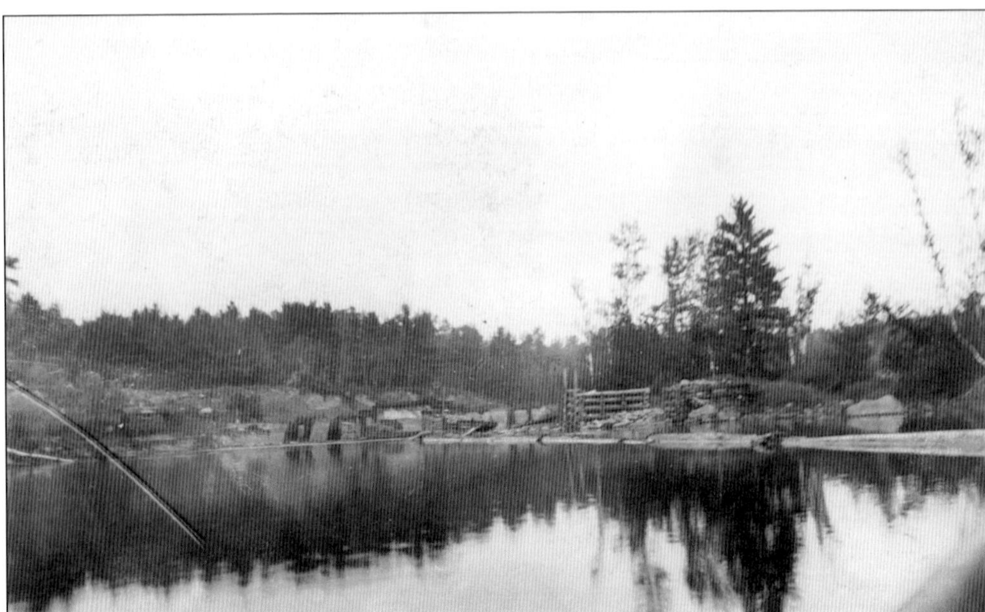

Shown is a dam on the Dead River, one of the major tributaries to the Kennebec. Following the Dead River upstream from the Forks brought the angler to a number of remote waters holding great numbers of large trout. The Dead River originates to the northwest, near the Canadian border.

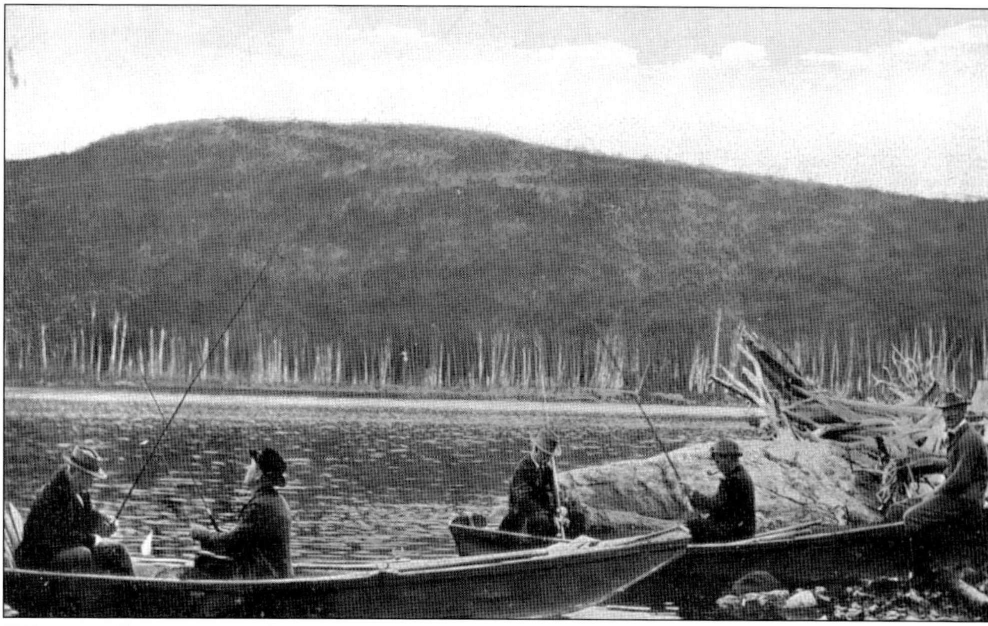

Whenever big trout are discussed, sooner or later someone mentions Pierce Pond. This water has long held a great reputation for both trout and salmon, with some very impressive fish being taken. Even today, many anglers eagerly await ice-out and others are challenged by reliable trout fishing in nearby ponds.

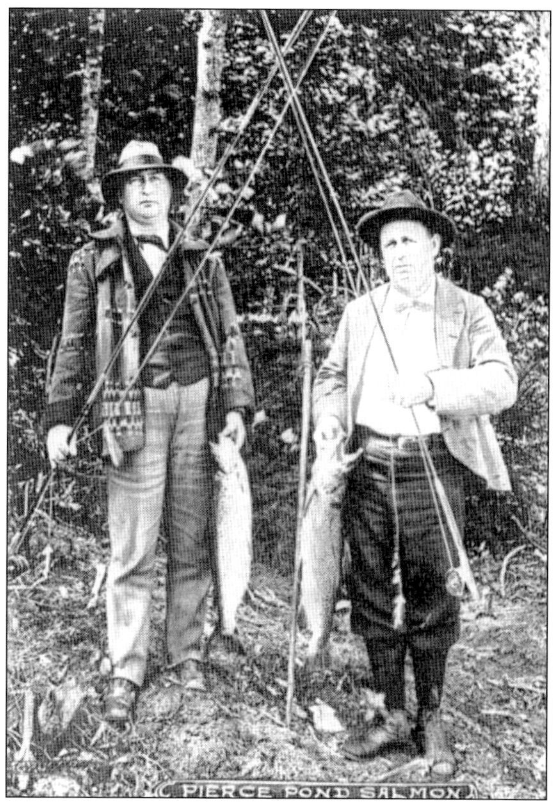

These two Pierce Pond salmon look to be in the 6- to 8-pound class.

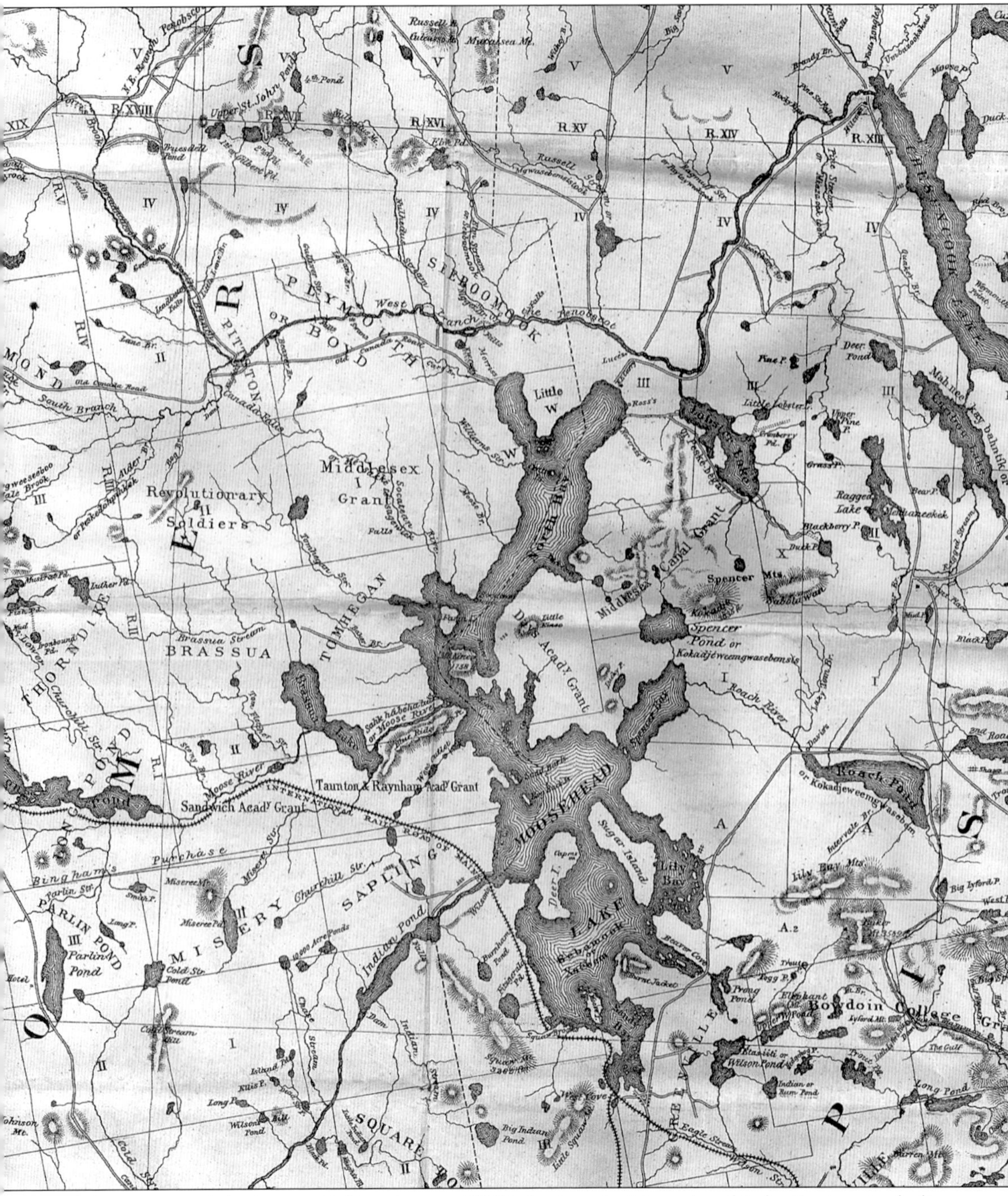

This portion of the Lucius Hubbard map of 1900 depicts the Moosehead Lake Region, including the Moose River drainage, the West Branch of the Penobscot and Roach River.

Seven

THE MOOSEHEAD LAKE REGION

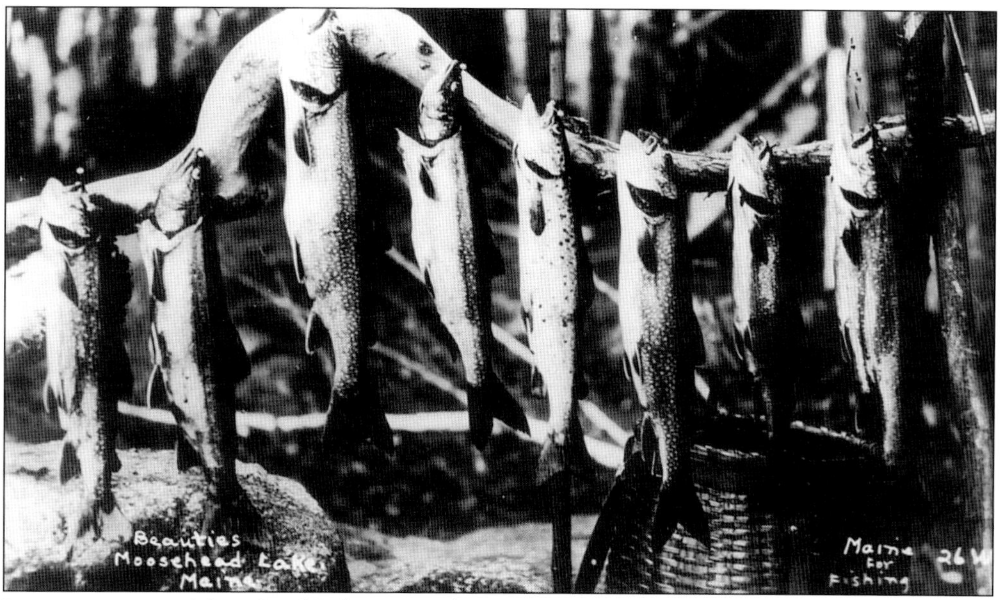

In some respects, Moosehead Lake meets the most exacting requirements of the nature-loving critic. It is the perfect field of the fly or bait angler, the deep-water fisherman, the genuine sportsman, or the lover of nature in pursuit of health and recreation. It is also the most famous outing resort within the entire Atlantic states' section of our country. As early as 1853, Moosehead Lake was visited by both James Russell Lowell and Henry David Thoreau. Moosehead cannot be compared with any other lake in New England or in the Atlantic states, for it is in a class by itself. In its extent, beauty, and diversity, in the landscape of forests and mountains that surrounds it, and in the lake itself with its islands, bays, and coves, Moosehead is easily beyond comparison. (From *In the Maine Woods*, 1907.)

Coburn Steamboat Company

U. S. MAIL STEAMERS

Moosehead Lake, Maine

STEAMERS:

"KATAHDIN"	"MOOSEHEAD"	"LOUISA"	"MARGUERITE"
"COMET"	"TWILIGHT"	"REINDEER"	"PRISCILLA"

First Class Passenger and Freight Service between GREENVILLE JUNCTION and DEER ISLAND (Capen's), Kineo Station, Kineo (Mt. Kineo House), Northeast Carry, Northwest Carry, Sugar Island and Lily Bay from opening until close of navigation. Direct connection made with B. & A. R. R. trains at Greenville Junction, and with Somerset Ry. trains at Kineo Station, where company has ferry service between Kineo Station, Rockwood, Kineo and West Outlet sporting camps.

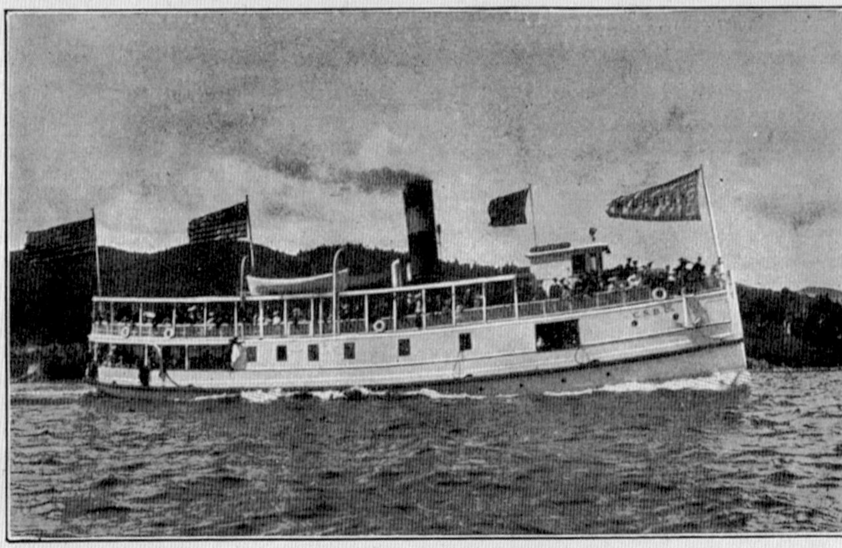

STEAMER "KATAHDIN"

Offices and Waiting Room on B. & A. R. R. Wharf at Greenville Junction, on Company's Wharf at Kineo, Ticket Offices at all regular landings

Parties wishing to remain over night at Greenville can take regular steamer leaving Greenville every morning (Sundays excepted) for Kineo and the head of the lake, returning same night. Regular Sunday boat during August and September leaving Greenville in morning for head of lake, returning same night.

The elegant steamer "**Katahdin**" (licensed for 600 passengers) can be chartered for Excursion Parties, and special boats for Fishing or Pleasure Parties can be secured at any time.

Coburn steamships, which sailed Moosehead for many years, took people from the railroad stations to their destinations at various camps and villages. One, the *Katahdin*, remains to take sightseers around the lake. (From *In the Maine Woods*, 1908.)

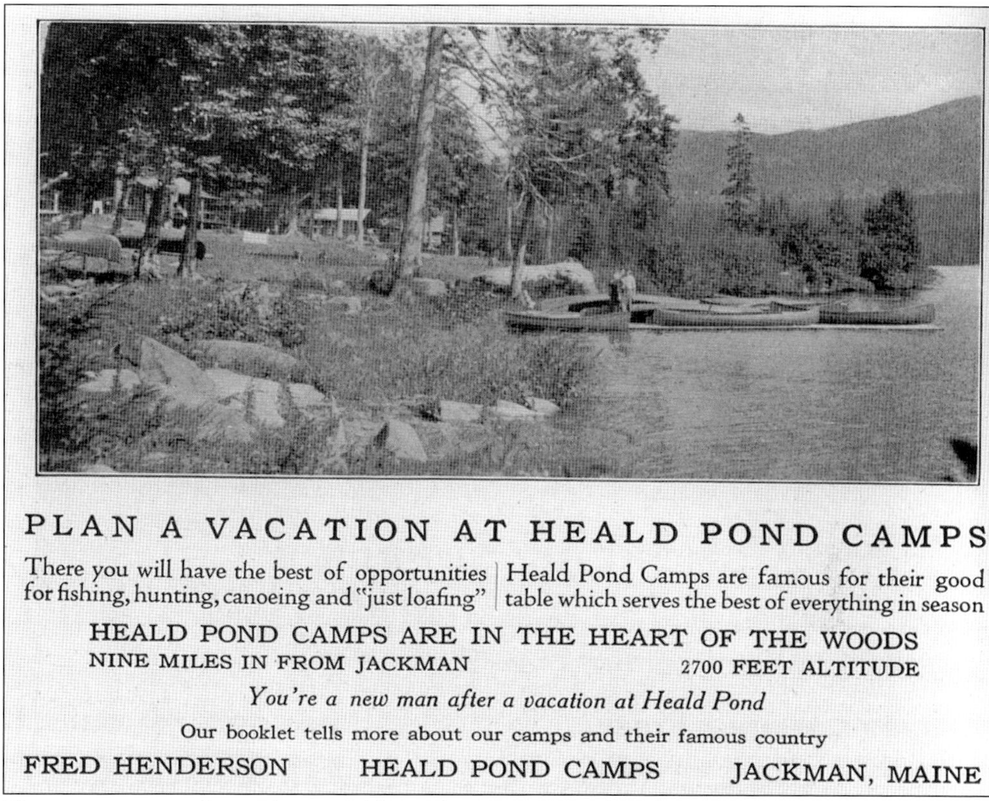

These camps were located on Heald Pond, just north and east of Jackman. (From *In the Maine Woods*, 1918.)

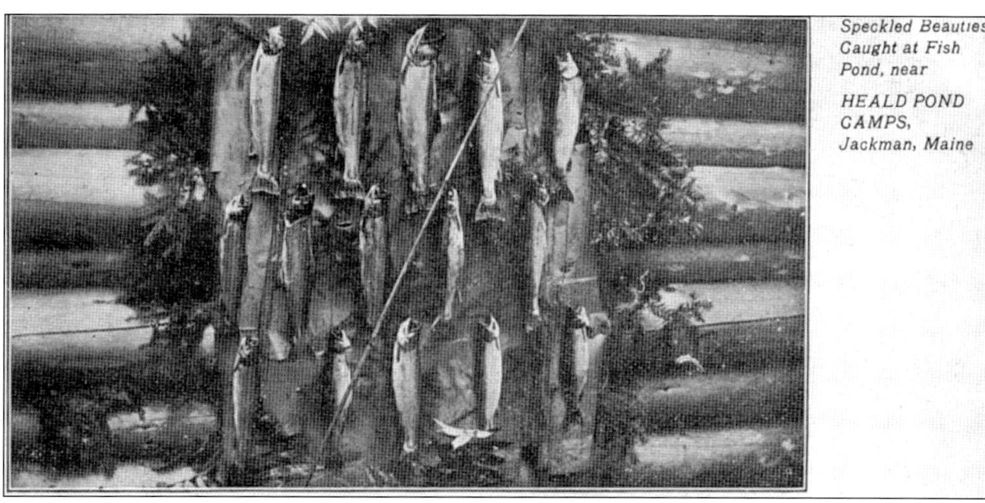

Here is an example of native brook trout found in Heald Pond and nearby waters. This area long enjoyed a good reputation for being consistent in producing large catches of decent-sized trout.

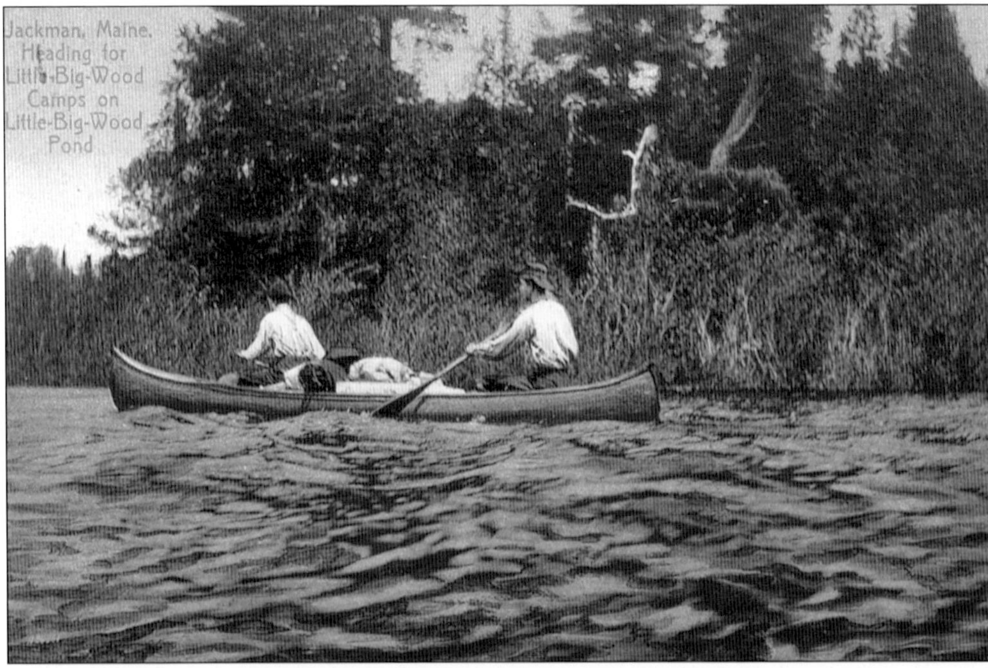

West of Jackman is the Big Wood Pond country, much of which even today requires transportation other than by vehicle. Here, two anglers paddle their 20-foot canoe loaded with gear from the railhead to the camps on Little Big Wood Pond.

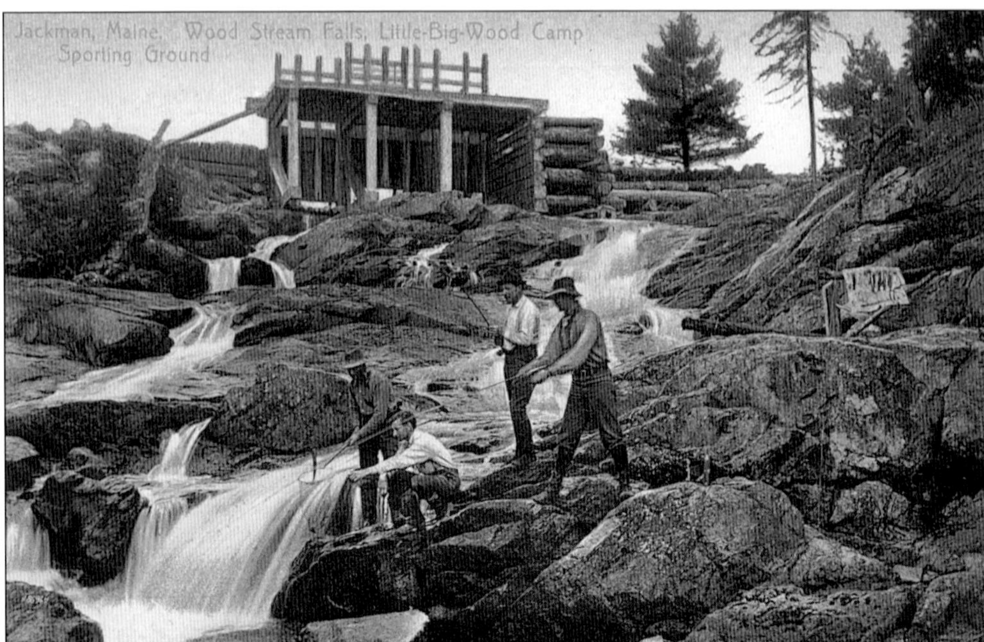

Anglers try their luck below the driving dam on Wood Stream. These dams provided excellent habitat and conditions for trout, and usually the waters nearby produced plenty of action for the angler.

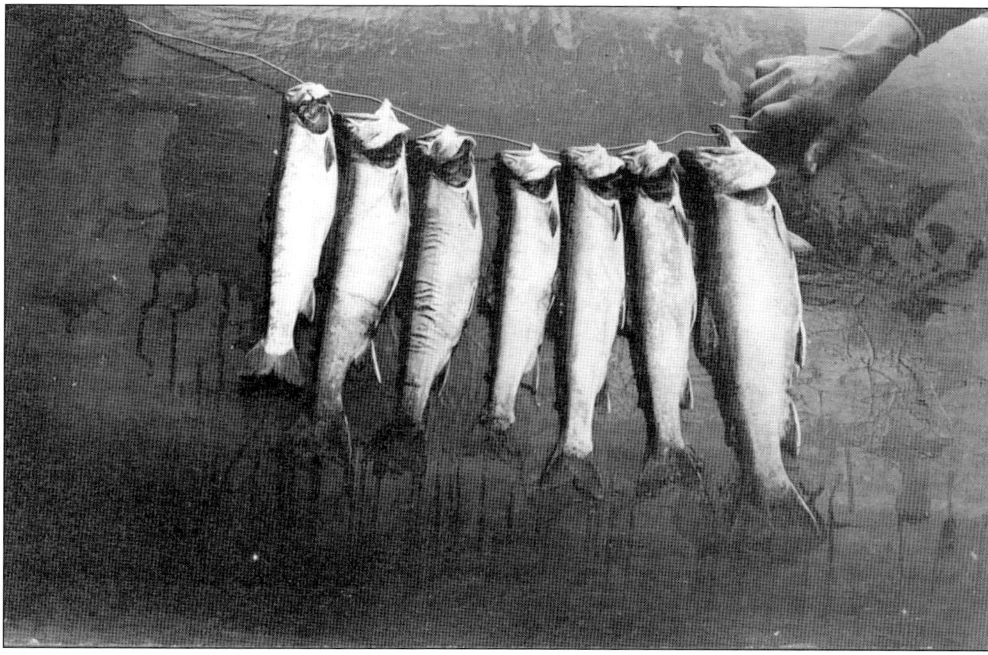

This nice string of native brook trout was taken from the waters near Holeb. The immediate area is the location of the famous Moose River Bow trip, so popular with canoeists today. By embarking the train at Holeb, the traveler has 70 miles of Moose River to follow to Moosehead Lake, with plenty of fishing along the way.

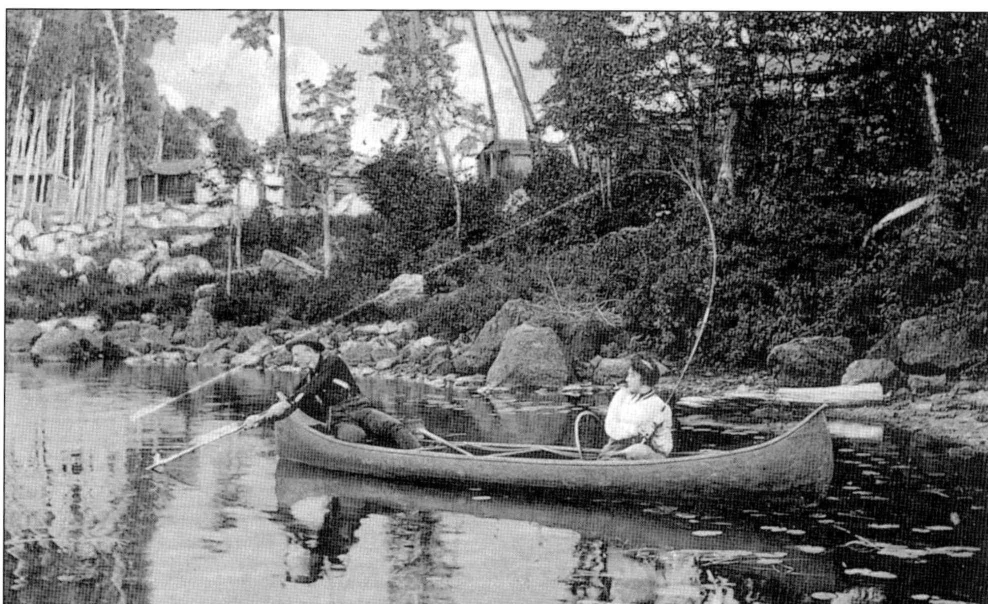

Here, the guide gets ready to net a fish for a lady angler. The two are fishing from a 20-foot canoe immediately in front of the Attean Camps, a popular spot.

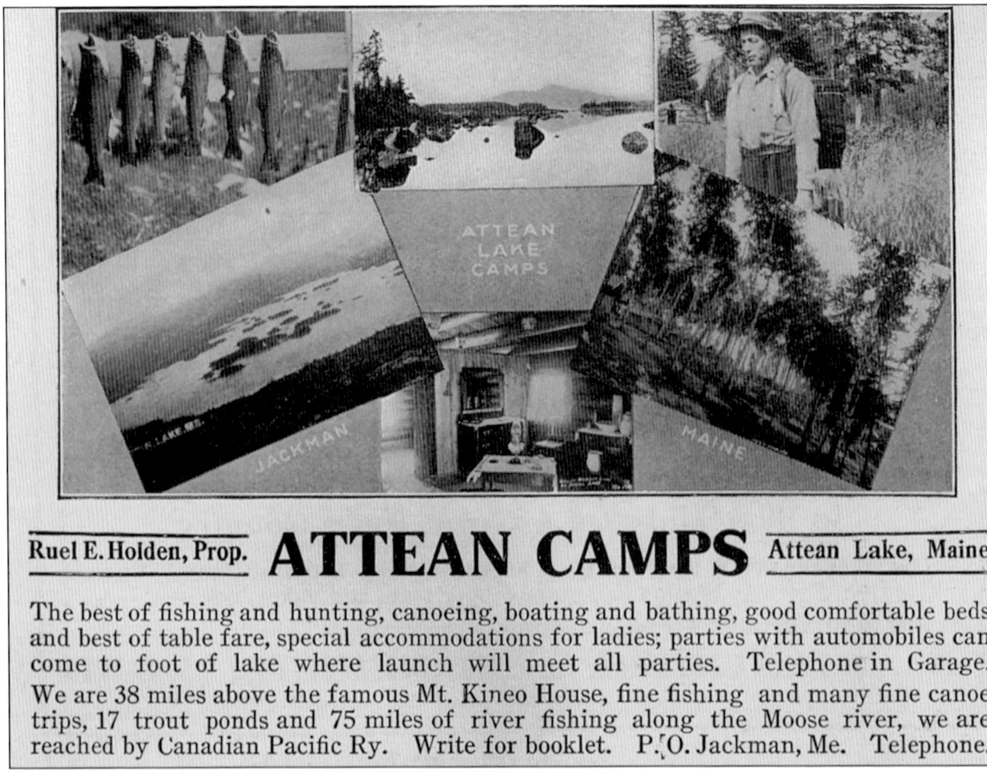

Attean Camps, located on Attean Pond, just east of Holeb and west of Jackman, were for years a popular location. This area is the upper end of Moose River, near the Canadian Border. (From *In the Maine Woods*, 1916.)

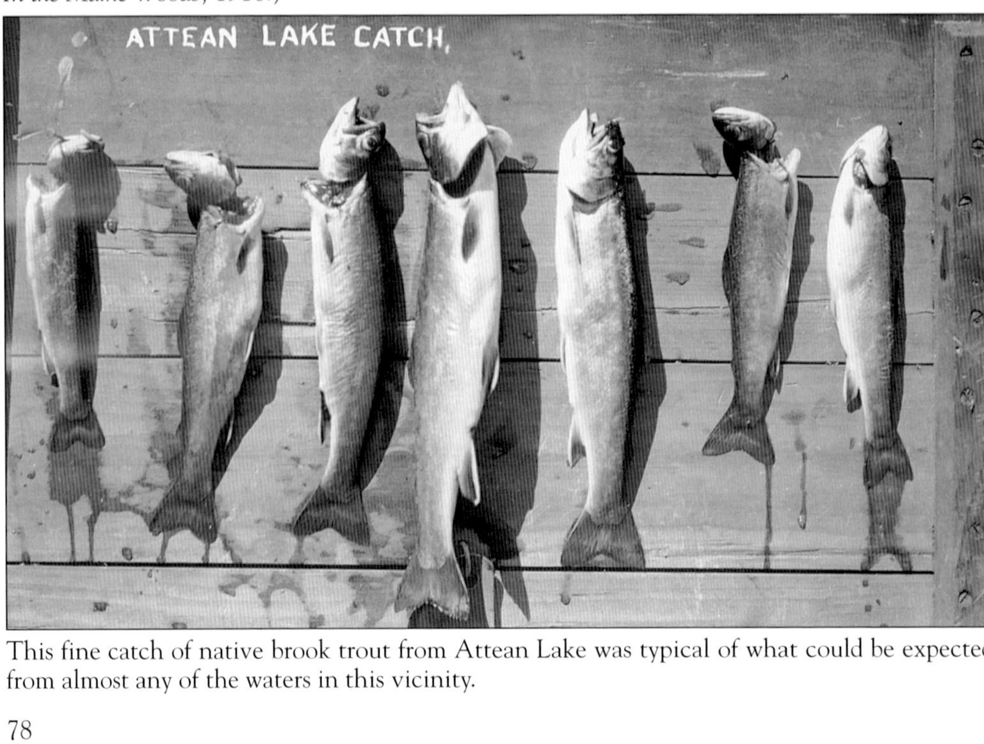

This fine catch of native brook trout from Attean Lake was typical of what could be expected from almost any of the waters in this vicinity.

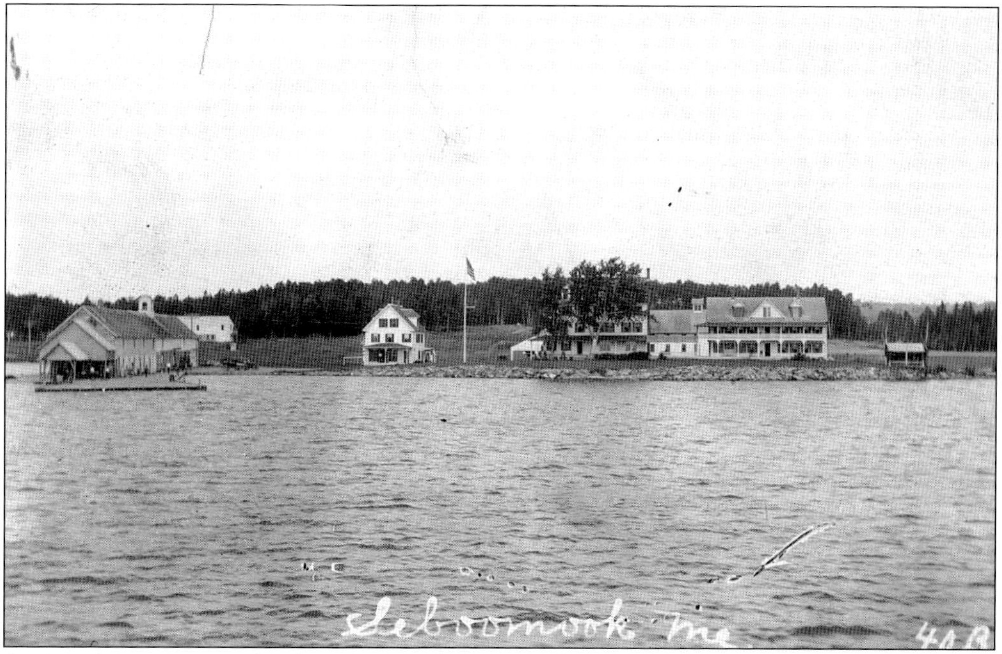

At Northwest Carry, also known as Seboomook, stood the Northwest Inn, a magnificent establishment at the head of Moosehead Lake. To the left was a major docking facility, adequate to handle even the largest steamers on the lake.

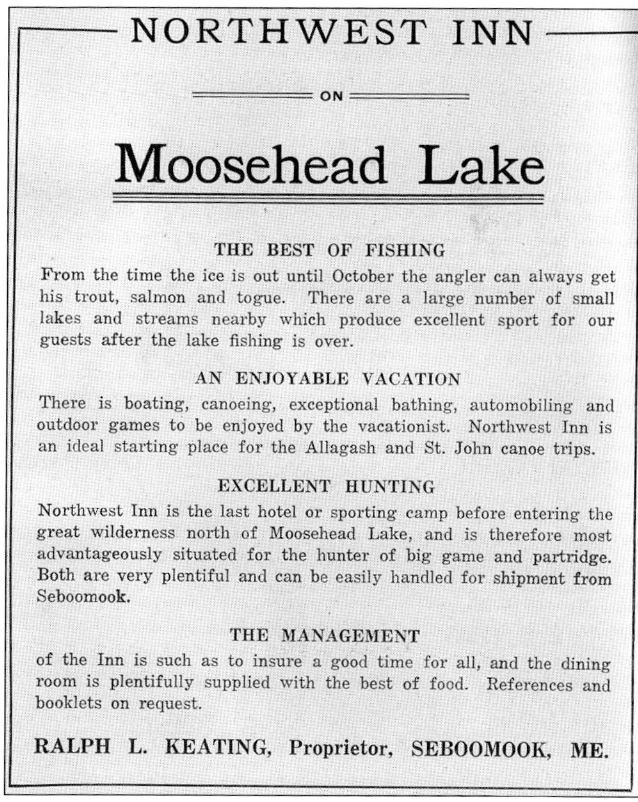

NORTHWEST INN

ON

Moosehead Lake

THE BEST OF FISHING

From the time the ice is out until October the angler can always get his trout, salmon and togue. There are a large number of small lakes and streams nearby which produce excellent sport for our guests after the lake fishing is over.

AN ENJOYABLE VACATION

There is boating, canoeing, exceptional bathing, automobiling and outdoor games to be enjoyed by the vacationist. Northwest Inn is an ideal starting place for the Allagash and St. John canoe trips.

EXCELLENT HUNTING

Northwest Inn is the last hotel or sporting camp before entering the great wilderness north of Moosehead Lake, and is therefore most advantageously situated for the hunter of big game and partridge. Both are very plentiful and can be easily handled for shipment from Seboomook.

THE MANAGEMENT

of the Inn is such as to insure a good time for all, and the dining room is plentifully supplied with the best of food. References and booklets on request.

RALPH L. KEATING, Proprietor, SEBOOMOOK, ME.

Known for its good food and magnificent views, the operation continued from 1849 until the spring of 1943, when it burned to the ground. (From *In the Maine Woods*, 1922.)

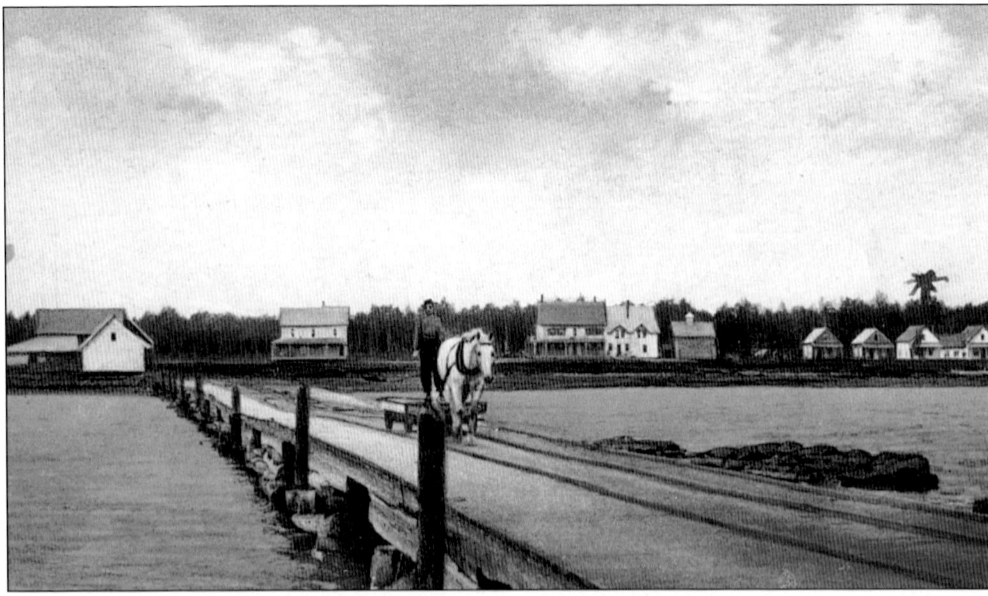

At Northeast Carry there was another large establishment, known for many years as the Winnegarnock. This was a popular stopover for travelers going across the carry to journey down the west branch of the Penobscot, just a couple of miles away. The long pier was used by steamers to off-load canoes and duffel for travelers taking the Allagash trip and starting from Moosehead. The pier shown here contained a set of railroad tracks.

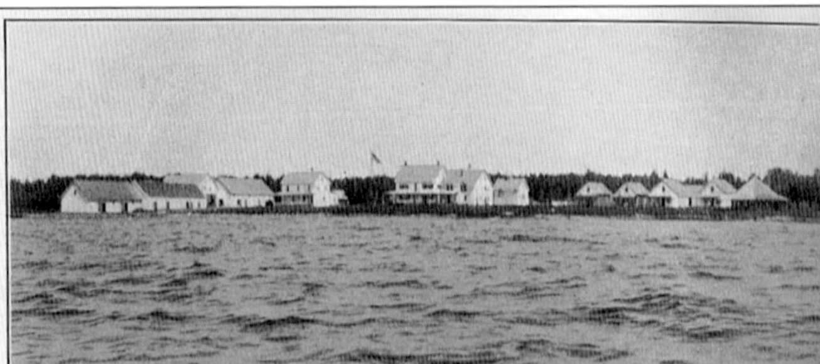

NORTHEAST CARRY—MOOSEHEAD LAKE

IS A

RESORT OF NATIONAL FAME

FOR CANOEISTS

Northeast Carry is the starting point for the famous Allagash and West Branch canoe trips. We make all arrangements for these trips. Write us and we'll have guides, canoes, camping outfit and provisions ready for the day you designate.

FOR THE SPORTSMEN

Northeast Carry is in the center of one of the biggest fish and game sections of the Maine woods. Besides Moosehead Lake, nearby are Lobster Lake, Russell Stream and numerous other fishing waters. If you want good deer hunting, come to Northeast Carry.

Seboomook Lodge, five miles up the picturesque West Branch by canoe or motorboat, is an attractive spot for private parties. Comfortable sleeping camps and a kitchen camp ready to use.

FOR THE VACATIONIST

Men and women seeking a delightful resort for their vacation can find no more attractive spot than Northeast Carry. Exceptionally good table, separate cabins, a central assembly cabin and up-to-date service are some of the attractions offered in addition to the natural charms of the Northeast Carry country.

Our booklet gives full information

THE WINNEGARNOCK, Northeast Carry, Maine

T. B. SNOW, Manager

The view in this advertisement shows the extent of this establishment. Even though at a remote location, accessible only by water until after 1919 when the Great Northern Paper Company began a road into this area from Rockwood, the resort offered much to the sportsman, or the vacationist. (From *In the Maine Woods*, 1918.)

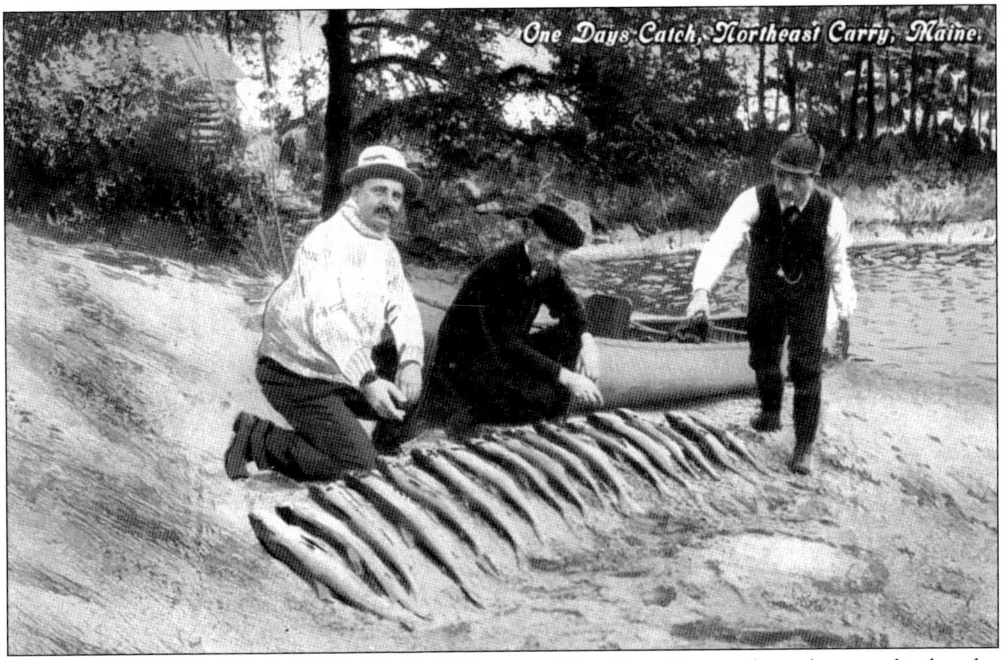

Here is an example of the fish taken from this part of the lake. The guide and sports display the day's catch.

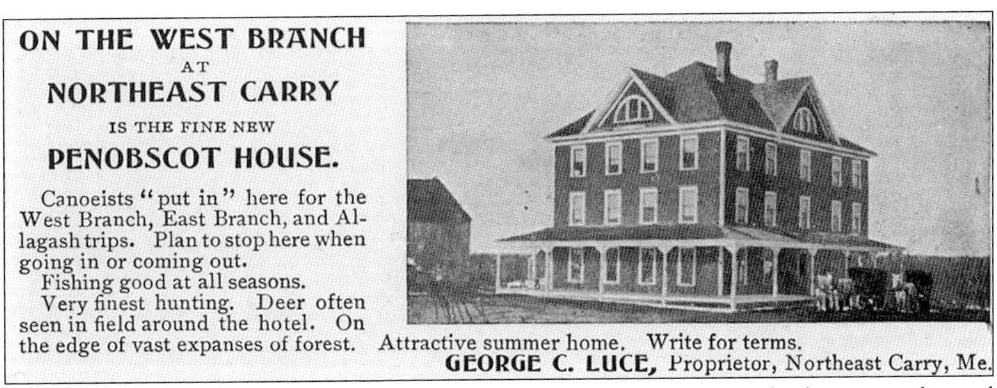

Located on the west branch was the Penobscot House, new *c.* 1900. The house was located at the north end of the carry near the bank of the river and was a convenient stopover for travelers on the river or those crossing the carry, "going in or coming out." (From *In the Maine Woods*, 1900.)

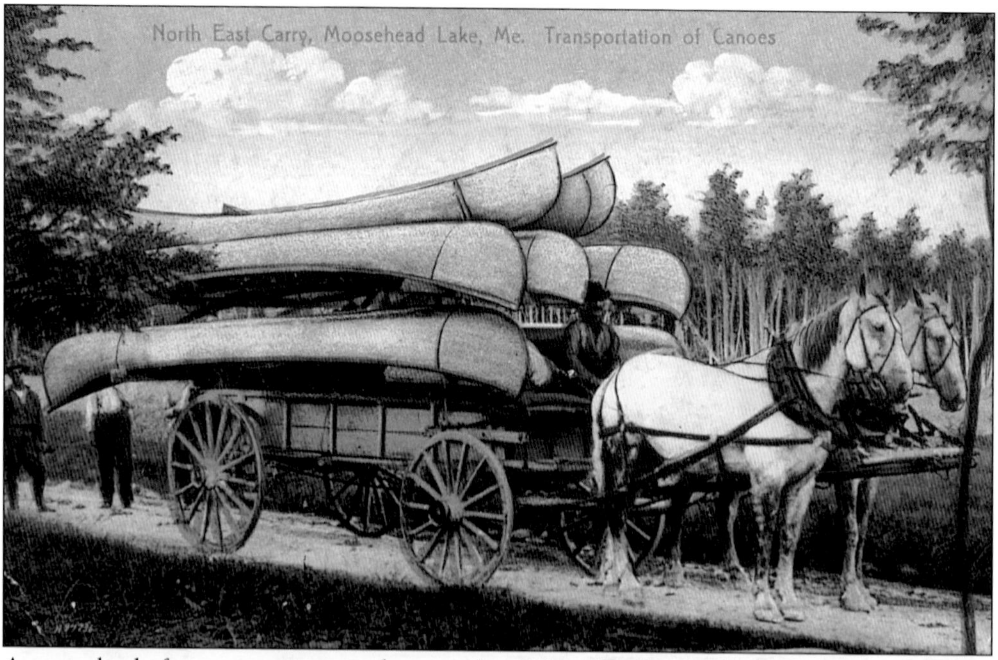

A wagonload of canoes goes across the carry from Moosehead Lake to the West Branch of the Penobscot River. For a modest fee, the transportation took the traveler from one body of water to the other. This was the usual accommodation on many carries throughout the north woods. This carry replaced an ox railroad that moved men and materials from Moosehead Lake to the west branch, or vice versa.

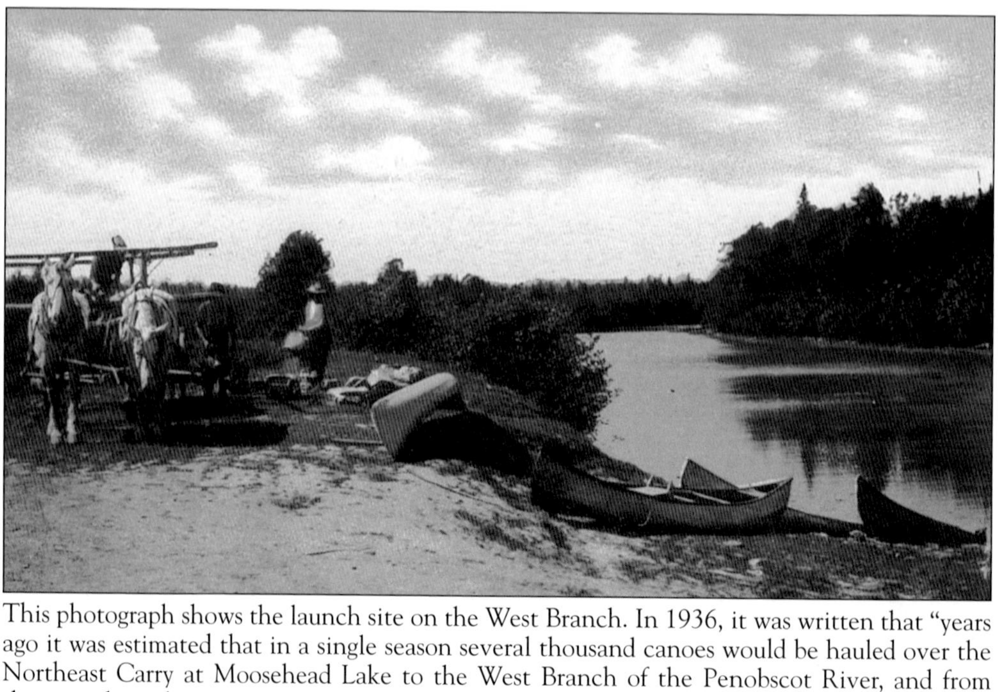

This photograph shows the launch site on the West Branch. In 1936, it was written that "years ago it was estimated that in a single season several thousand canoes would be hauled over the Northeast Carry at Moosehead Lake to the West Branch of the Penobscot River, and from there go their chosen journey through the network of waters, comprised in the Maine woods. The heyday of the canoeing era was *c.* 1909." (From *In the Maine Woods*, 1936.)

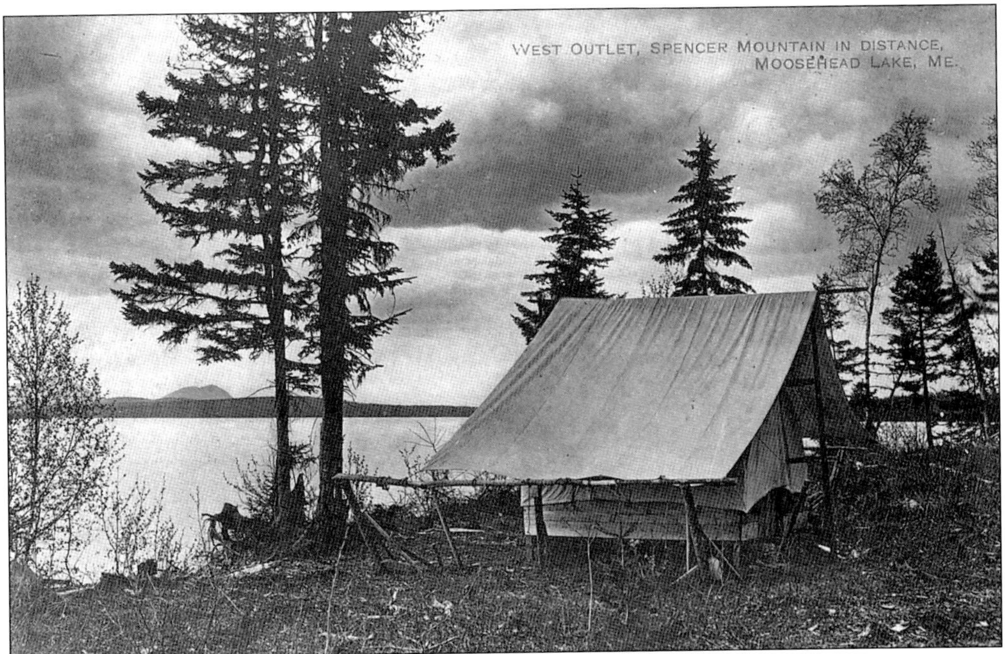

At the West Outlet of the Kennebec River on Moosehead Lake was a set of camps with a popular tenting area. This view is from that location looking nearly east toward Spencer Bay.

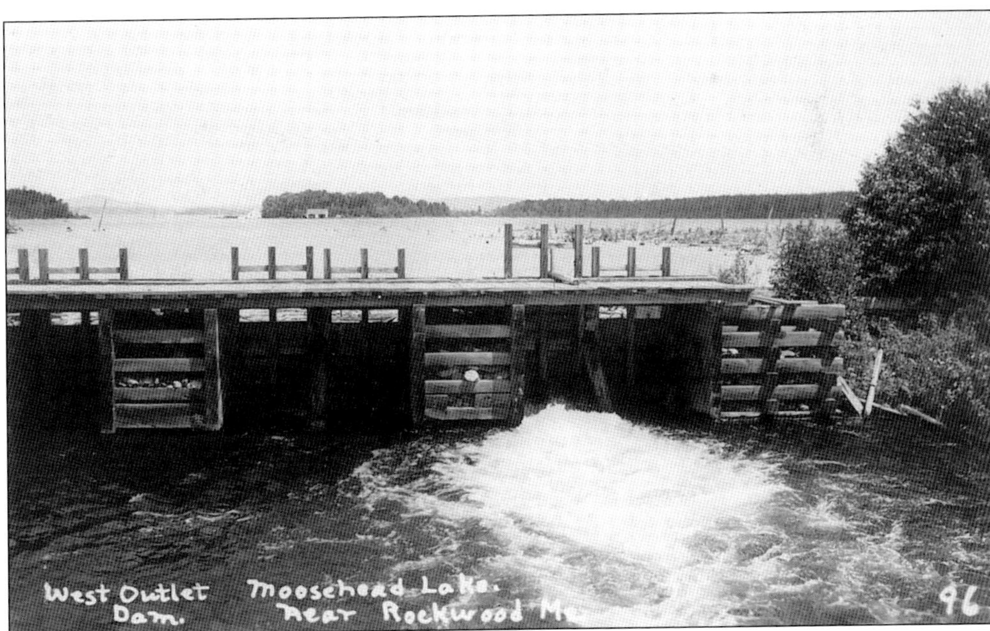

This dam at the West Outlet, which was replaced with a concrete and steel structure *c.* 1934, has always been a popular fishing site. The background is Barrows Cove, and the island at the center of the photograph is the site of the West Outlet Camps.

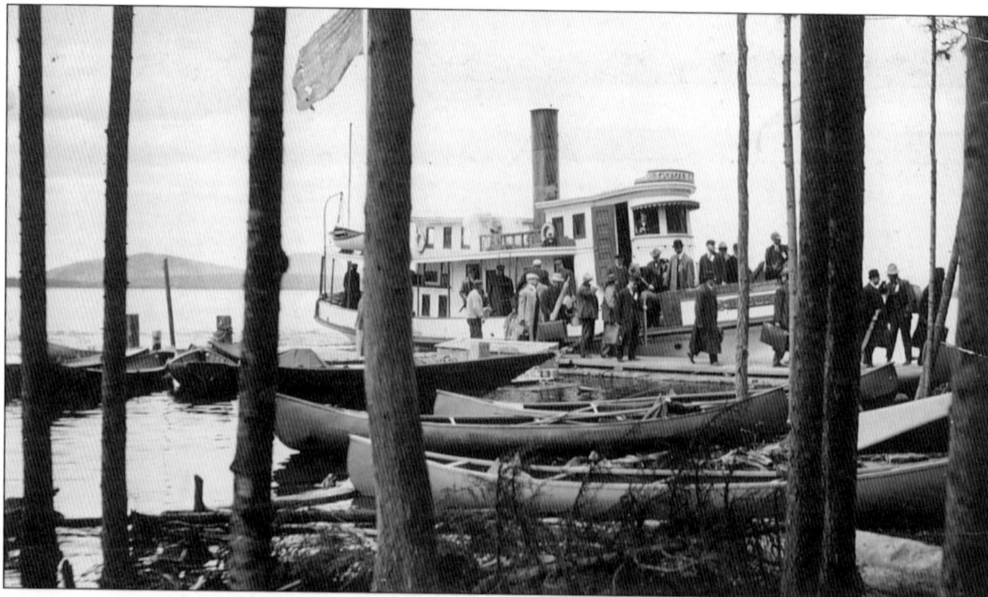

There is a lot of activity at West Outlet Camps as the steamer *Louisa* drops off a party who probably arrived at the lake by train, landing either at Rockwood or Greenville. Note the variety of boats and canoes; the one in the center is a bateaux.

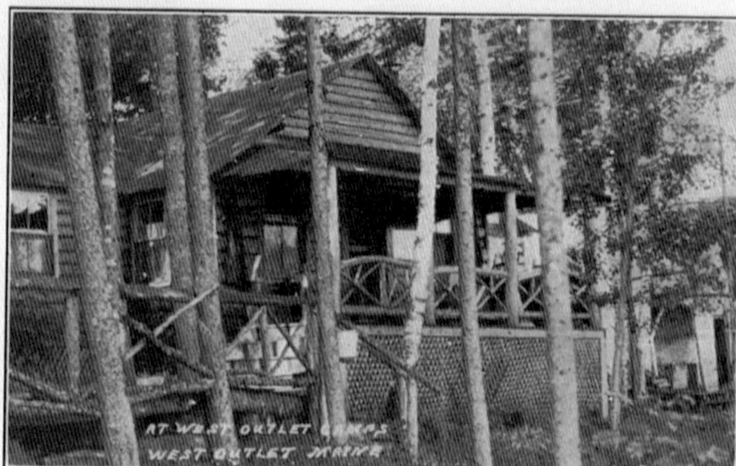

West Outlet Camps

All the conveniences of the city in the heart of the big woods

SITUATED on the shores of Moosehead Lake with a magnificent combination of lake and mountain view, visible from every part of the grounds, are grouped twenty log cabins, each one large enough to house a family comfortably, having two and three sleeping rooms, living room and bath room, with modern plumbing and a continuous supply of hot and cold running water. Electric lights in every building. A large main camp contains dining room to accommodate 100, a comfortable meeting room with fireplace, a library containing 1000 volumes, piano, victrola. The dining room service and foods need no praise from me here as W. O. C. became famous by attending properly to having the best foods procurable, cooked properly. Best Trout and Salmon fishing and ideal vacation conditions. Reached via B. & A. Railroad to Greenville Jct., thence by steamer to camp. Or by Maine Central Ry. to Kineo Station, all trains being met by launch. ***Descriptive booklet on request.***

FRANK A. MacKENZIE, Proprietor - - West Outlet, Maine

An advertisement for West Outlet Camps shows one of the typical cabins and describes the establishment. (From *In the Maine Woods*, 1930.)

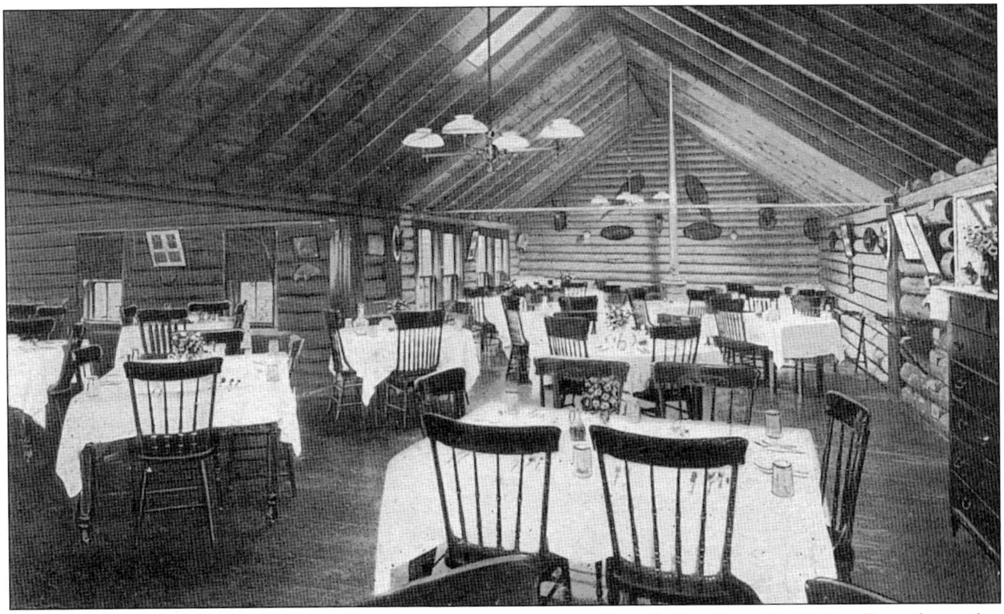

The dining room at West Outlet Camps is an example of the fine facilities found at the large establishments. In these dining rooms, arrangements were semiformal, patrons generally dressed for dinner, and the menus offered a variety of choices. It was common for patrons other than guests to dine at these locations, since restaurants were a rare entity except in the villages. A support staff of cooks and waitresses was necessary to service these facilities. Dining facilities became less popular after the 1950s as resorts in general converted to housekeeping accommodations.

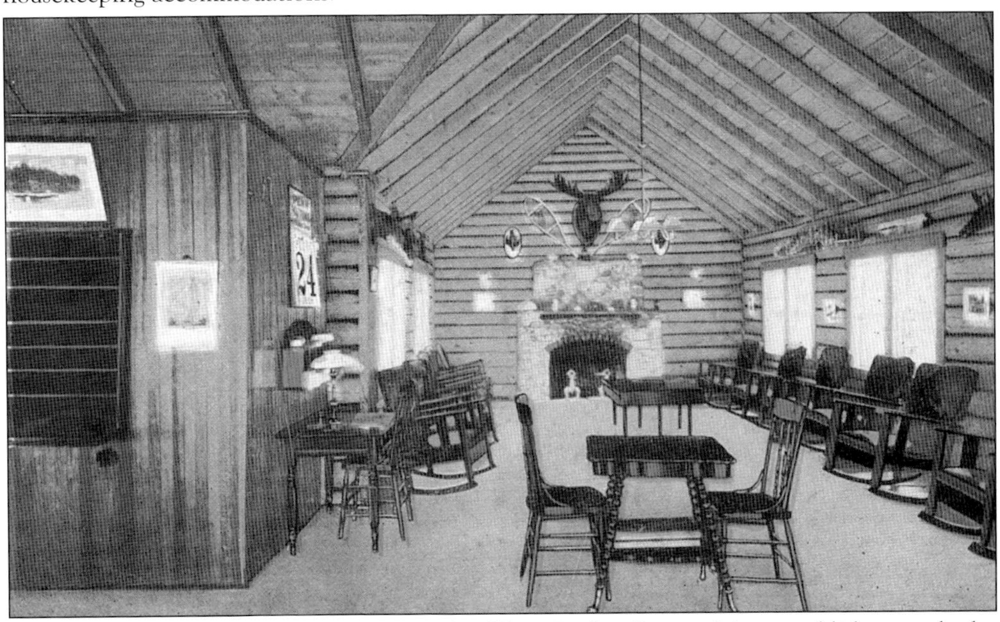

This is the office and relaxation area at the West Outlet Camps. Most establishments had a guide's room or a place where folks could gather after dinner to swap stories of the day's fishing, tell tall tales, and play games; cribbage and forty-five were the most popular. Probably more big fish were caught here than on the lake.

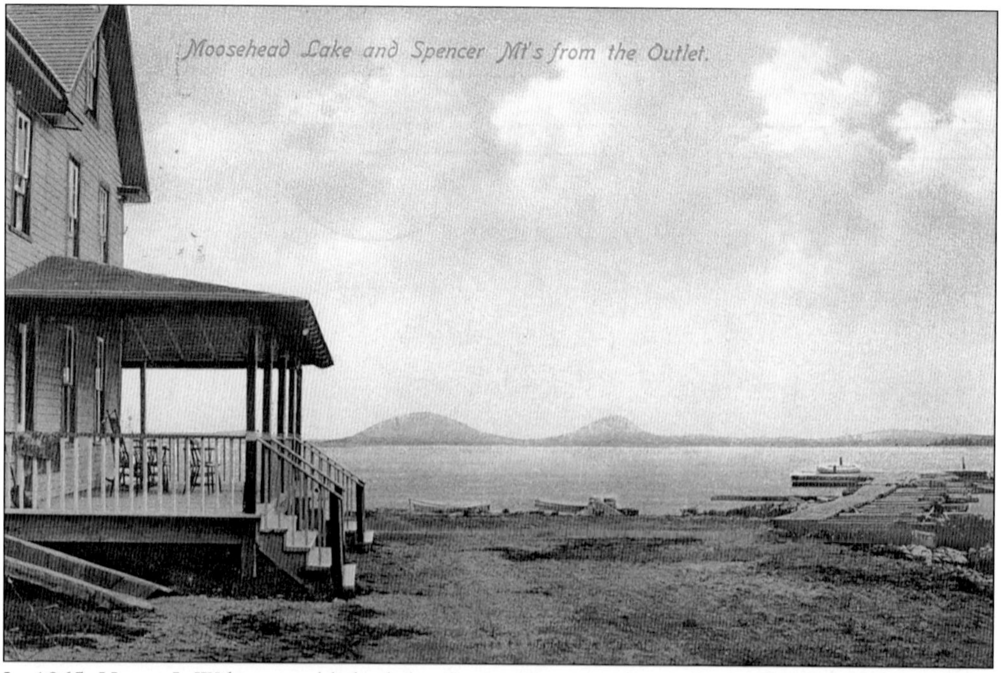

In 1865, Henry I. Wilson established the Outlet House and cottages at the East Outlet of the Kennebec River. The establishment later became known as Wilson's and operated through four generations until it was sold in 1974. The complex was once 40 buildings with a 60-seat dining room and a staff of guides. This photograph shows the view across the widest part of the lake. Some 20 miles separate this spot from the mountains.

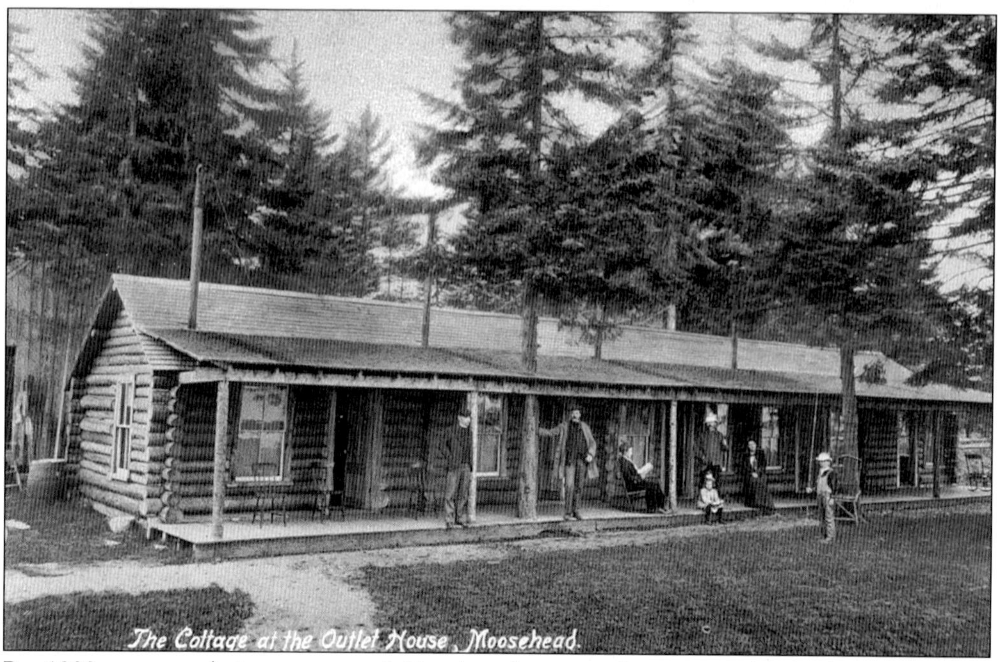

Pre-1900 accommodations were much like this, the original cottage at the Outlet House. Note that the person at the far right is dressed for fishing.

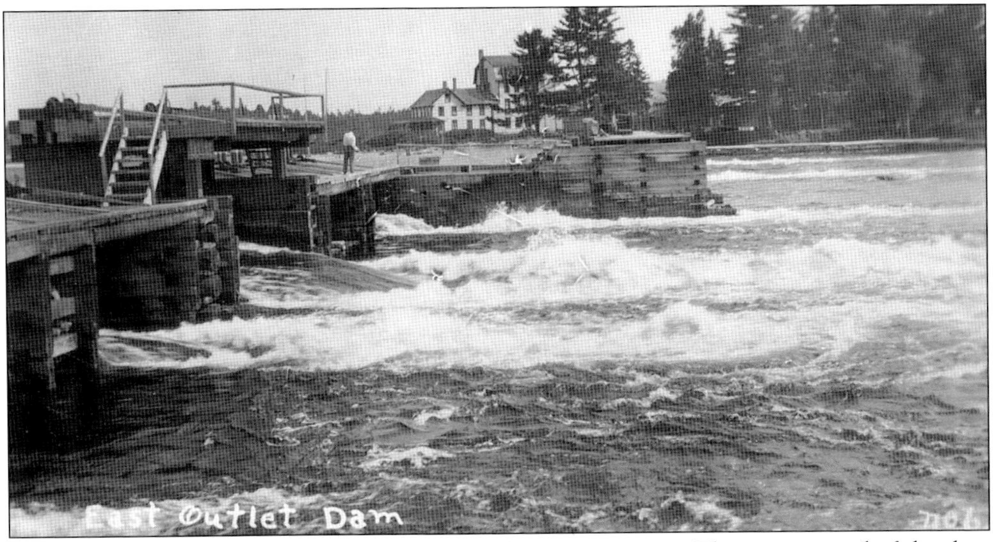

This is how the East Outlet Dam looked more than 50 years ago. The western end of the dam was replaced with a concrete structure c. 1947; the eastern section was rebuilt in the mid-1950s. Since the dam was moved downstream, the pool below the dam was much larger than it is today. Salmon and trout fishing here were known far and wide.

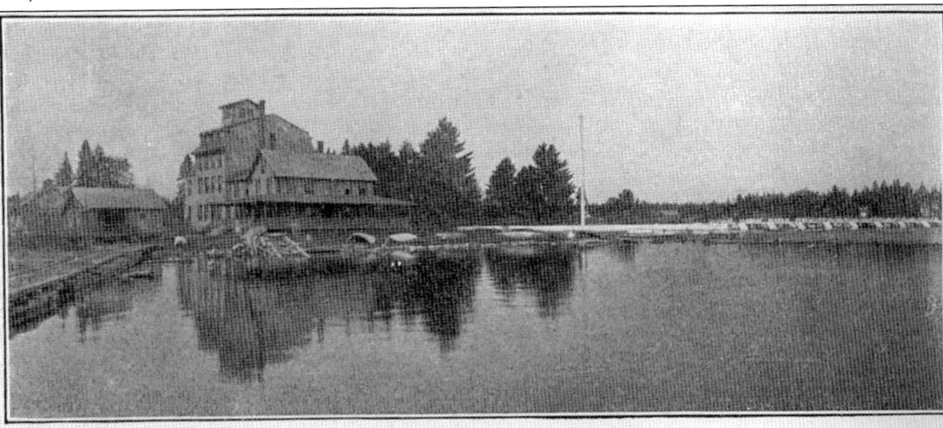

Outlet House and Camps

Moosehead, Maine, 11 miles from Greenville by C. P. R'y or by steamer.

HERE'S FISHING, HUNTING AND HEALTH IN PLENTY!

Best fishing in Moosehead Lake—earliest and latest—is had here; big game is also abundant. The house is newly furnished; has hot and cold water and baths. The grounds are attractively graded, with plots for tennis and croquet, and several attractive woods roads are laid out. No guide needed at our house, although we furnish guides, boats and canoes when desired. Rates $2.00 to $2.50 per day. On notification by mail or wire, we will meet parties at Greenville Jct., with our own private steamer.

CHAS. E. WILSON. Proprietor, **MOOSEHEAD, MAINE.** Write for descriptive booklet. . . . . . .

The Outlet House is situated at the eastern end of the dam. Establishments around the lake, such as this one, could be reached only by boat or train until the road was put in. Early travel was by stage, since guests were met at the railroad station and brought to the resort. Many places had their own steamboat to transport their patrons. (From *In the Maine Woods*, 1908.)

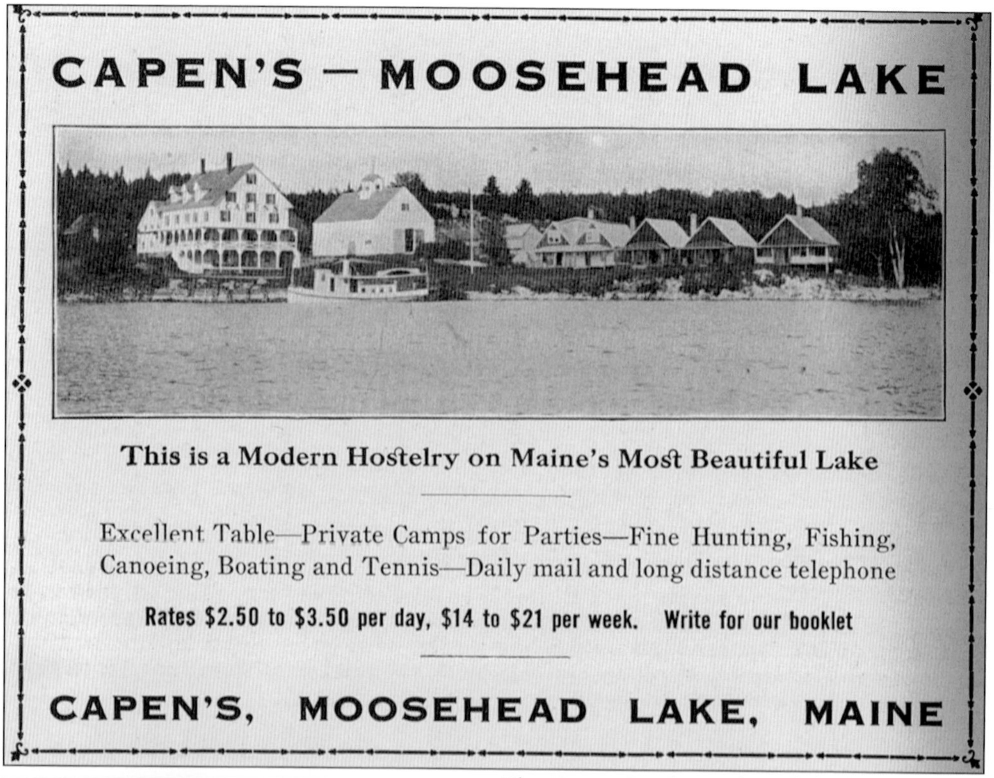

The Capen family purchased the land on Deer Island *c.* 1832 and cleared a farm. The coming of the railroad in the late 1800s substituted for lake travel. Henry Capen remodeled the property and changed the name from Deer Island House to Capen's. The first hotel burned in 1853, and the hotel shown here burned on November 17, 1953, putting an end to the famous establishment. In the photograph, Capen's steamer *Tethys* is docked in front of the place. (From *In the Maine Woods*, 1915.)

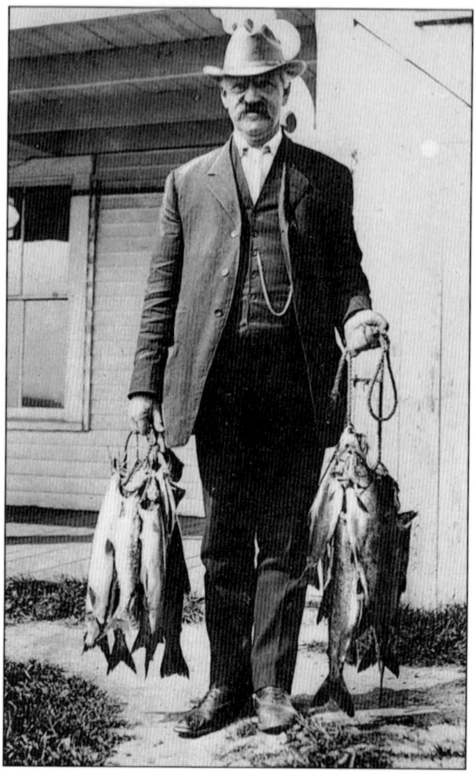

Catches like this were commonplace until the late 1950s or early 1960s. About this time the limit was changed from 15 pounds of fish to 7.5 pounds; fishing was good, so nearly everyone had bunches of fish like these in cold storage to take home.

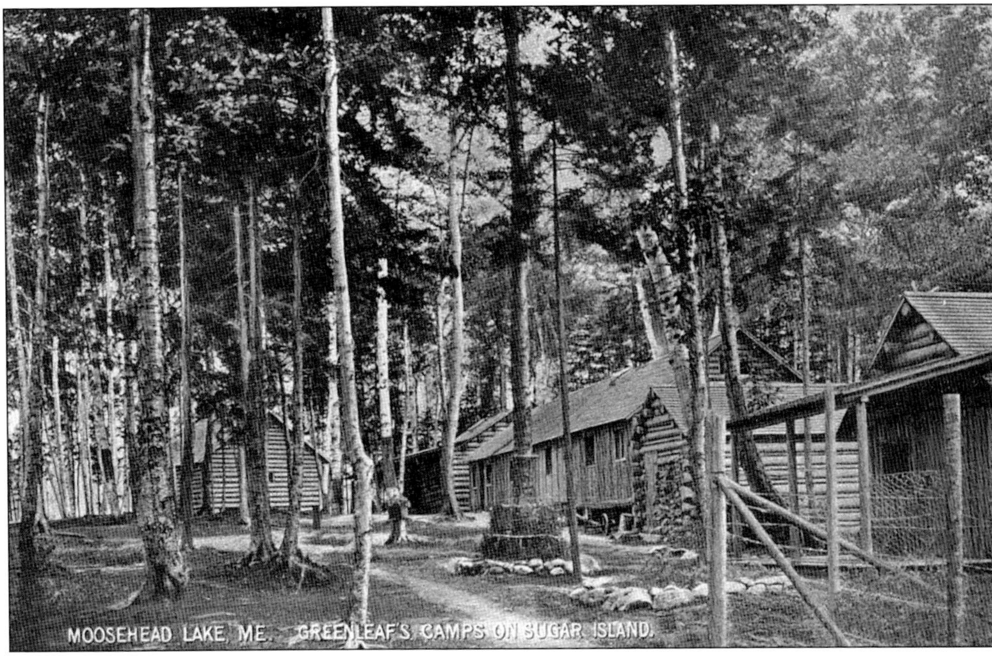

The Greenleaf Camps were located on a beautiful birch point at the southern end of Sugar Island.

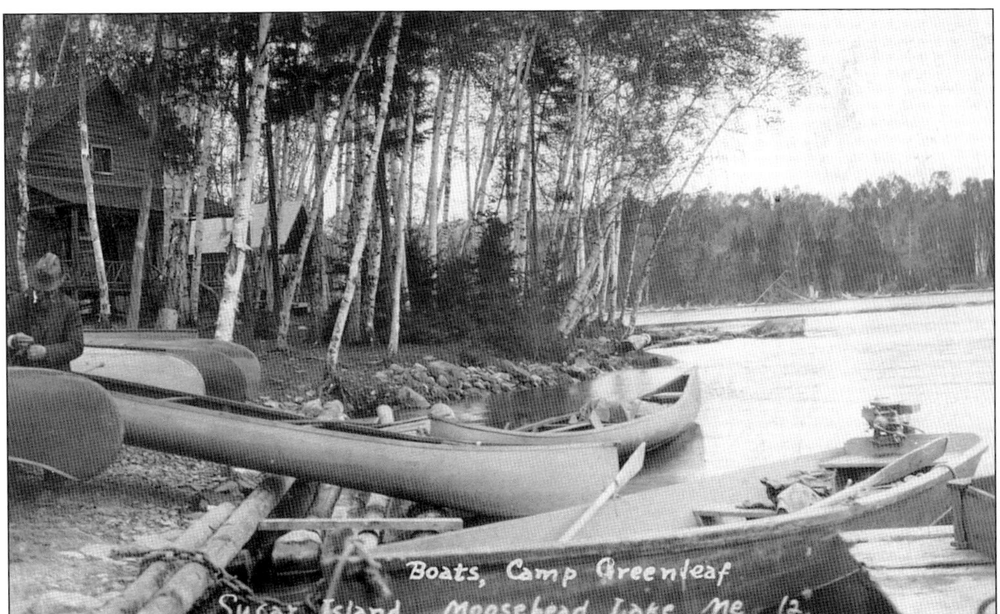

For the most part, strictly canoes were used for fishing, although one flat-bottom boat with an early motor is docked here at the waterfront of Camp Greenleaf.

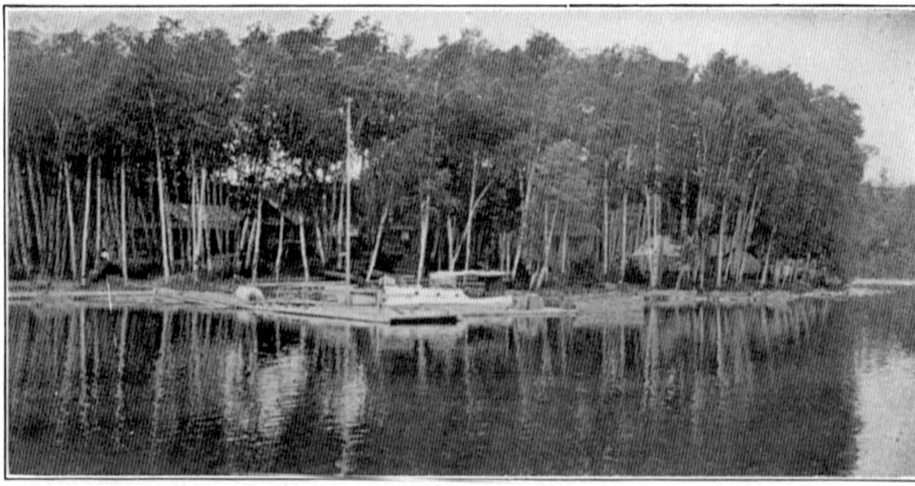

CAMP GREENLEAF Sugar Island
Moosehead Lake, Maine

Ten log cabins, with open fires, modern plumbing, situated on Island which is six miles long and three miles wide, with good trails. Bathing and tennis. Mail boat daily except Sunday, connecting with trains at Greenville Junction. Post office and long distance phone at camp. Noted for its togue, trout and salmon fishing. Partridge, deer and bear hunting in season. Motor boats, row boats and canoes for hire. Excellent cuisine. Fresh Vegetables. Milk and Cream from tested cows. Hay Fever unknown. Auto road one mile from camp at Ellis Tent Ground. Motor boat to camp. *Send for booklet and rates.*

WILLIAM C. MESERVEY SUGAR ISLAND, MAINE

This early advertisement for Camp Greenleaf leaves no doubt as to the beauty of the waterfront. (From *In the Maine Woods*, 1936.)

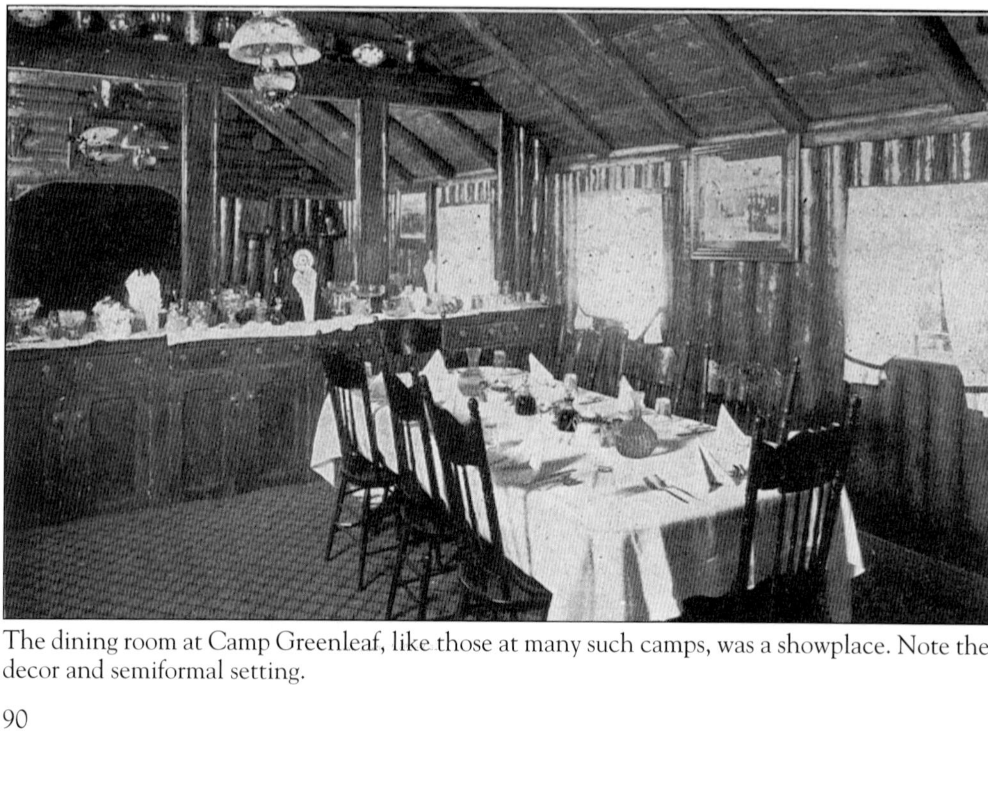

The dining room at Camp Greenleaf, like those at many such camps, was a showplace. Note the decor and semiformal setting.

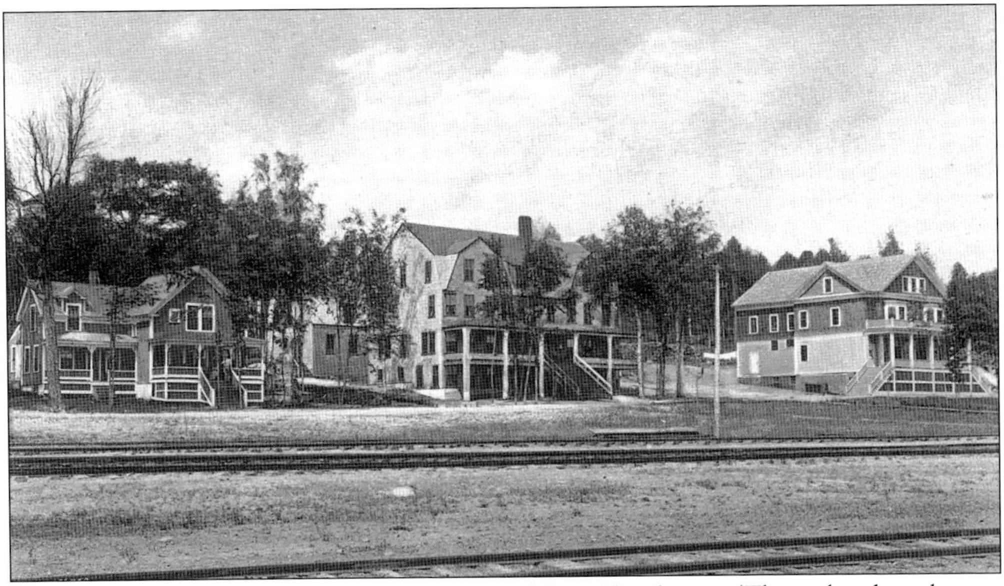

Rockwood was the end of the line for the railroad from Skowhegan. (This railroad was known as the Somerset Railway, the Maine Central Mountain Division, or the Kineo Branch, since it primarily serviced the Mount Kineo House, although smaller establishments along the line took advantage of it.) The line was established in 1907 and discontinued in 1933. This photograph was taken at Kineo docks, looking across the tracks to the Hotel Rockwood and the Rockwood Store, both built shortly after the railroad came into town.

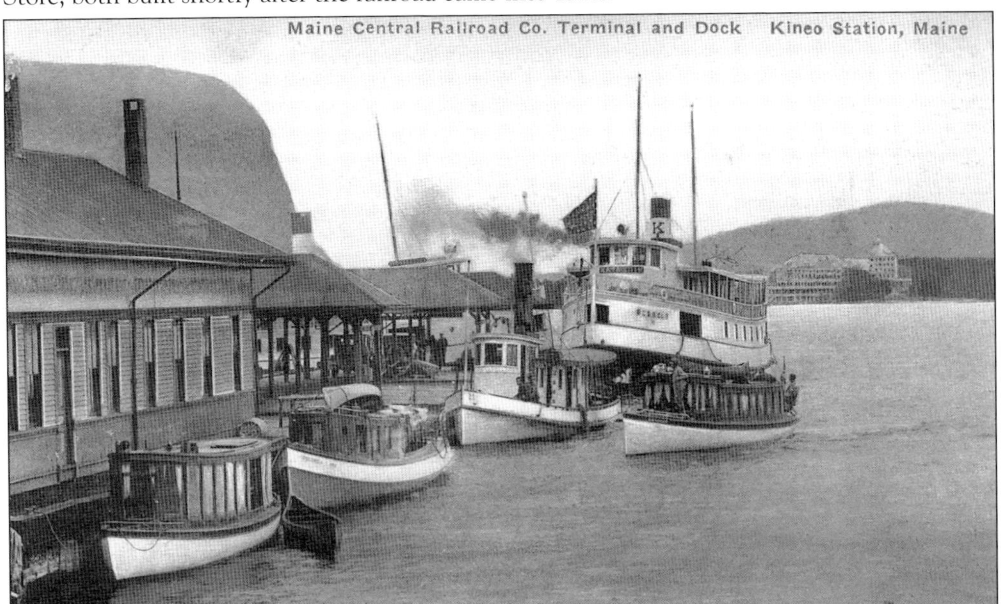

The Kineo docks were where steamers from all over the lake came to meet their parties. The *Katahdin* is docked at the rear of smaller, private craft belonging to places such as West Outlet Camps (the *West Outlet*) and Wilsons (the *East Outlet*) and to guides or individuals such as George Masterman (the *Neptune*). For years, the Mount Kineo House (seen in the background) ran a regular ferry service for its visitors back and forth to the mainland, using a boat similar to those in the foreground.

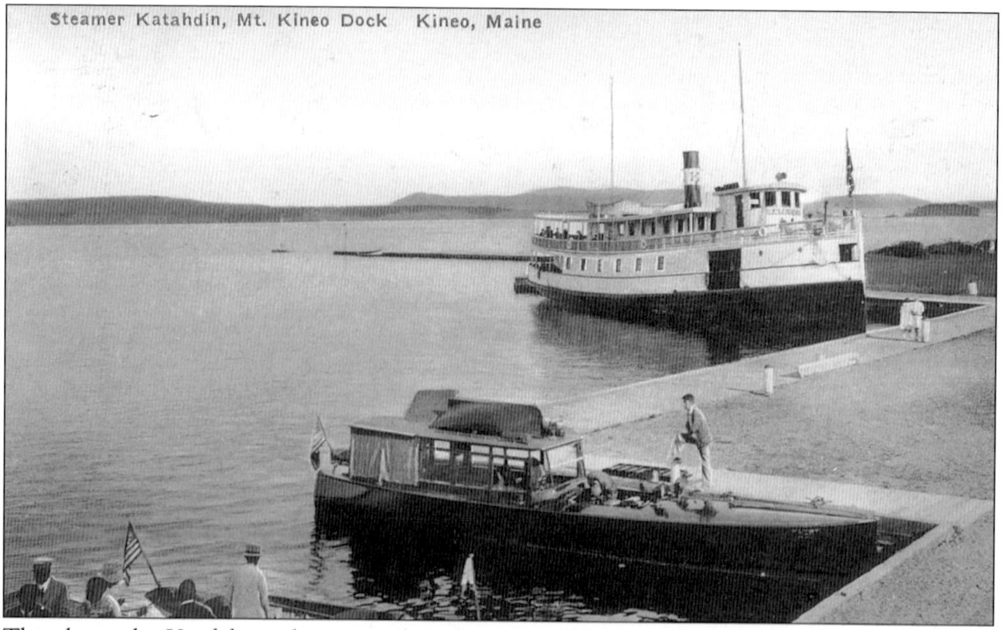

This shows the *Katahdin* and a private boat launch at the Kineo dock in front of the hotel.

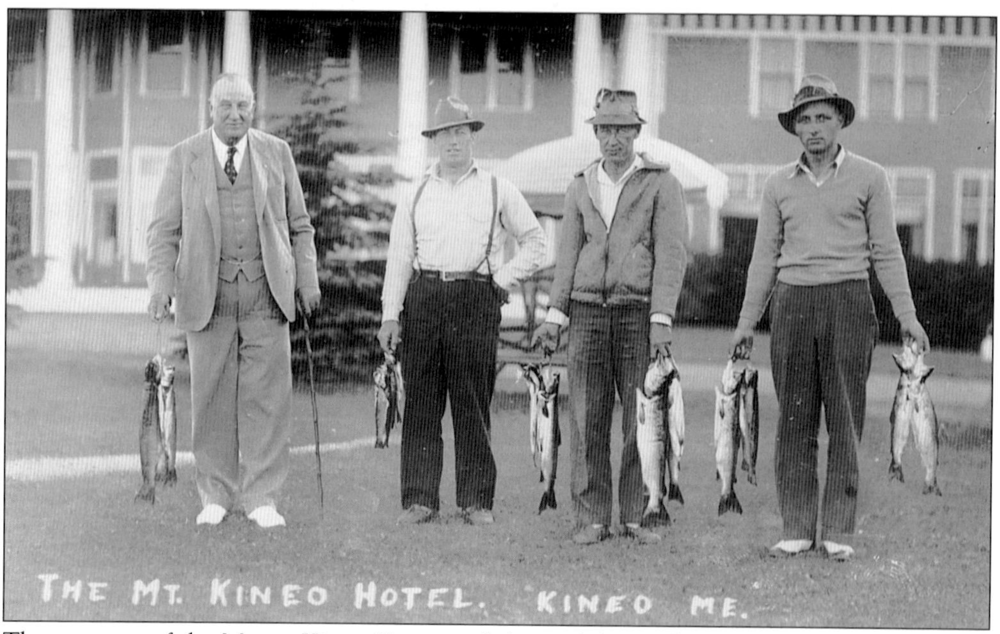

The manager of the Mount Kineo House and three of the guides stand in front of the hotel showing off some of the fish caught that day. Several of the salmon look to be in the 5- or 6-pound class or better.

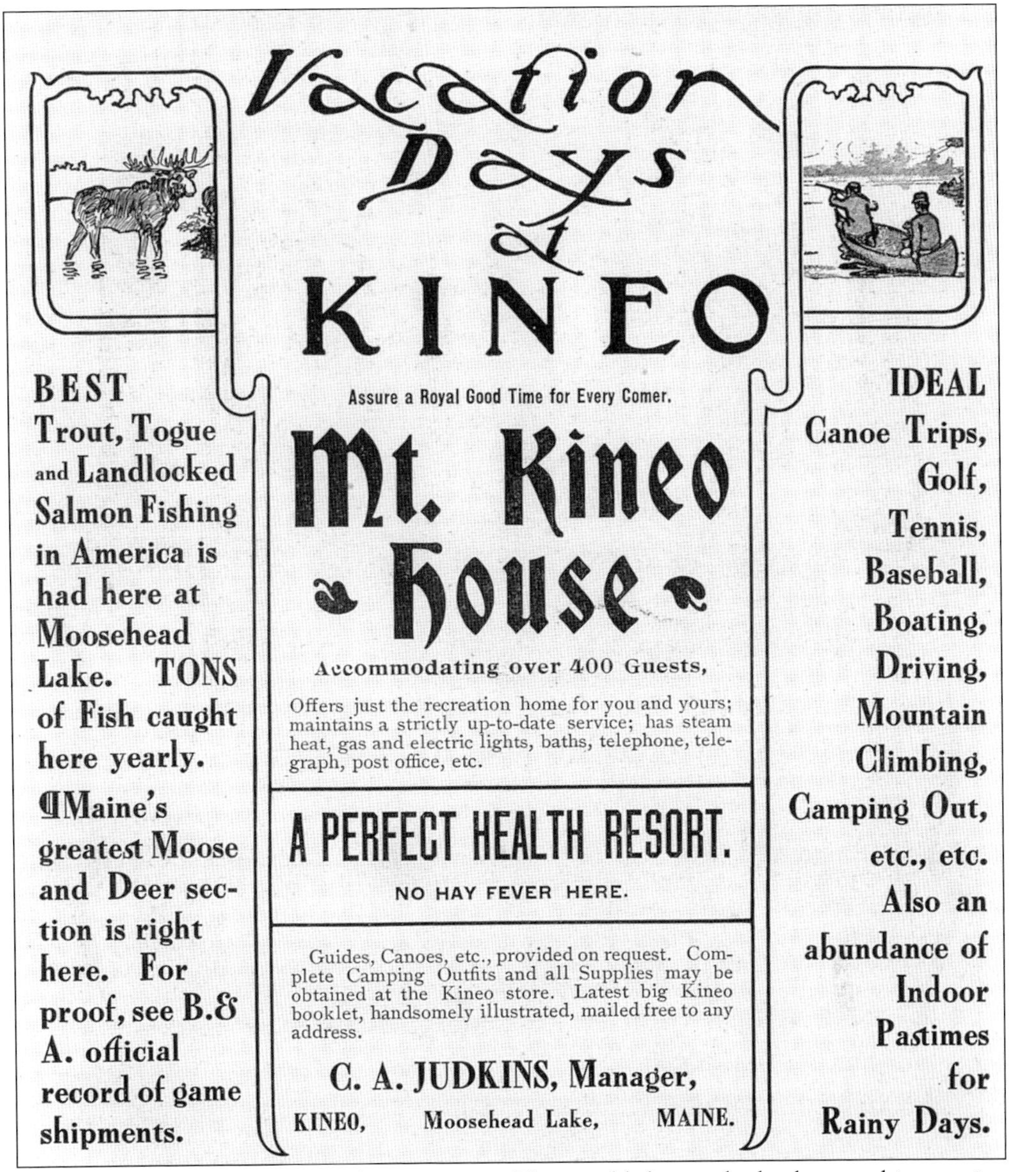

This is one of Mount Kineo's advertisements. This establishment had a long and interesting history. The first building and tavern was operational by 1844, with the Mount Kineo House built in 1848. After an 1868 fire, the guest house was rebuilt in 1871. A second fire struck in 1882, and the house was rebuilt again in 1883. By 1884, it had 200 rooms accommodating 500 guests. By 1900, the dining room could seat 400 people; by 1911, it could seat 500. In 1914, the hotel had 431 employees and 62 registered guides, who charged $3 a day for their services. Another major fire in 1938 resulted in the rebuilding of a much smaller structure, accommodating 120 people. The final demolition took place in 1995. (From *In the Maine Woods*, 1906.)

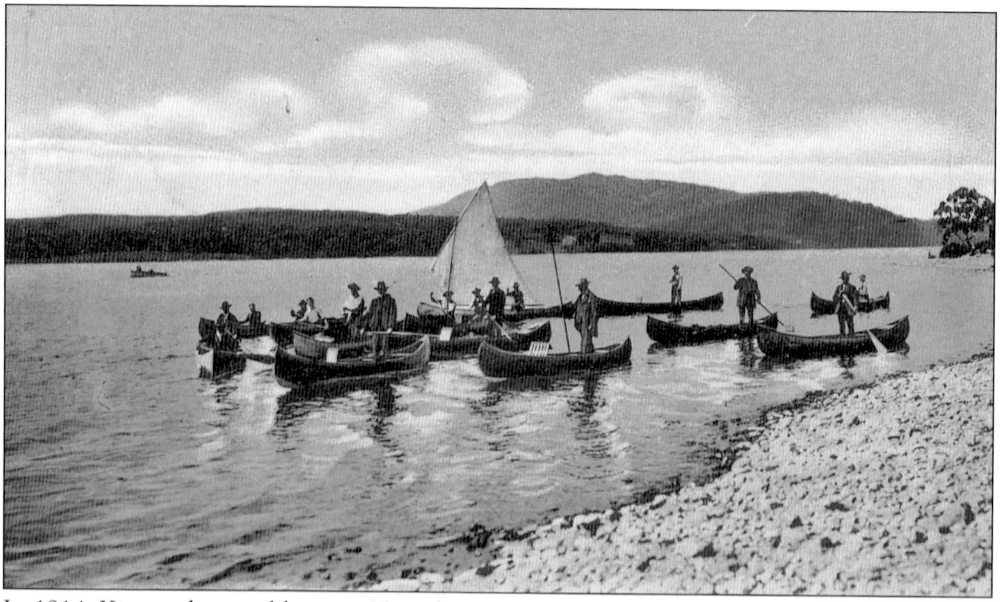

In 1914, Kineo advertised having 65 guides on staff to accommodate its guests. At that time, the establishment could serve 500 guests. The fishing pressure of that magnitude from this one resort alone must have been tremendous. Despite the pressure exerted throughout the early part of the century, fishing seems to have held up well until after World War II, up to c. 1950.

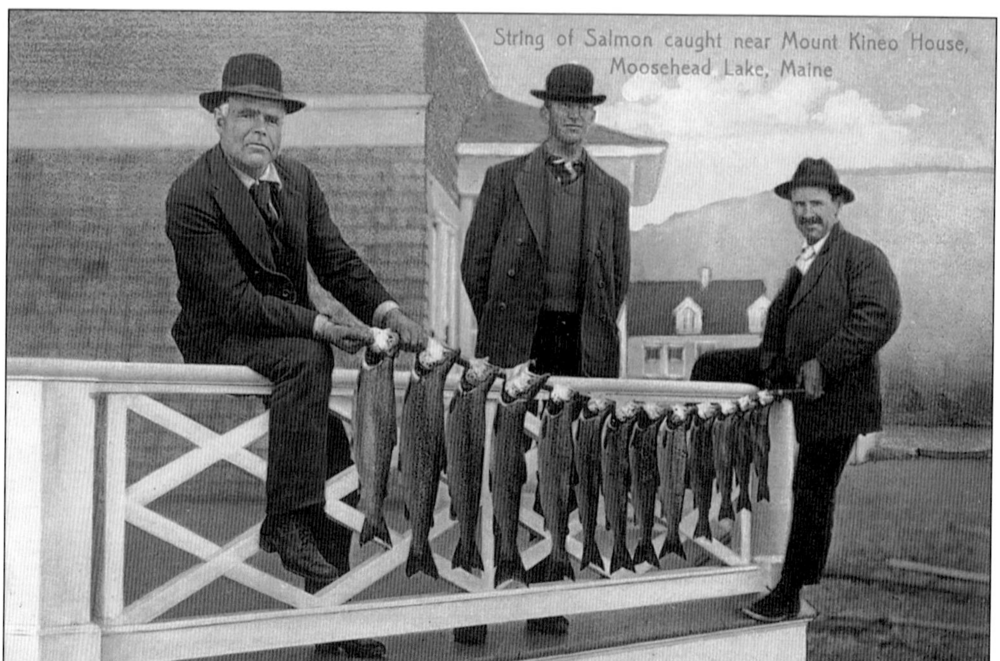

Here is another example of a large catch by fishermen, this one consisting of salmon, the largest being in the 6- to 8-pound range.

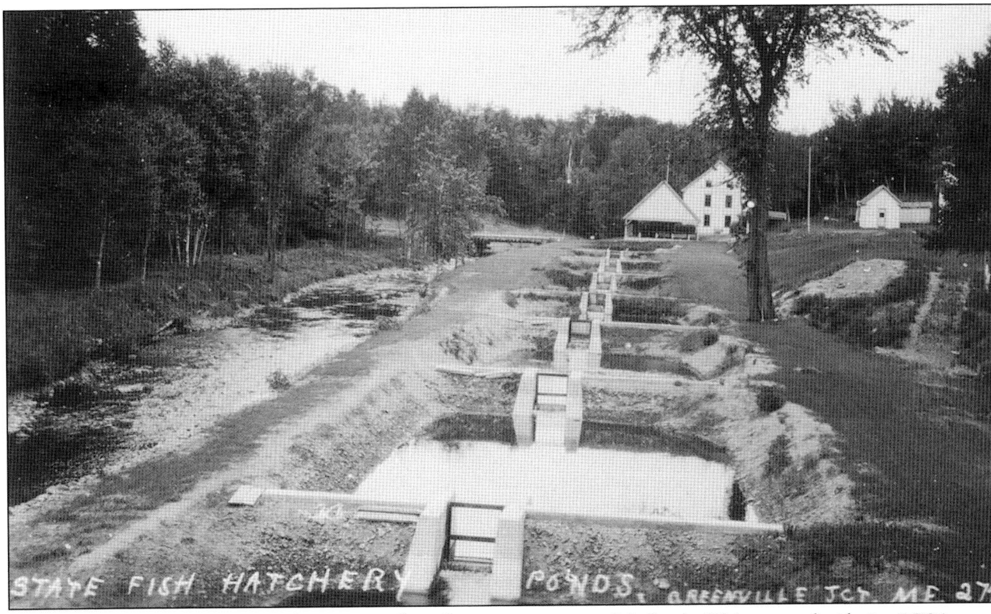

To support Moosehead's fishery, two hatcheries were established. This one, built in 1901, was located at Lower Squaw Brook on the Greenville-Rockwood Road. The bridge in the center of the photograph is on Route 15, which bisected the hatchery property before being relocated to the west. Old Route 15 now services this site. The hatchery was closed in the mid-1950s, but a Maine Forest Service campsite remains.

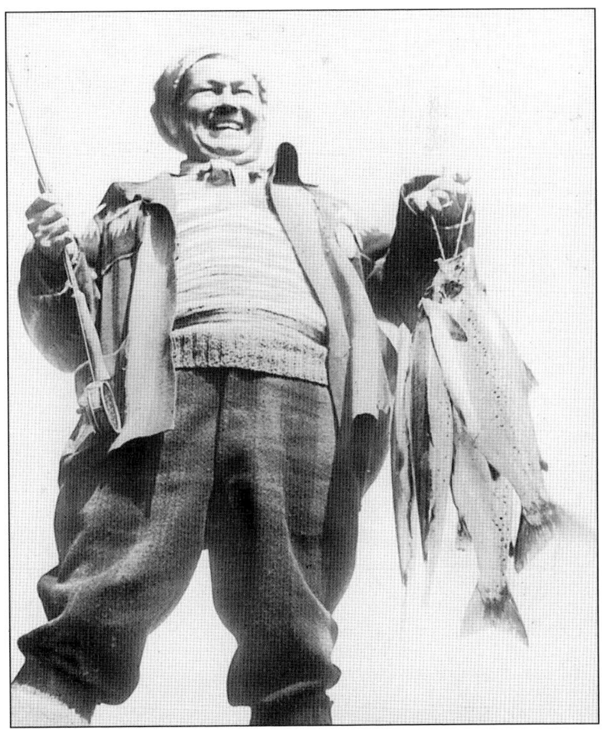

One of the most famous of all the guides, Chief Needahbeh, was of the Penobscot tribe. Born Roland Eugene Nelson, he owned a summer cottage at Harford's Point, between the Squaw Brook Hatchery and Greenville Junction. Until his death in 1954, the chief was a frequent attraction at sportsmen's shows, sometimes as the master of ceremonies. He was famous for his loon calls and remembered by the streamer fly named in his honor.

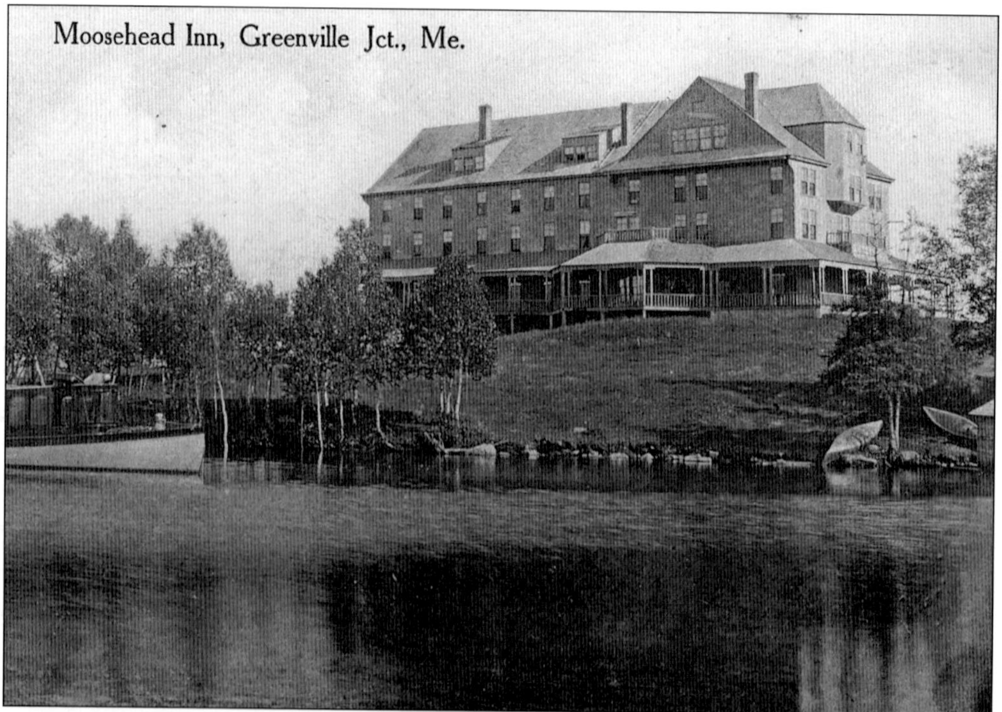

The Moosehead Inn was situated at a prime location on the lake and within walking distance of two railroad stations, the Bangor & Aroostook and the Canadian Pacific, both of which arrived in the 1880s. At its door, the inn offered ferry service to anywhere on the lake. The hotel burned in 1912.

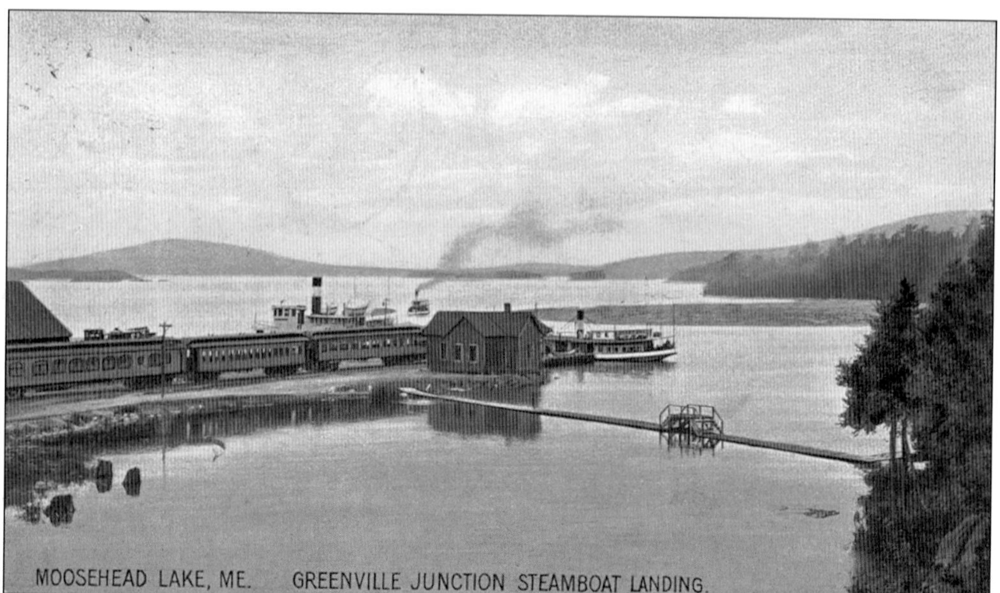

A steamer lands directly in front of the Moosehead Inn. The Bangor & Aroostook station was located here as well, so railroad service directly to steamboat service was possible at this location. This arrangement made it possible to have a ride directly from points south to destinations on the lake.

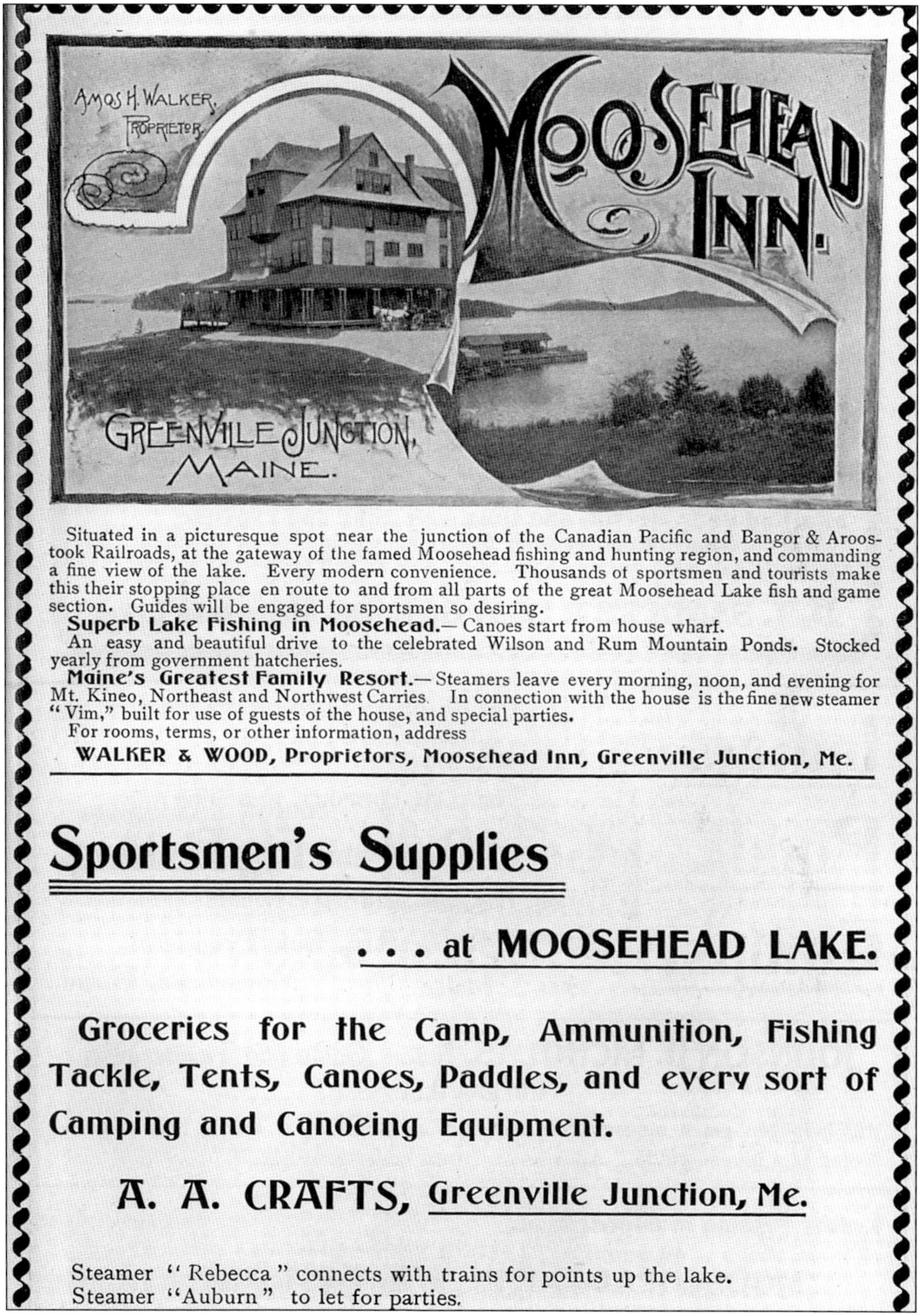

In an advertisement for the Moosehead Inn, one can note the detail concerning the services offered and the fact that at this early date, local ponds were stocked with fish. The accompanying advertisement demonstrates that camping supplies were available in the immediate neighborhood. (From *In the Maine Woods*, 1900.)

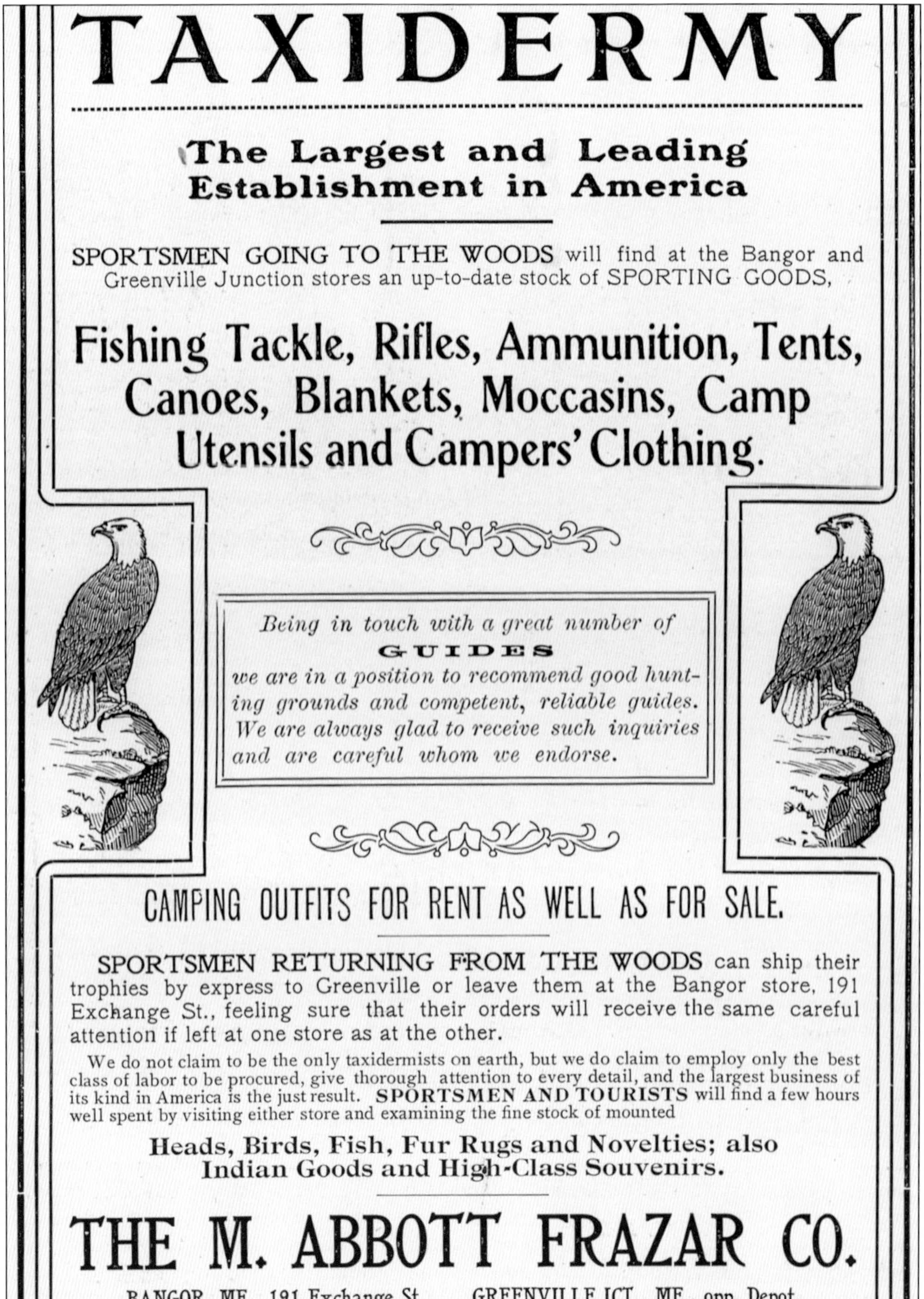

Since so many fish were in the trophy category, many anglers were interested in taxidermy services. Studios were located all over Maine, with branches at all the key hubs where sportsmen frequented. The advertisement speaks of other services such as guides and equipment. Many taxidermists offered a variety of goods and services.

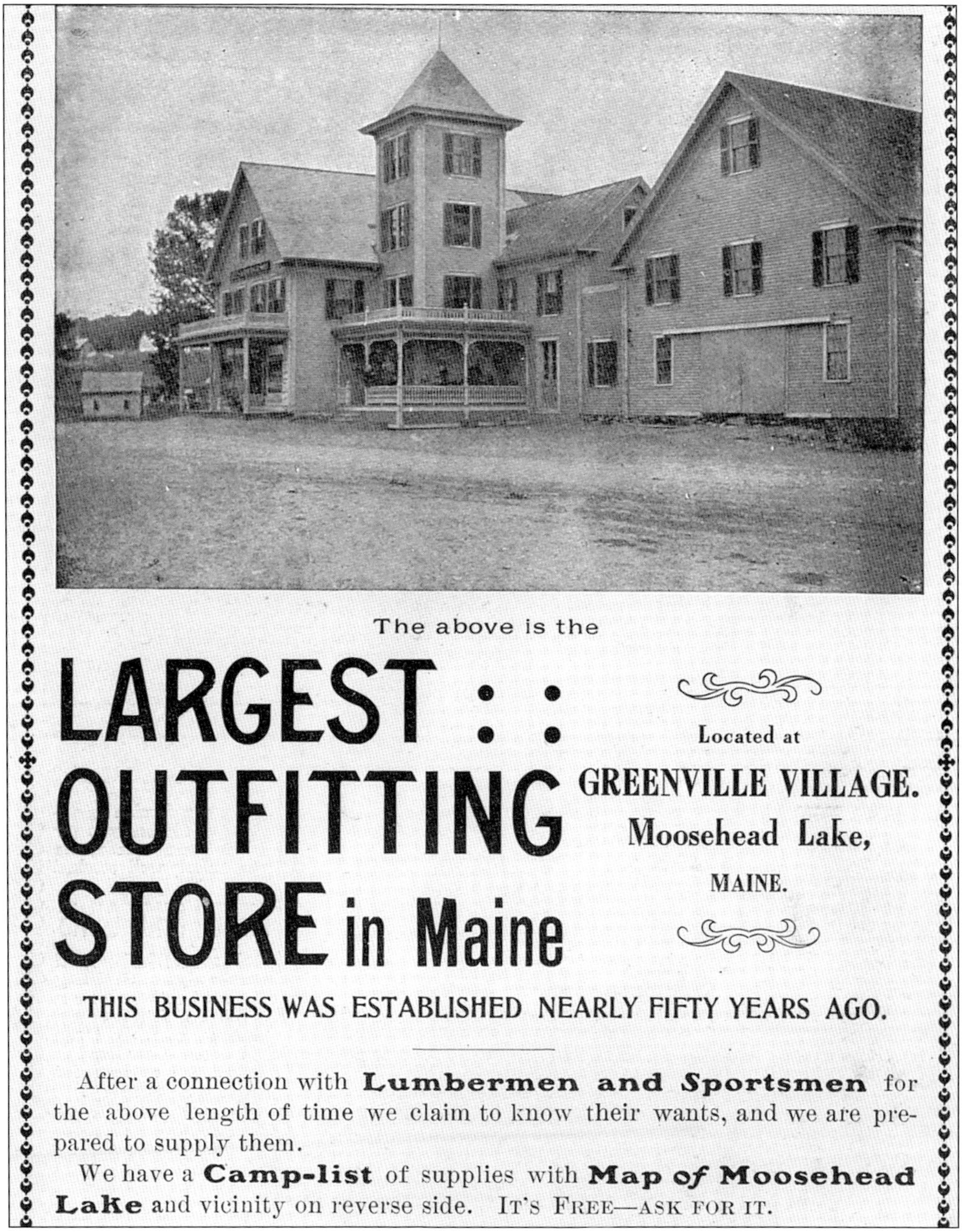

Sanders Store was founded by David T. Sanders in 1878. Many Allagash and other north woods trips began at Sanders Store, where fishermen and adventurers equipped themselves with clothes, food and other supplies, and tackle. Sanders sold everything from real estate, canoes, and outboard motors to clothing, food, and hunting, fishing, and camping equipment. In fact, the store's first sale was a gallon of molasses to an Indian guide named Lewis Annance. For a long time, Sanders advertised having "Maine's largest display of mounted fish." The display was representative of the region, not including warm-water species, and consisted of very large examples of salmon and trout, along with whitefish, eel, and cusk. (From *In the Maine Woods*, 1906.)

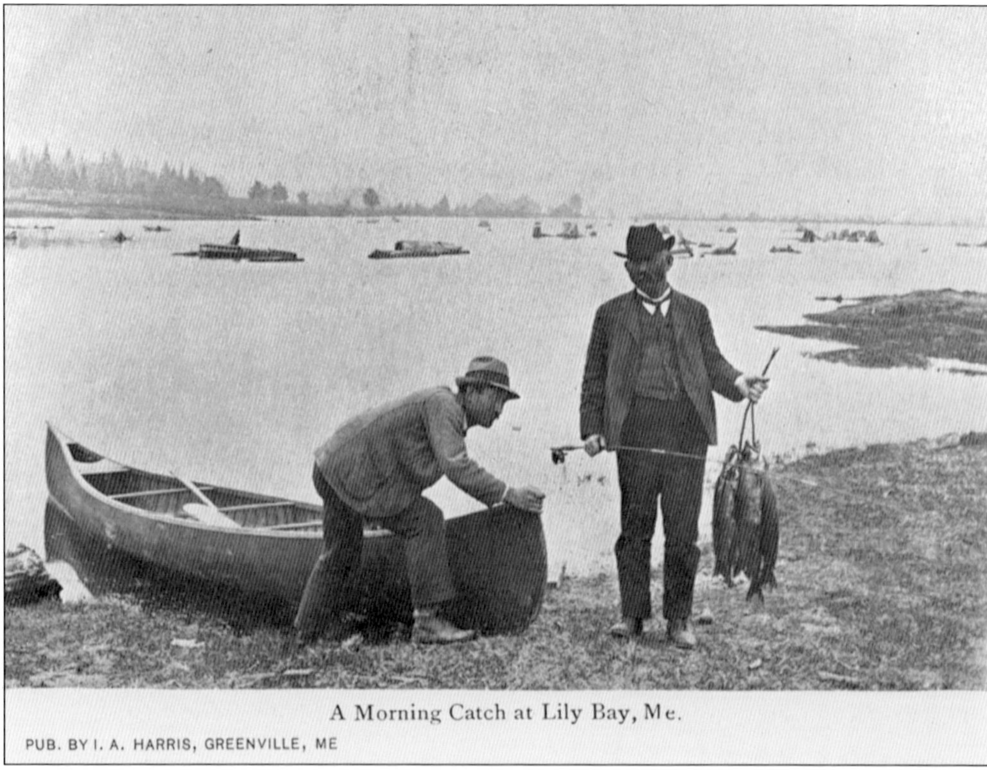

Lily Bay, situated on the east side of the lake, was a halfway point between Greenville and Kokadjo. Many lumbering operations were based in this area, and a few sporting facilities were built nearby. This area of the lake itself and the numerous surrounding streams and ponds were well known for producing impressive catches of fish, as this photograph demonstrates.

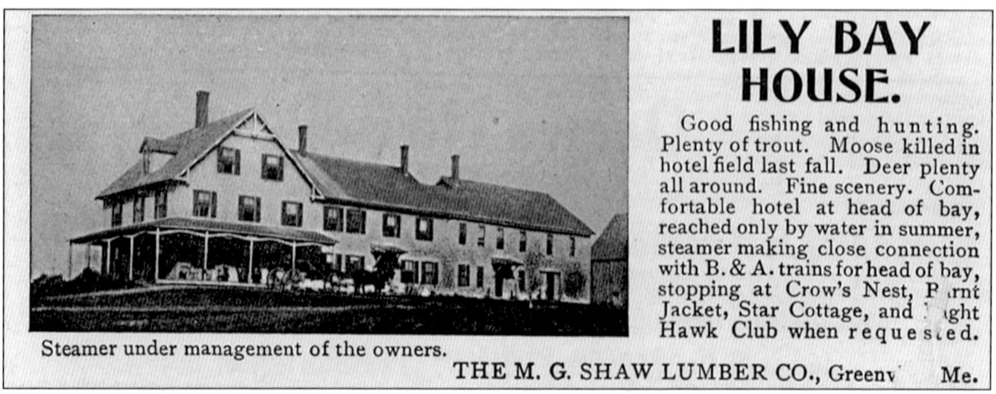

What eventually became the Lily Bay House began as a farm, which was sold to Milton G. Shaw & Sons, who remodeled and enlarged it in 1876. The Shaws sold to the Hollingsworth & Whitney Company in 1904. Although there was a stage operated by the Shaws, the Greenville–Lily Bay Road was not built until 1919, linking Greenville with the road already built from Lily Bay to Ripogenous Dam. One of Shaw's advertisements boldly stated that the Lily Bay House was located "right on the spot for the best trout, togue, and landlocked salmon fishing to be had in America." In 1955, the Lily Bay House was closed, and the buildings burned a few years later. (From *In the Maine Woods*, 1900.)

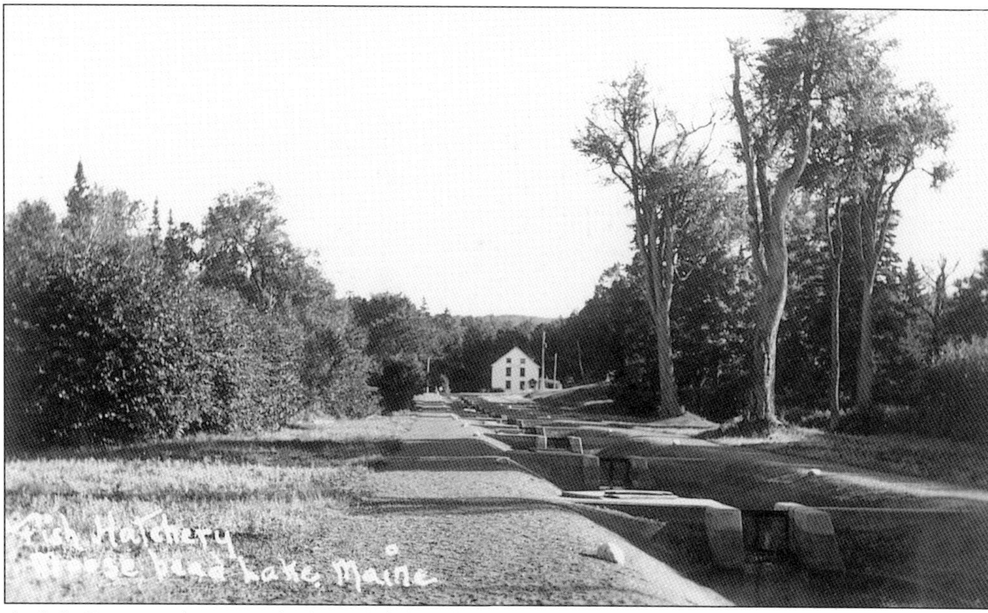

At Lily Bay was the second of two fish hatcheries used to support the fishery of Moosehead Lake and nearby waters. This one built in 1930 more than doubled the capacity of fingerlings and by 1932 allowed Moosehead to boast one of the largest and best-equipped hatcheries in the East. In later years only brook trout were reared here and in 1967, the hatchery was closed.

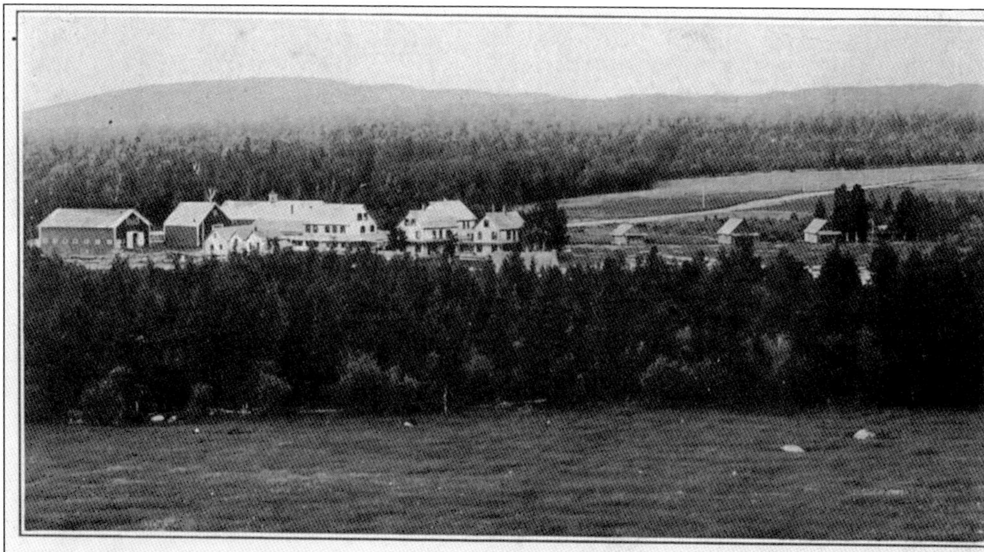

Kokad-jo Inn and Spencer Mountain in Distance

Although there were farms here beginning in 1844, it was not until 1894 that the establishment at this site was operated as an inn. Until 1914, Kokadjo was reached either by steamer from Greenville to Roach River or by woods trail from Lily Bay. This resort was later known as the Kokadjo Inn.

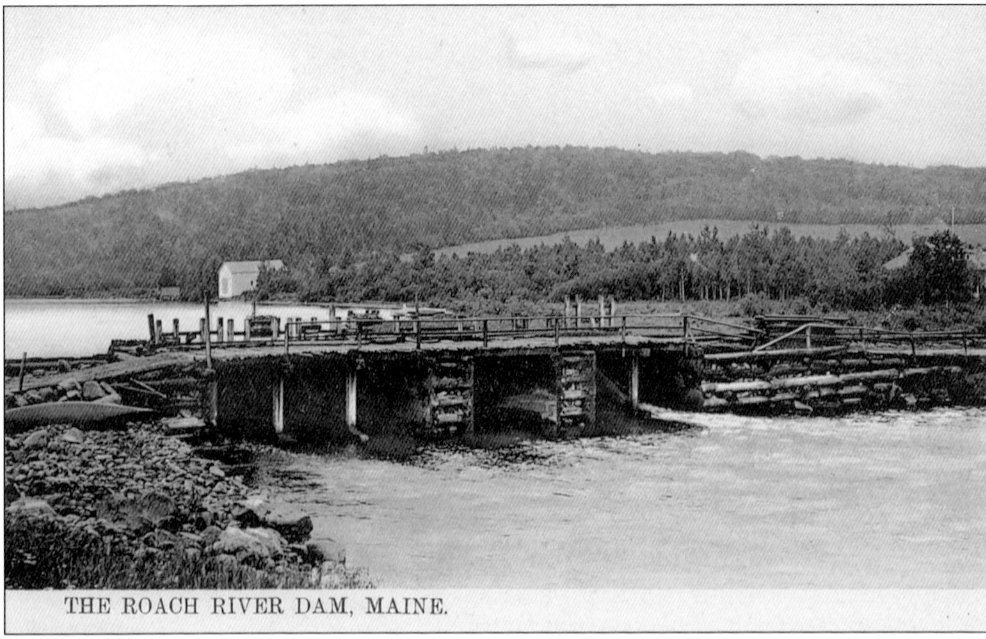

Featured here is one of the earlier dams at the outlet of First Roach Pond, at the head of the Roach River. In later years the dam had a wooden fishway and until only a few years ago, the main road crossed on the dam. The village here is known as Kokadjo, which today boasts a population of "not many."

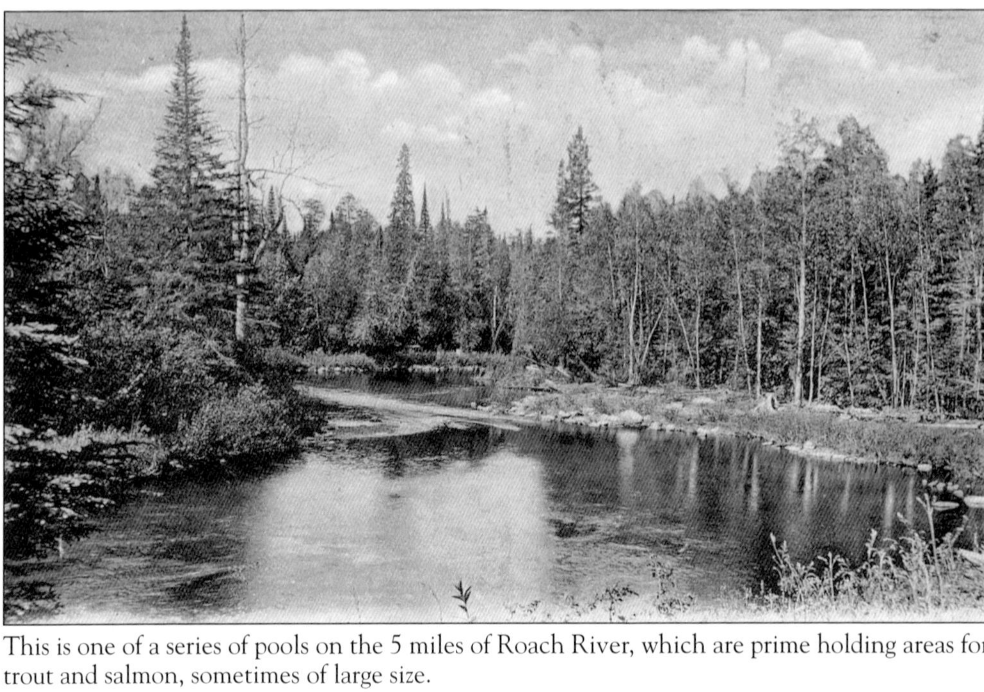

This is one of a series of pools on the 5 miles of Roach River, which are prime holding areas for trout and salmon, sometimes of large size.

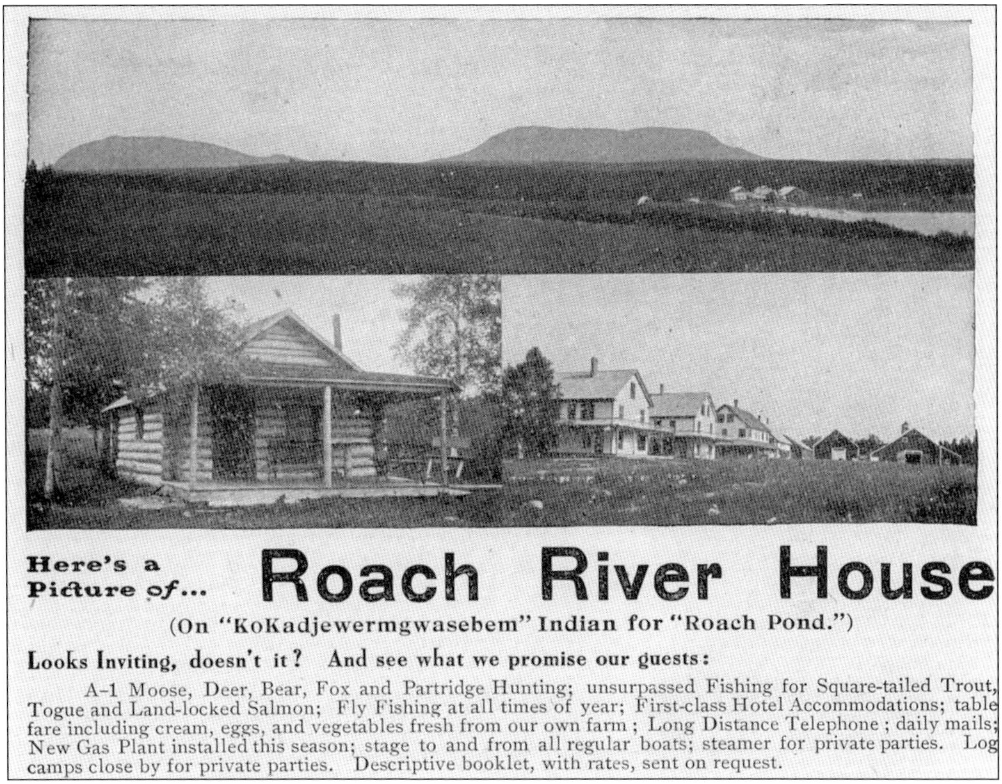

This advertisement for the Roach River House demonstrates its remote and picturesque setting. (From *In the Maine Woods*, 1907.)

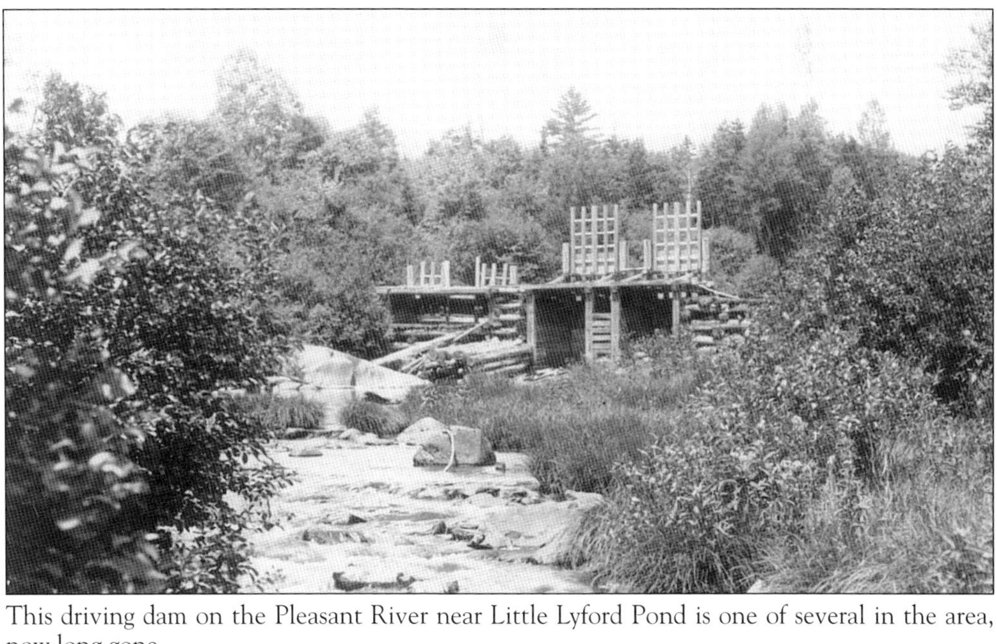

This driving dam on the Pleasant River near Little Lyford Pond is one of several in the area, now long gone.

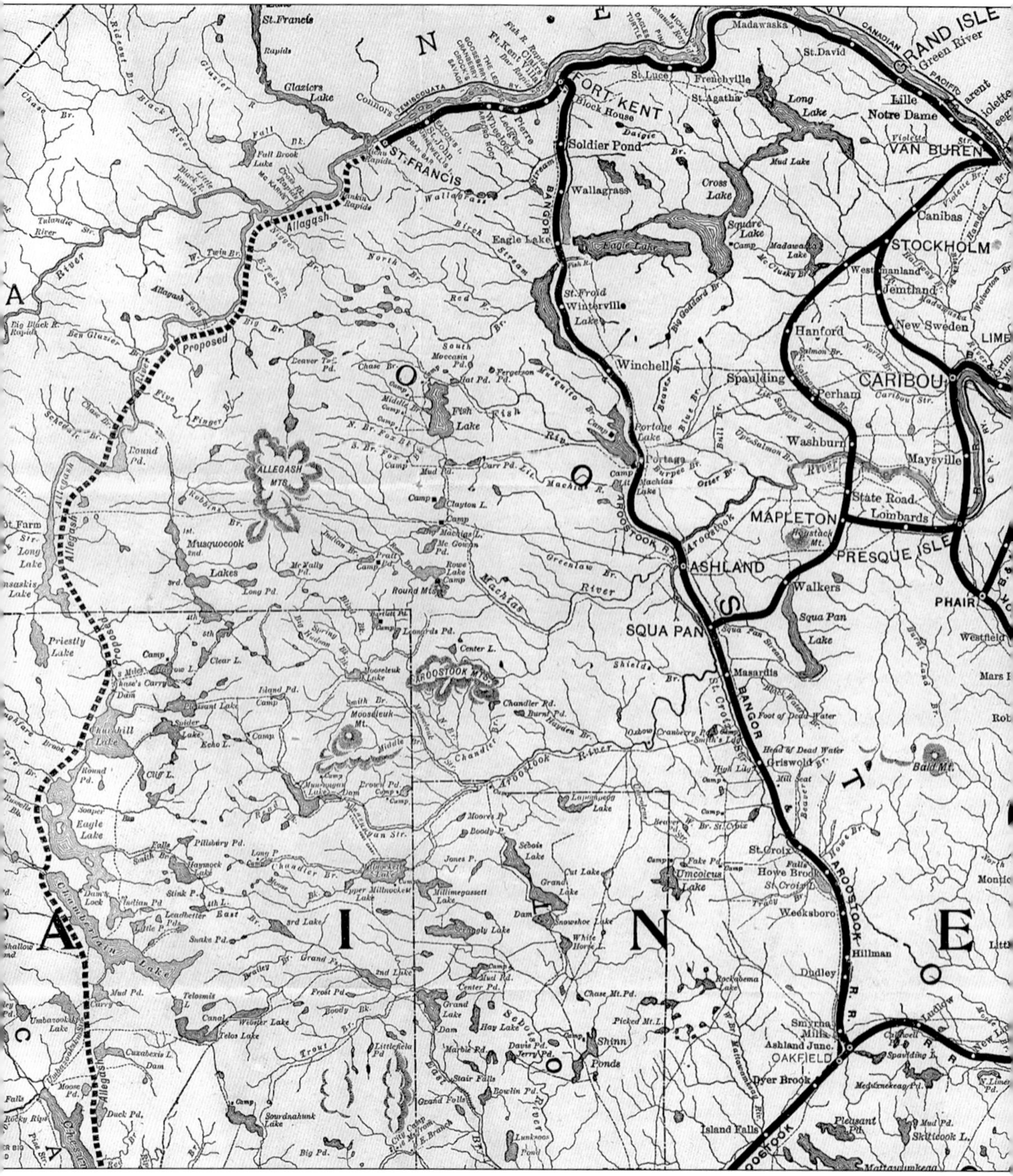

A section of the 1915 Bangor & Aroostook Railroad map of northern Maine shows most of Aroostook County and the Allagash region. Note the proposed Allagash railroad running alongside the Allagash River.

Eight

NORTHERN MAINE

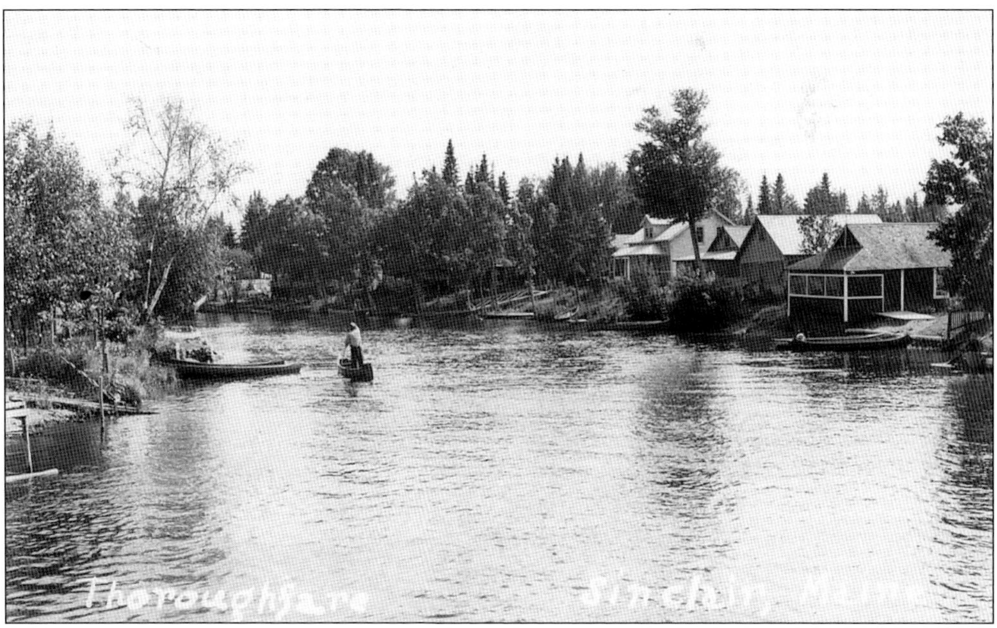

A canoeist maneuvers in the half-mile-long thoroughfare between Cross Lake and Square Lake. This site was justly famous for large catches, primarily salmon.

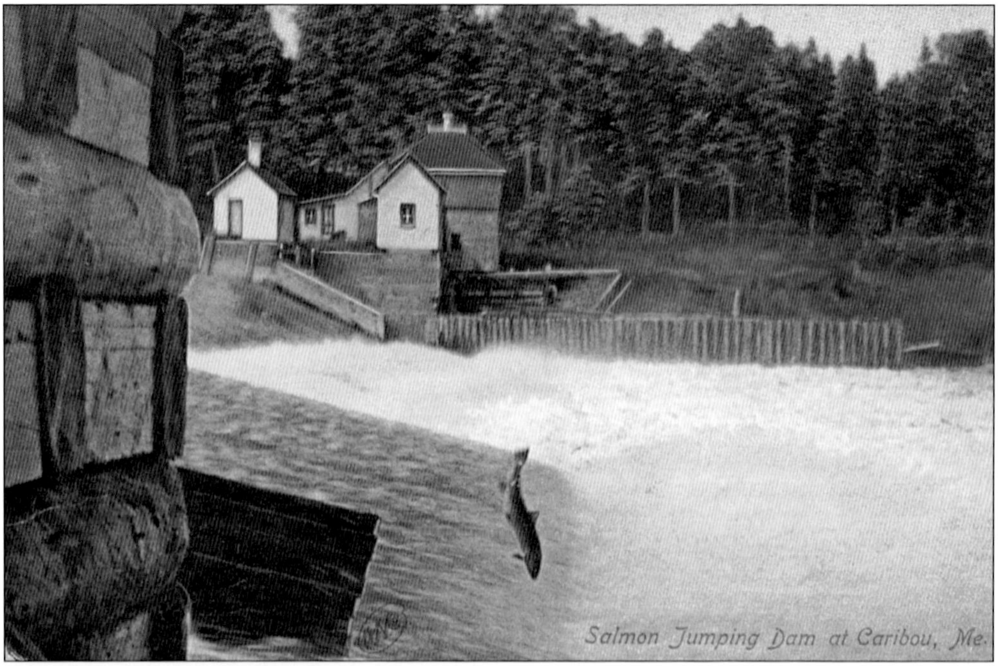

The salmon pool at the Caribou Dam on the Aroostook River was a famous location for big salmon in large numbers. A 1908 article states that "salmon of magnificent size are captured here." (From *In the Maine Woods*, 1908.)

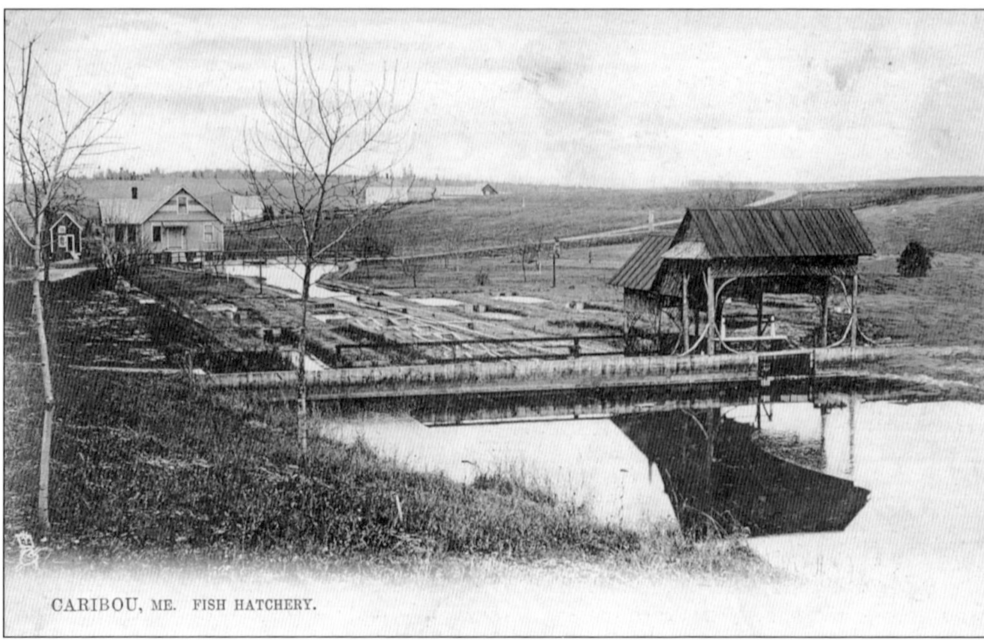

This fish hatchery, located in Caribou, was devoted almost wholly to the rearing of salmon.

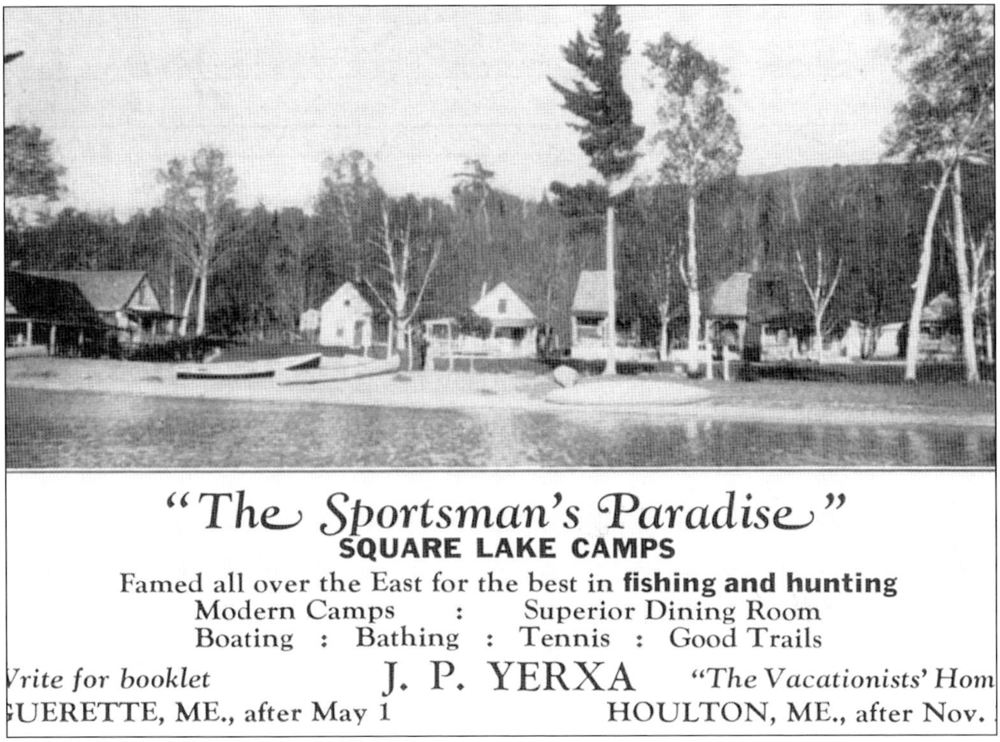

Yerxa's Camps were a popular place for Maine governors and a gathering place for the outdoor writer's groups. Gov. Lucius Barrows was a frequent visitor and an accomplished angler. He was recognized by having a fly named for him. The establishment was founded and operated by Jack Yerxa and his wife, c. 1912, and stayed open until the former's death in 1950. Jack Yerxa himself originated the Yerxa Bucktail in 1928, a streamer fly that accounted for more than 100 salmon that year. (From *In the Maine Woods*, 1936.)

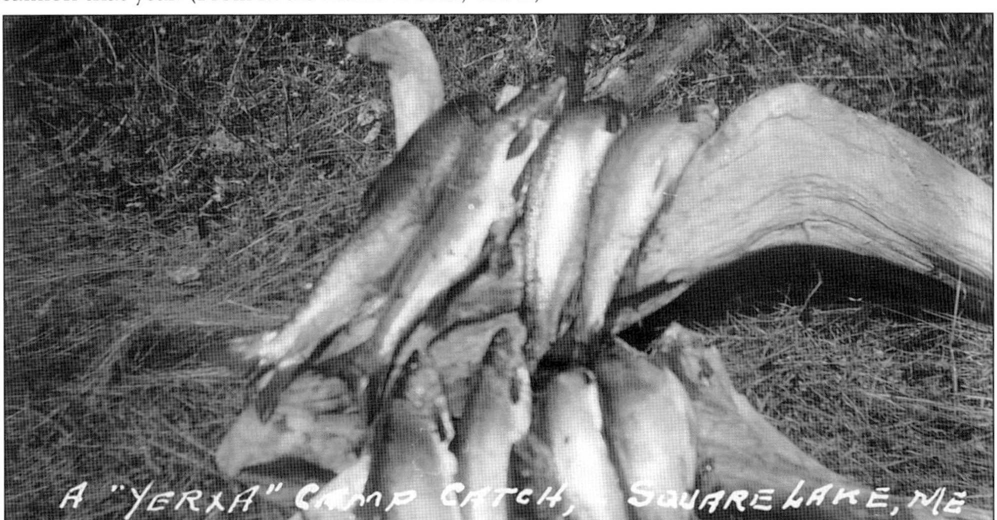

Trout in Square Lake were said to have run from 3 to 7 pounds, with 4- or 5-pounders being the rule rather than the exception. Salmon ran from 2.5 pounds up, with the largest on record weighing 21.75 pounds.

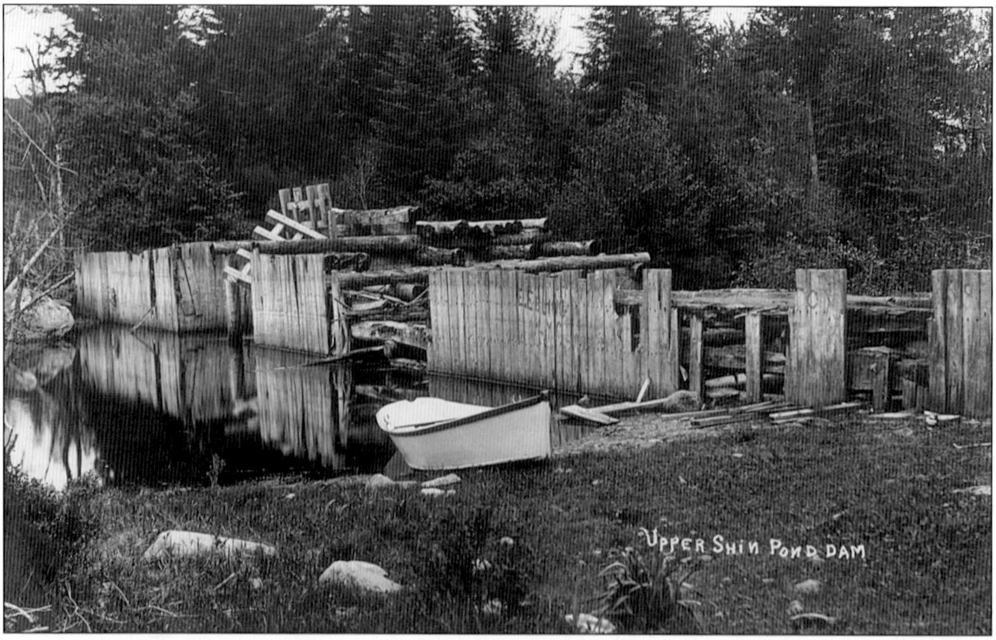

Shin Pond was a popular wilderness area that was advertised heavily in the Bangor & Aroostook publications. Guide Ross McKenney spent his early years here.

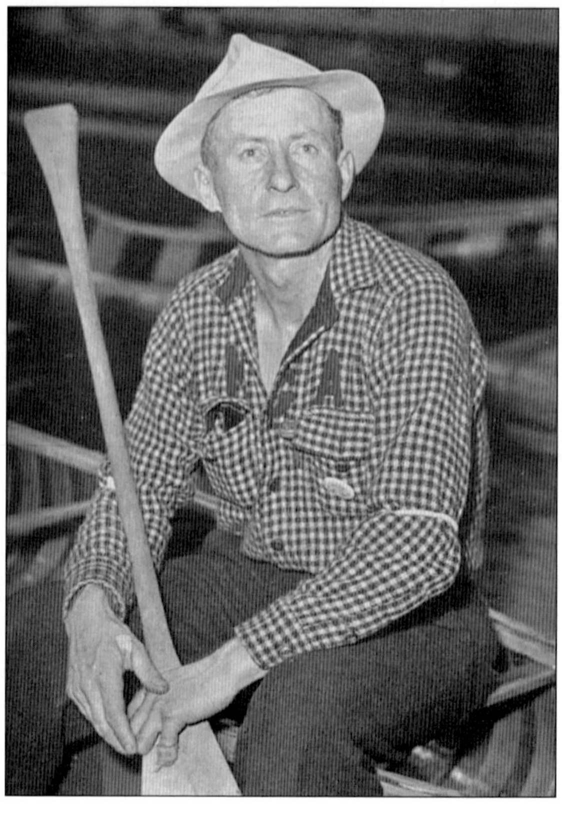

C. Ross McKenney, famous guide of sportsmen's shows, later became affiliated full-time with the Dartmouth Outing Club. He was known not only for his guiding ability but also for his storytelling, utilizing the French Canadian character Jean Baptiste. An effective salmon fly is called the Ross McKenney. (From *In the Maine Woods*, 1937.)

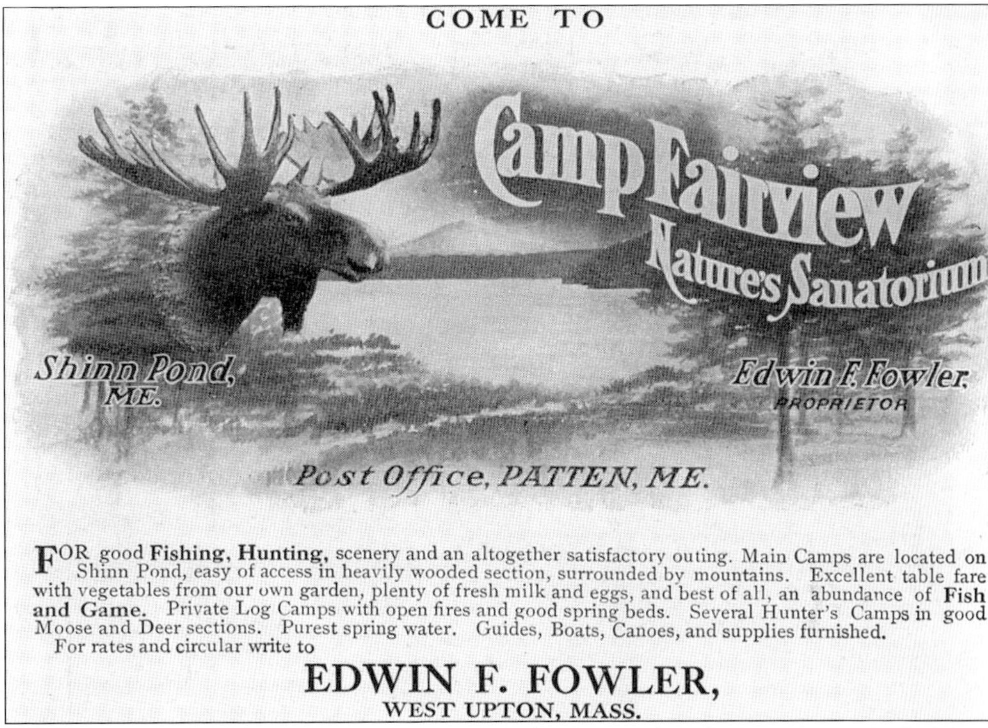

Camp Fairview was one of the prominent establishments in the Shin Pond area. *In the Maine Woods* for 1933 contained an article on Shin Pond, which read, "For those who wish seclusion and quiet, Camp Fairview should be recommended. This group of modern camps is situated at the lower end of Lower Shinn Pond, 3 miles from any kind of a road." (From *In the Maine Woods*, 1908.)

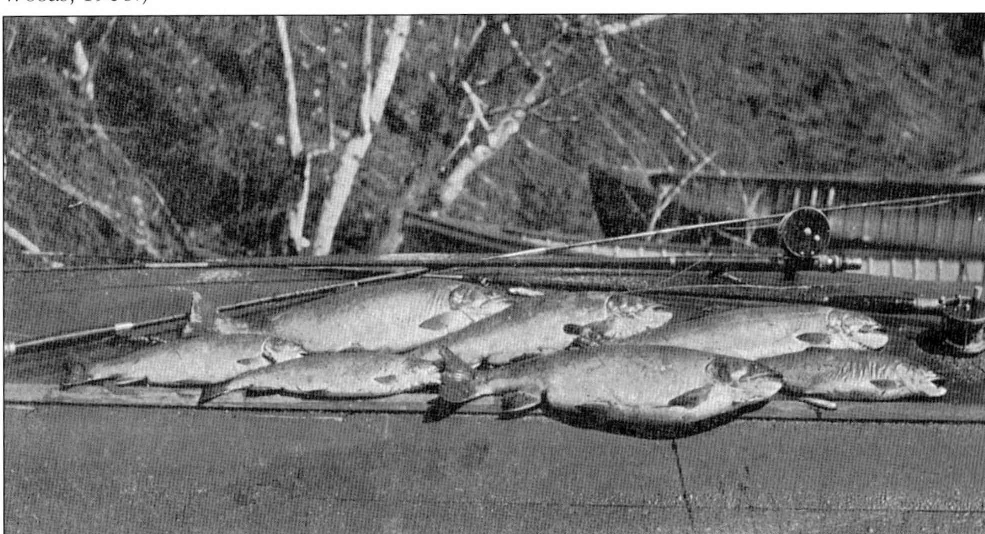

Shin Pond was described as having spring and fall fishing that was exceptionally fine, with the trout and landlocked salmon running very large and readily taken with either fly or bait. In 1933, there were 40 privately owned camps on the shores of Shin Pond. Note the style of fly rods in the background.

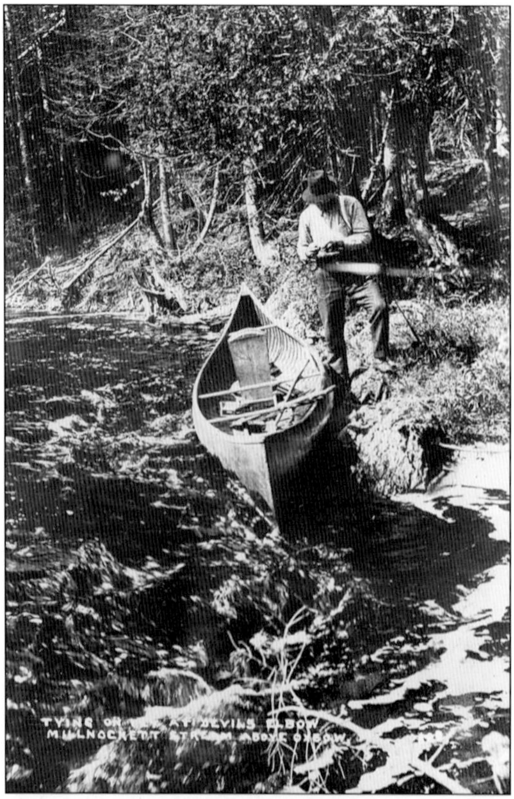

At Devil's Elbow on Millinocket Stream, an angler ties on a new fly.

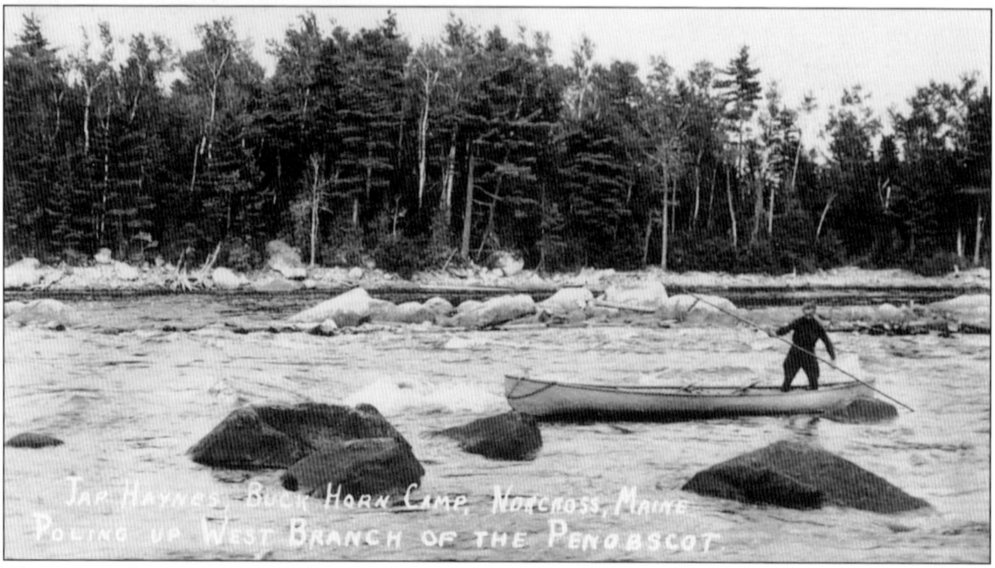

There is nothing prettier in the art of canoeing than to sit in the bow and watch a guide work his way down among rocks and rapids without a false stroke. In quick, shallow, rocky bottomed streams, no matter how swift, it is always the practice of the Maine guide to use a pole—never a paddle, and always to stand in the stern of the canoe. If the guide is in a tight place in a short rapid, he ropes down a canoe but generally resorts to the pole and the skillful art of "snubbing her down."

'E YOU GOING TO SPEND **Your Summer Vacation in th**

/oods? *If you are, write me.* I will plan for you ANY KIND OF A TRIP you want, (huntir fishing or canoeing,) and furnish everything necessary—food, canoes, tents, guides, e n thoroughly acquainted with all the best hunting and fishing regions of Maine and New Brunswick. T what you want to do and I'll tell you where to go and relieve you of all the trouble of the preparatio ite for references.

:ORGE EGAN, LICENSED GUIDE AND TRAPPER, ASHLAND, MAIN

This is an advertisement for licensed guide George Egan. Many guides offered a variety of services, and a few advertised in popular publications. Some, like most of the sporting camps, offered brochures or references. (From *In the Maine Woods*, 1909.)

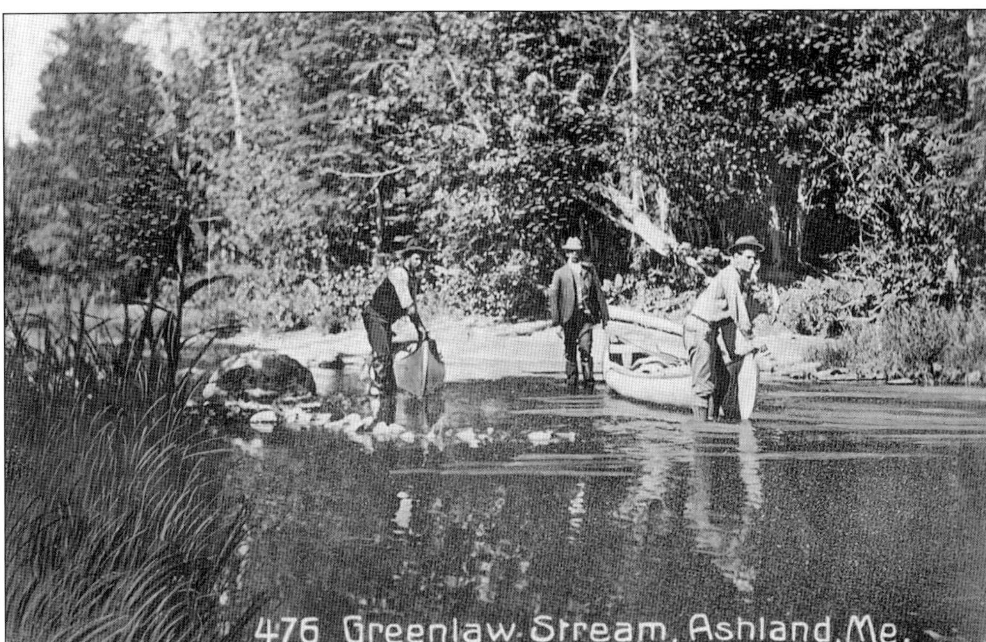

When low water is encountered, canoes must be pulled along by hand until deeper water is found in which to float again and be able to paddle. These conditions are typical of midsummer on most northern Maine streams and some rivers, as well as in periods of little or no rain. Any stream or river without a dam to control the flow is subject to low water during times of lack of rain.

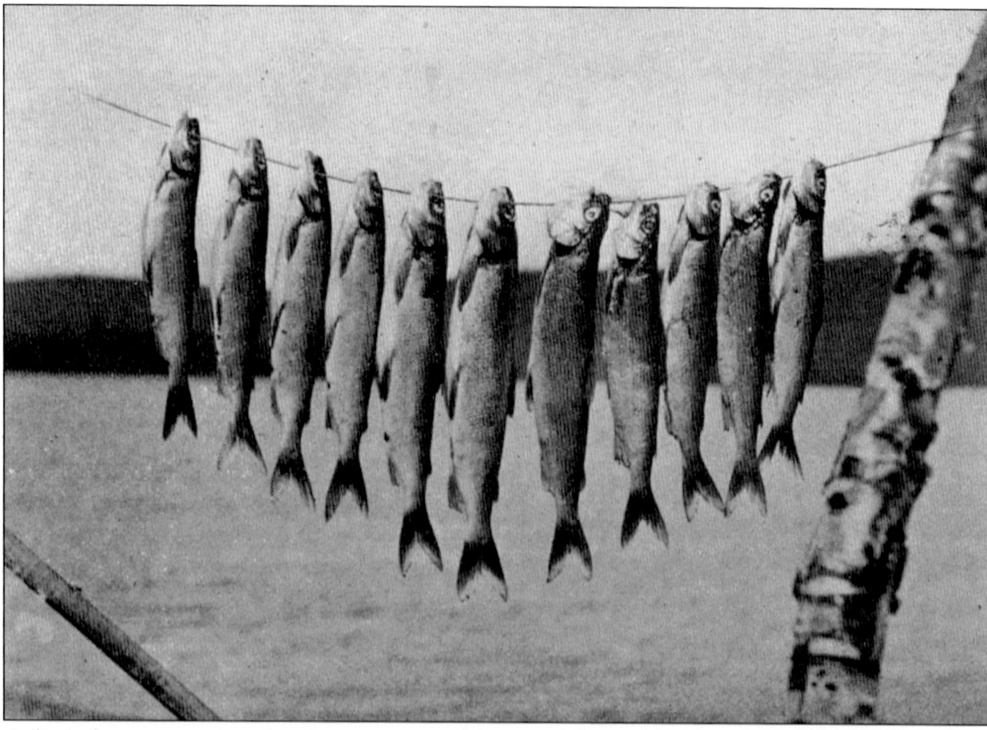

A little-known sport today, but once common, is fishing for whitefish. Many Maine lakes contain at least one if not two species, which provide an abundant food supply for game fishes, particularly large togue. Whitefish take a fly very well, especially small dries on flat, calm summer evenings. As table fare they are outstanding and were highly sought by anglers on some waters. Fish logs from sporting camps list the number of whitefish taken along with the salmon and trout. (From *In the Maine Woods*, 1924.)

GUIDE For any part of Northern Maine, for fishing and hunting, particularly the region around Norcross, outfits furnished
References given, **A. O. HALE, MEDWAY, MAINE**

GUIDE For Moose, Deer and Fishing Parties. Trips planned, Guides secured, and references given.
CHAS. BERRY, Katahdin Iron Works Maine

MOLUNKUS Camps Easy to get at—Special accommodations for ladies—Eight camps—Moose, Deer, Partridge and Good Fishing. Send for Booklet.
Rates $1.00 per day. Boats and Canoes free. **L. P. Swett, Molunkus, Me.**

GUIDE I Guide Hunting Parties, also Fish and Small Game Headquarters at Norcross, Me. Canoes and outfits furnished. References given.
P. P. FOWLER NORCROSS, ME.

Guide for any part of Maine Outfits furnished. Your Guides engaged. Supplies boxed and shipped. Trips planned.
References furnished. **FRED C. RAY, - Medway, Maine**

These are early advertisements for guide services in the northern part of the state. Note particularly that Molunkus Camps charged $1 per day and provided boats and canoes at no charge. (From *In the Maine Woods*, 1906.)

Nine

Atlantic Salmon

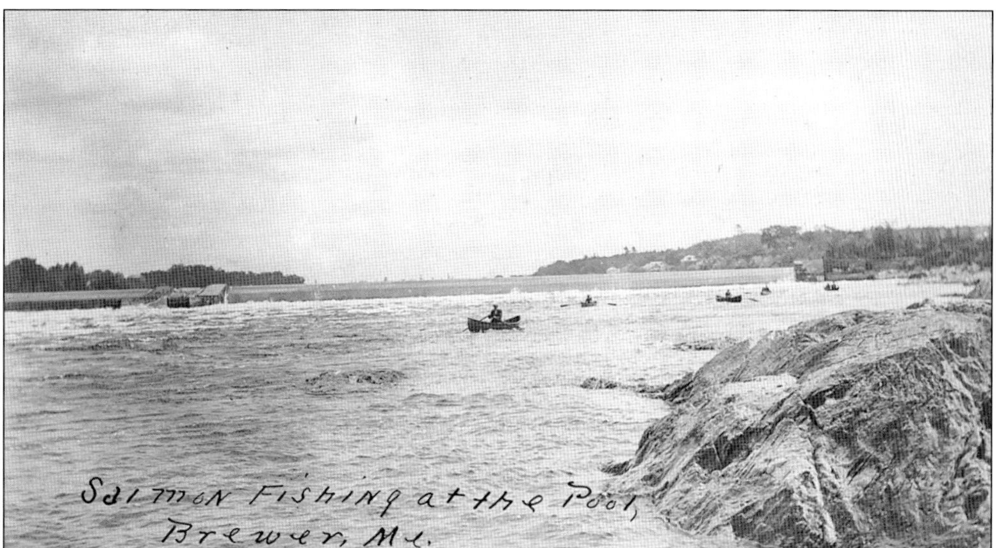

The Bangor Salmon Pool in the Penobscot River was famous for great numbers of large fish. Also, until fairly recently, the first salmon caught each season from here was given to the president of the United States. Several salmon clubs are located on both sides of the river.

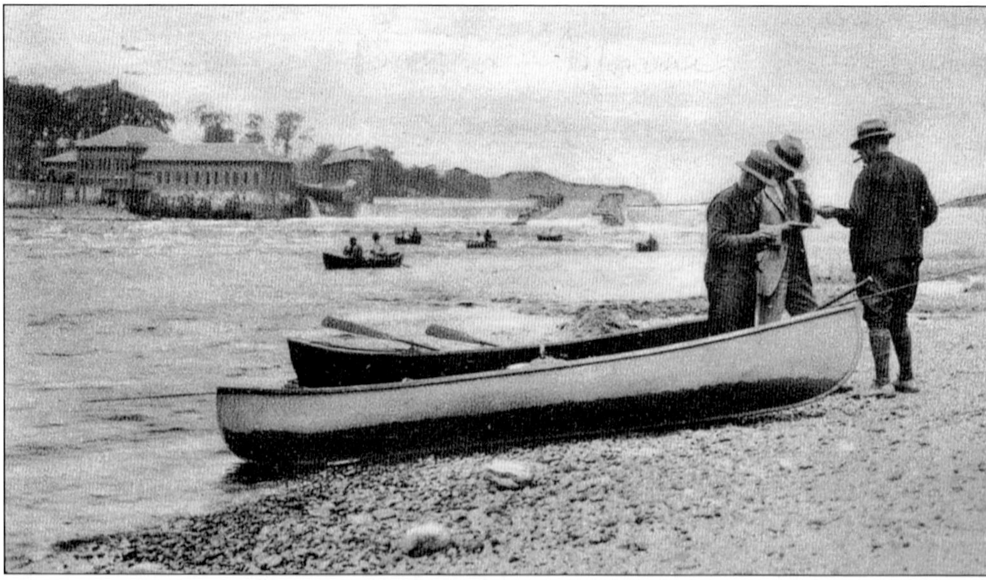

On the Brewer side of the river, anglers exchange flies as they compare notes and outline their strategy against the Atlantic salmon. Common fly patterns were Black Dose, Cosseboom, Blue Charm, and Jock Scott, fully dressed.

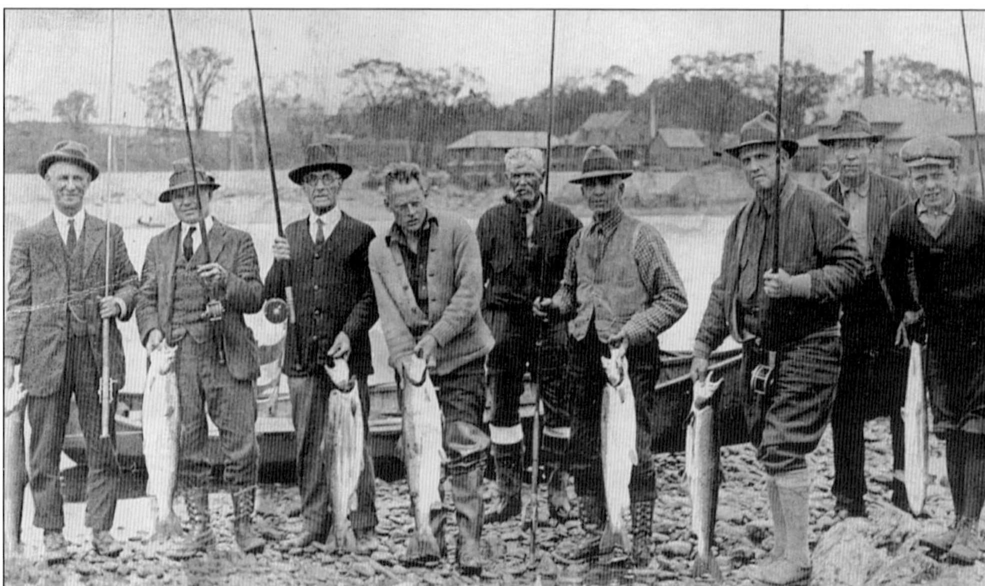

Also on the Brewer side of the river, nine anglers pose with seven salmon taken within a 30-minute period. Shown are, from left to right, Walter Crossman, William West, Fred W. Ayer, Horace Chapman, Frank Conan, Charles Bissell, Guy Peavey, Brian Hanson, and unidentified. Several of these anglers caught the first salmon: Crossman, 1927, 1933, 1937; Chapman, 1929, 1931; and Bissell, 1913, 1919, 1925, 1936.

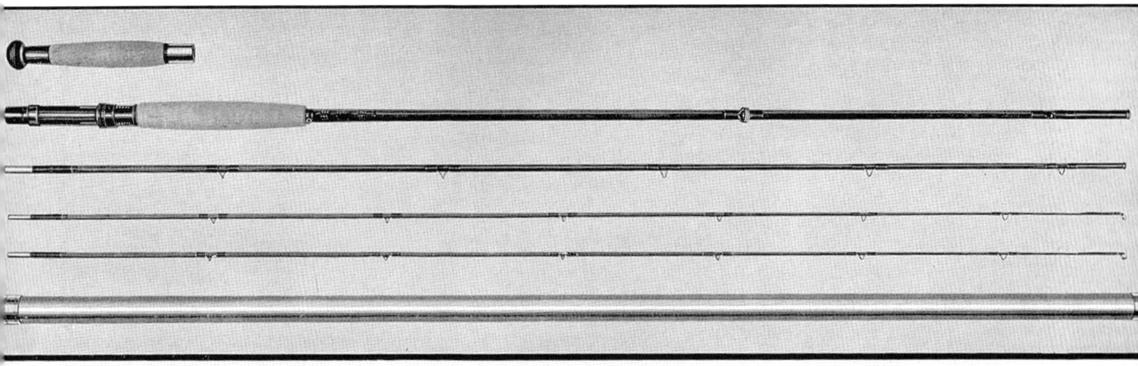

THOMAS *Brown Tone* DRY FLY SALMON OR GRILSE ROD

with Thomas Grip, Thomas Patented Solid Metal Locking Reel Seat and Extension Detachable Rear Butt Grip with Rubber Button

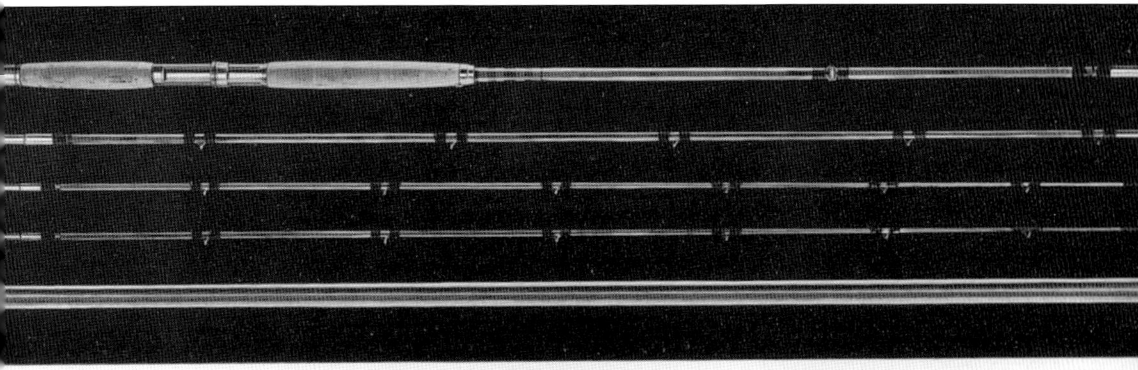

THOMAS *Special* SALMON FLY ROD

with Double Cork Grip and Thomas Patented Solid Metal Locking Reel Seat

The local manufacturer of the two-handed salmon rods that appear in the photograph at the bottom of page 114 was the F.E. Thomas Company. The company advertised salmon rods in two grades, Brown Tone and Special; four lengths, 9, 9.5, 10, and 10.5 feet; and with four distinct actions, powerful wet fly, medium dry fly, fast dry fly, and very fast dry fly. The advertisements claimed that "in the hands of an experienced angler, one of these rods, because of the extreme power for its length and weight, will kill fairly large salmon without an undue amount of effort."

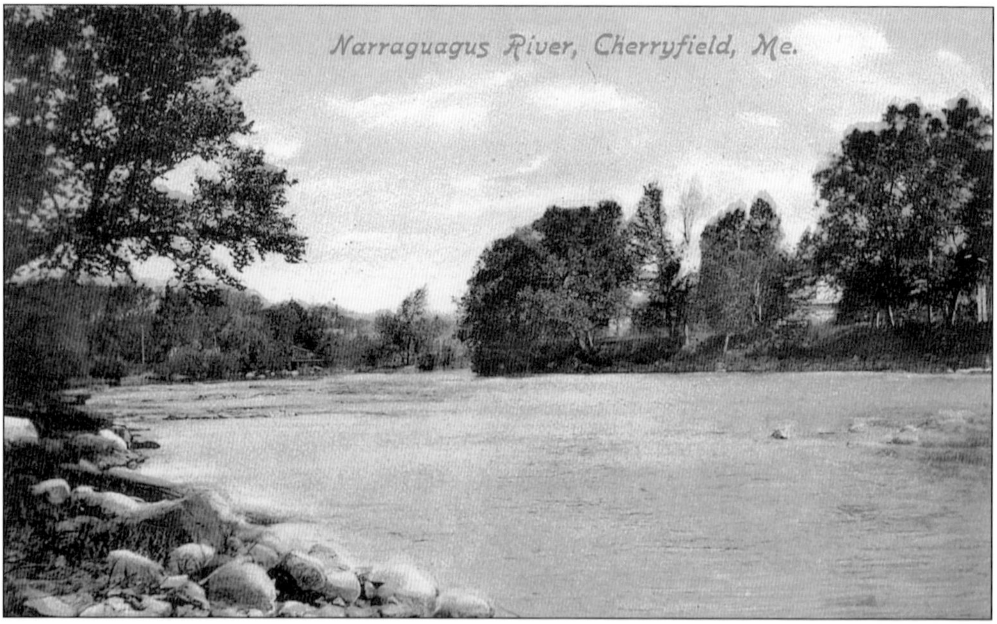

Next to the Penobscot, the Narraguagus River is an area probably the best known for Atlantic salmon.

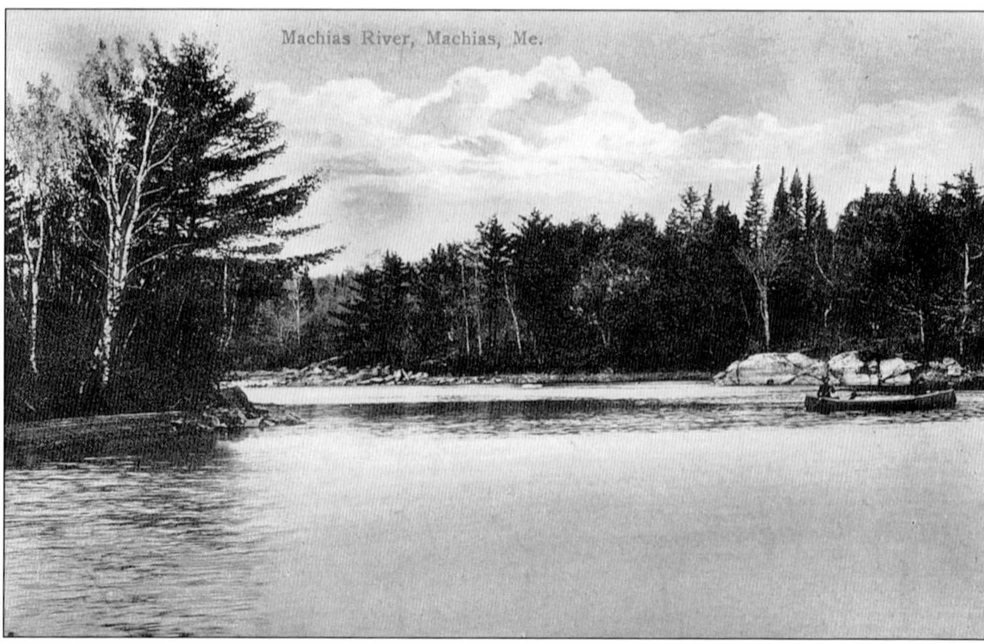

Anglers try their luck on the Machias River. Other Maine rivers known to have Atlantic salmon are the Aroostook, the St. Croix, the Dennys, the East Machias, the Pleasant, the Union, the Ducktrap, the Sheepscot, the Kennebec, the Androscoggin, and the Saco.

Ten

EQUIPMENT

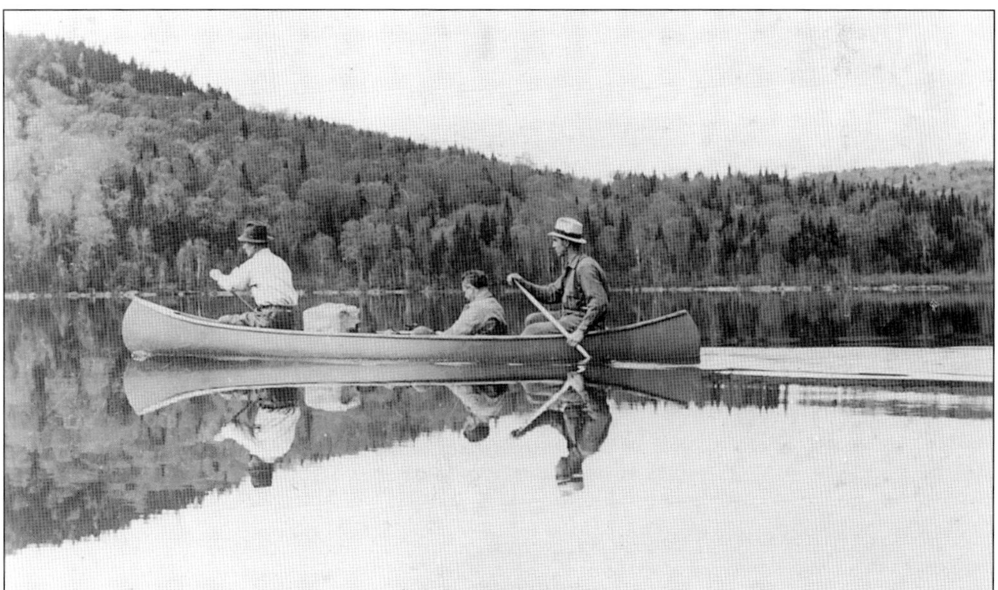

A canoe loaded with fishing and camping equipment heads for good fishing spots.

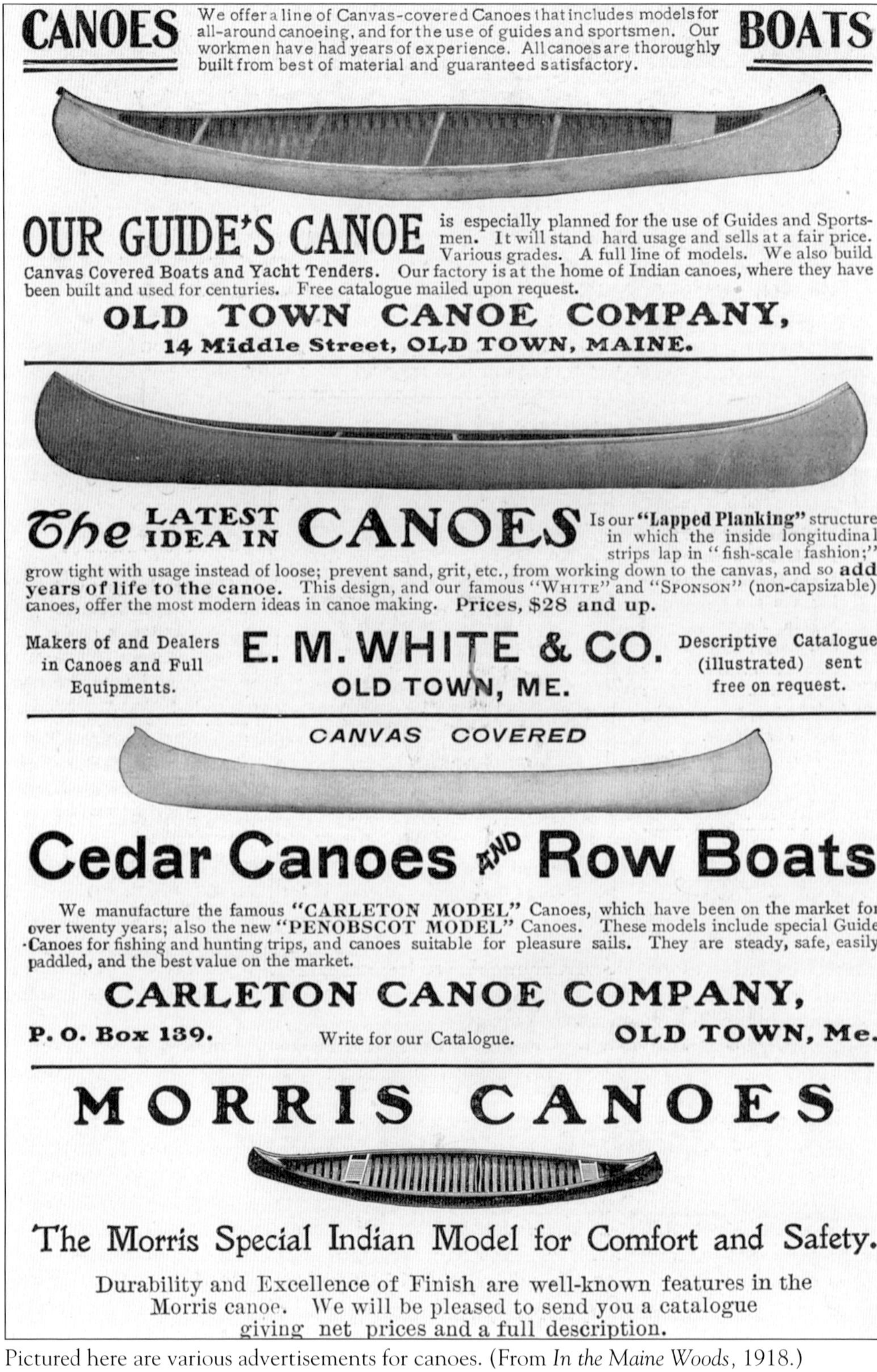

Pictured here are various advertisements for canoes. (From *In the Maine Woods*, 1918.)

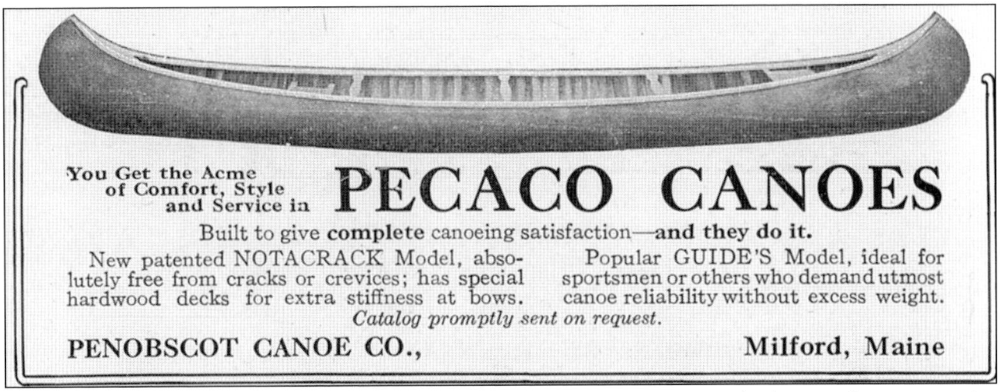

Much of the on-the-water fishing was done from canoes. Canoes were the best and most popular mode of travel for river and stream trips and were widely used for trolling, particularly before the outboard motor became popular. Strings of canoes were towed by large craft carrying sports and their guides to the fishing grounds where guide and sport fished the surrounding waters until it was time to return to camp. This way a motor launch could take the anglers anywhere to fish, saving a long and sometimes arduous paddle from and back to the camp. This practice continued until *c.* the early 1950s.

The first commercial wood-canvas canoe builder was Evan H. Gerrish, who lived in Bangor in 1875. He was formerly a guide who manufactured fishing rods and canoe paddles but turned to canoe manufacture after 1878. By 1884, he was producing 50 canoes a year. The Old Town canoe is by far the most famous of all the Maine canoes. The company was begun in the late 1890s by the Gray family, who had a variety of businesses in the area. The family hired Alfred E. Wickett who, by that time, had a lot of experience in the manufacture of canoes, including having worked for the E.M. White Company and perhaps also having run a business of his own at one time. By 1900, the company was producing 400 canoes a year and by 1910, employed 50 men. Wickett left that company and in 1915, he opened the Penobscot Canoe Company in Milford, across the river. The company manufactured not only canoes but also rowboats. Wickett invented a spearhead-shaped deck, which he added to the tips of his canoes, claiming that it added strength and rigidity; he patented the idea in 1916. The company did well until 1917, when personal problems and fires caused the business to fail. Wickett moved to St. Louis, founded the St. Louis & Meramec Canoe Company, and manufactured the Arrowhead canoe, which had a deck in the shape of an arrowhead. He joined with his son and the business prospered until his death in 1943. In 1885, E.M. White began his business, producing canoes from his home in Pushaw. He expanded his business; one of his builders being Alfred Wickett. In 1896, business was so good that White moved his operation to Water Street in Old Town, near the rail yard. By 1910, the business employed nine men and for many years was a strong competitor of the Old Town Canoe Company.

Guy Carleton of Old Town built bateaux for the log drivers and birchbark canoes beginning in the 1870s. He eventually added a wood-canvas canoe to his offerings. By 1910, Carleton employed 20 men, when they were acquired by the Old Town Canoe Company. In Veazie, on the Penobscot River between Bangor and Old Town, Bert Morris founded the Veazie Boat and Canoe Company in 1882. He soon named his business the Morris Canoe. By 1910, the company employed 30 men and 1 woman. S.L. Ingalls began his business in Old Town in the 1890s. He sold his bateaux business to Carleton and concentrated on canvas-covered canoes. In addition to numerous small, local canoe builders, other commercial manufacturers of note are the Kennebec Canoe Company of Waterville, the Skowhegan Boat & Canoe Company of Skowhegan, the Chestnut Canoe Company of Fredericton, New Brunswick, and the Charles M. Partelow Boat & Canoe Company of Boston.

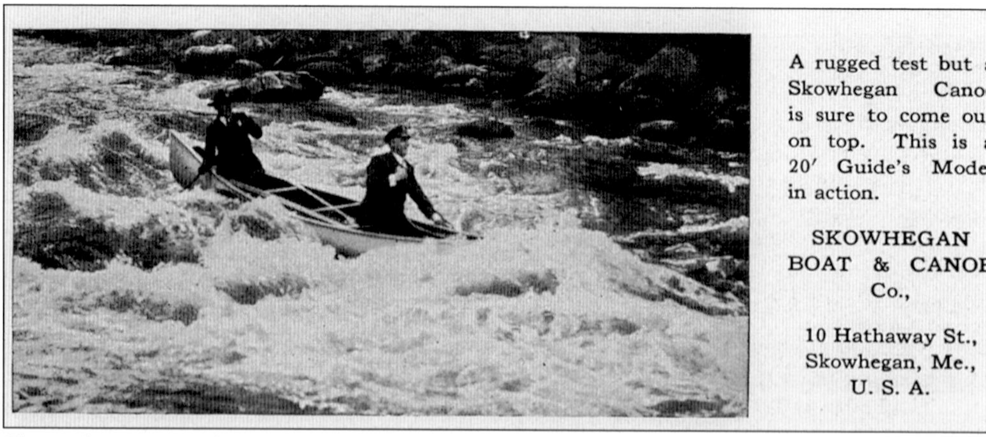

Shown here is an advertisement for one of the smaller canoe companies. (From *In the Maine Woods*, 1936.)

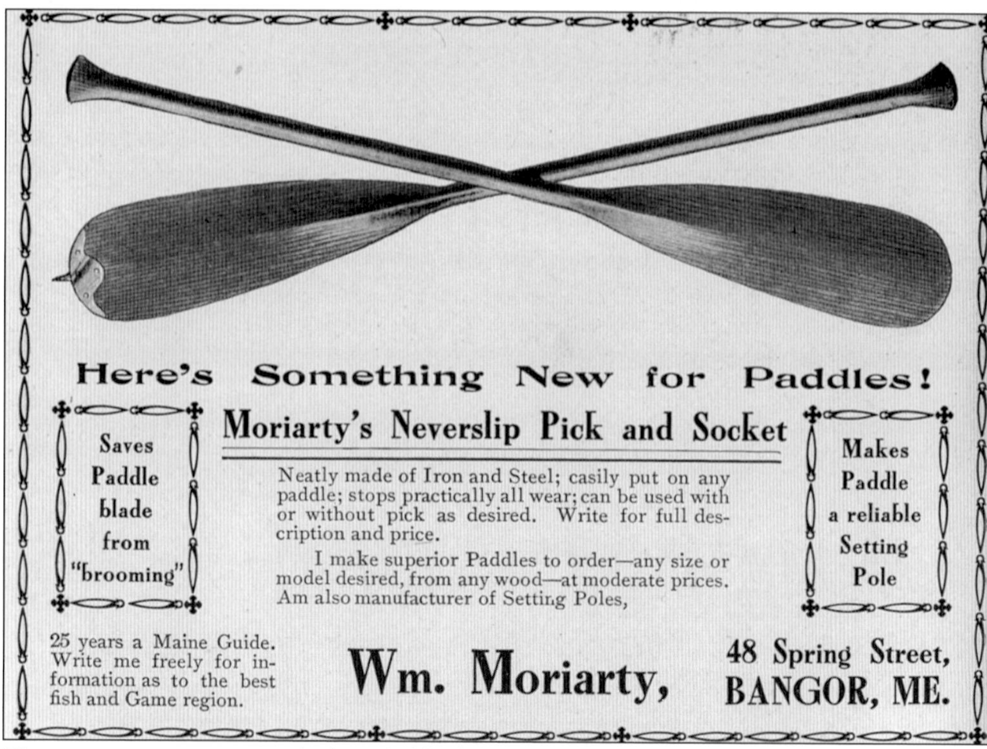

This was a new invention, which probably did not last too long, as there do not seem to be any of them around. However, it was a unique idea. (From *In the Maine Woods*, 1907.)

While most rod companies were manufacturing and promoting bamboo rods, the Bristol Company for years produced steel rods. In many ways, the steel ones were more durable. They provided a practical fishing tool produced from a fabricated material—the true precursor to fiberglass and graphite. Horton's patents were from 1887 to 1912, and the company advertised in *Field & Stream* in 1918 that their prices ranged from $3.50 to $25 and that their rods were available in 16,000 stores. (From *In the Maine Woods*, 1909.)

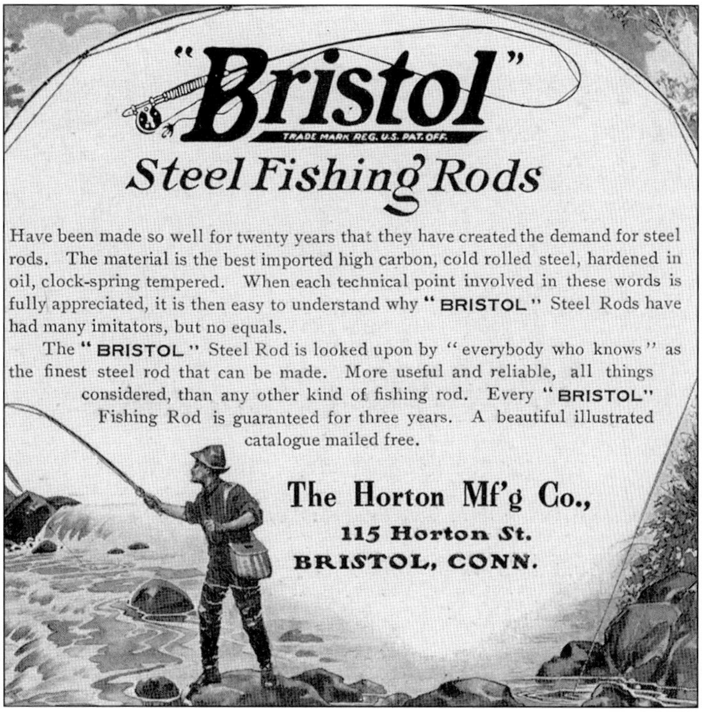

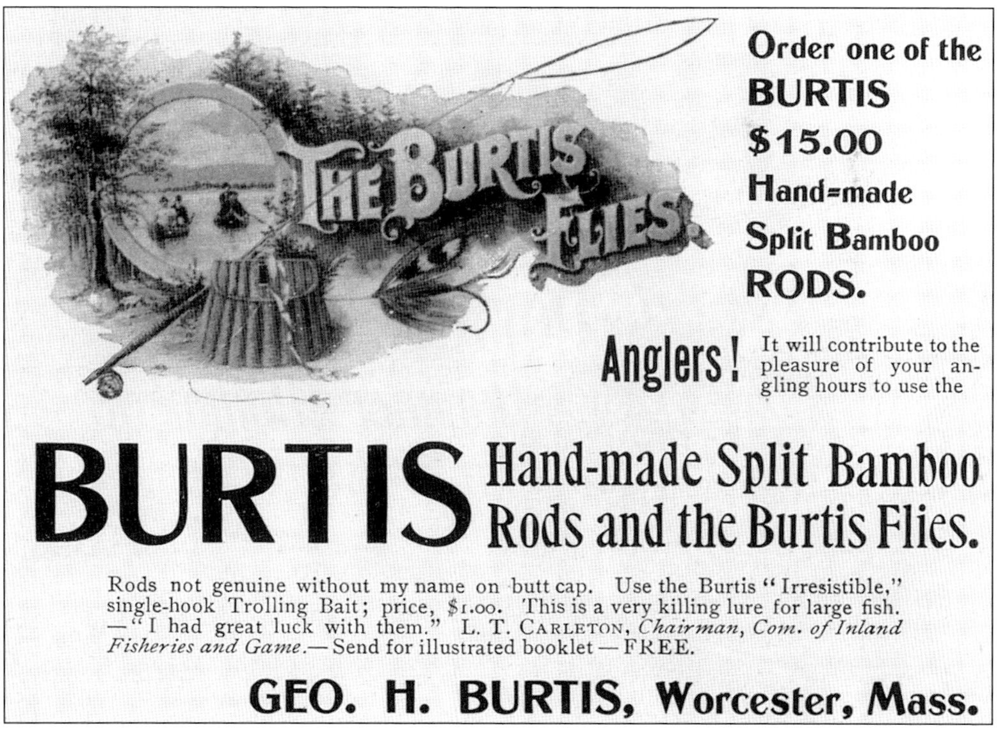

This is a fancy advertisement for one of the bamboo rod manufacturers who also marketed fishing flies and lures. (From *In the Maine Woods*, 1900.)

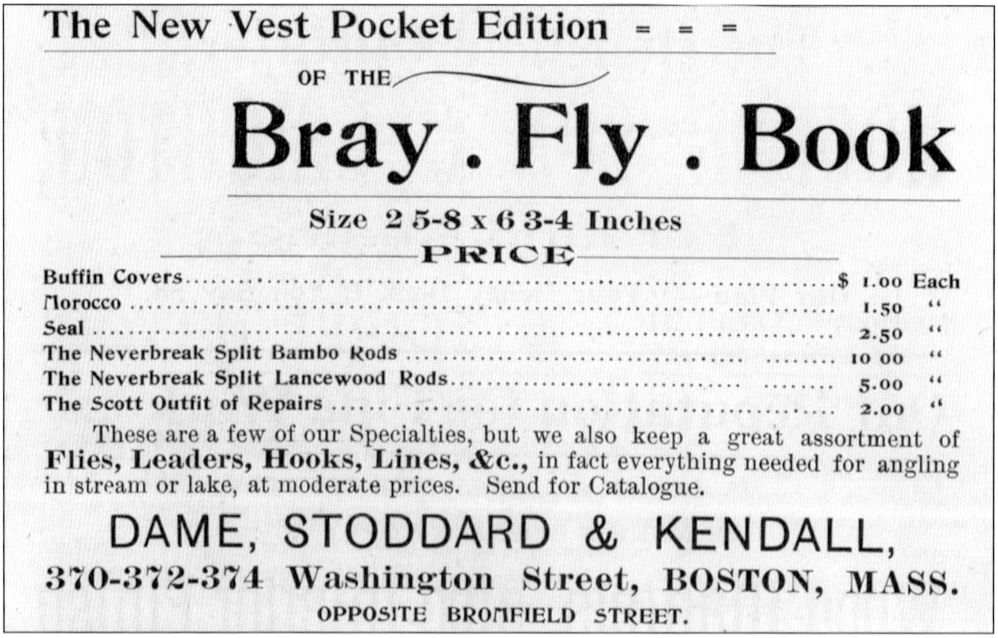

Dame, Stoddard, & Kendall was a large supplier of fishing materials. (From the *Maine Central*, *May*, 1896.)

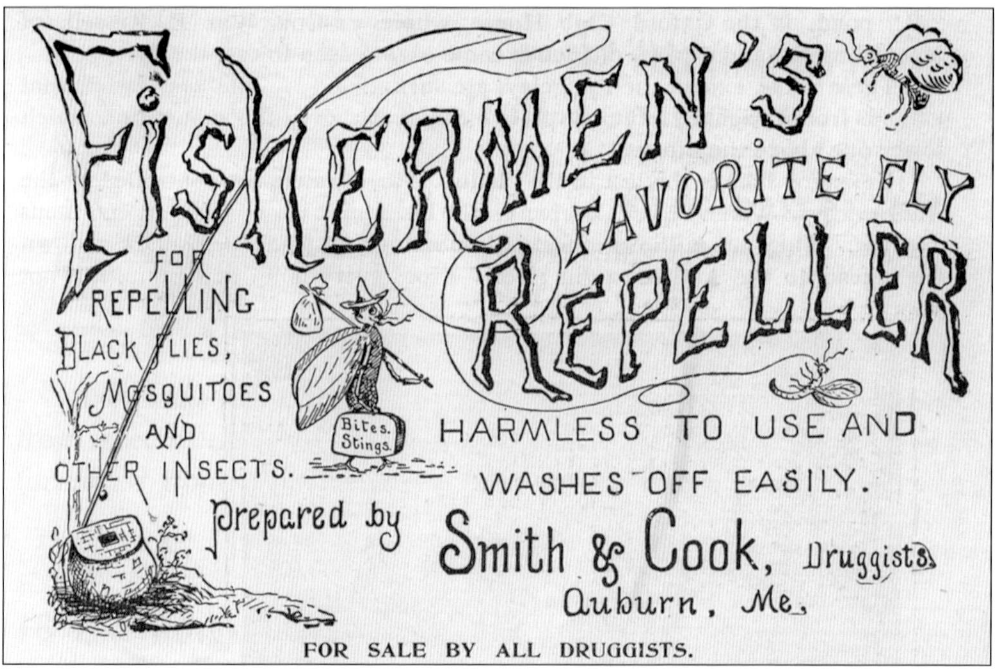

Despite what some of the advertisements stated about there being no troublesome insects, the Maine woods was, still is, and always will be infested with mosquitoes, blackflies, and no-see-ums. There were a number of repellents on the market, one of which is described here. Some camp operators and guides manufactured their own fly dope, containing mainly citronella, in both liquid and salve form; these repellents did work. (From the *Maine Central*, May 1894.)

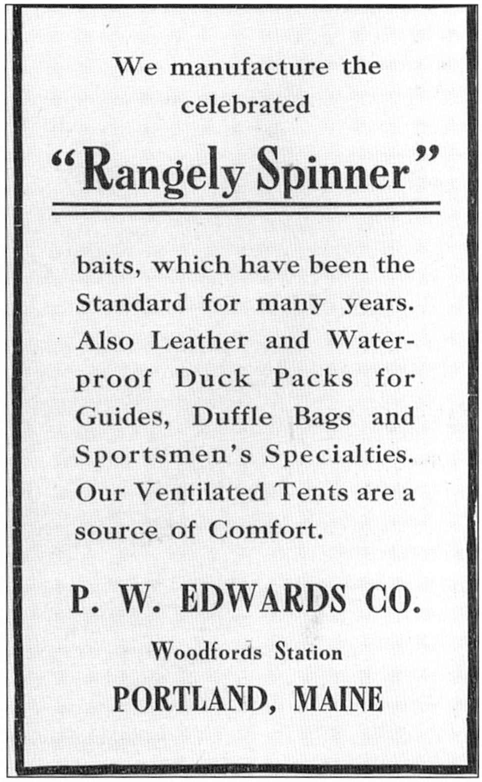

The Rangeley Spinner was one of the most popular and effective fishing items ever invented for use in trolling for trout, landlocked salmon, and togue. It is useful with flies, bait, or worms. (From *In the Maine Woods*, 1909.)

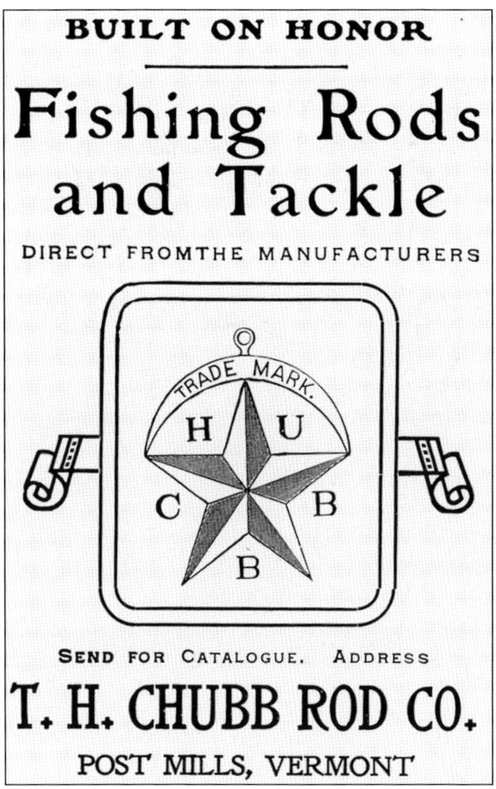

Thomas H. Chubb produced large numbers of well-built rods and is credited with a number of innovations that were patented in the late 1800s. Just after 1900, the Chubb Company was purchased by the Montague Rod Company, located in Montague City, Massachusetts. (From *In the Maine Woods*, 1904.)

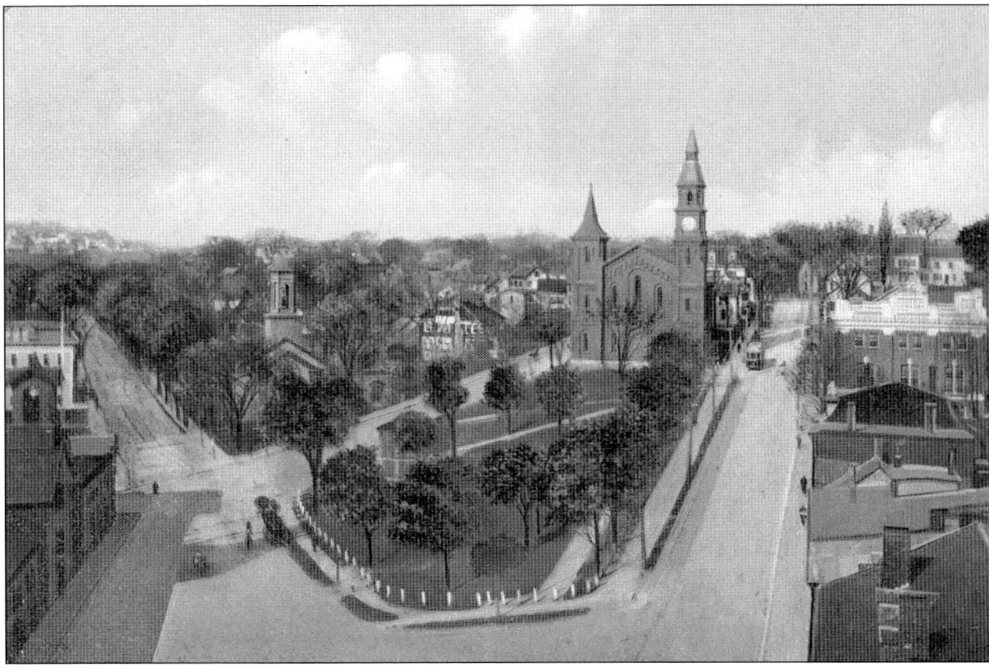

In 1923, F.E. Thomas moved his shop to a new building constructed to his specifications at Park and Center Streets, a corner on the left side of the above street just beyond the church. The business remained there until it closed in 1958.

THOMAS RODS

The Thomas hand-made split bamboo fishing rod has been perfected to meet both the all round and the various special requirements of the modern angling sport. Made of the finest bamboo, light, resilient, perfectly jointed and balanced. In the Thomas rod the acme of perfection has been obtained.

Send for our interesting booklet THOMAS ROD CO. 168 Park St., Bangor, Maine

Thomas rods became very famous and were prized by many fly fishermen. Among the long list of proud owners were Carrie Stevens, Cornelia "Fly Rod" Crosby, and Herb Welch. (From *In the Maine Woods*, 1930.)

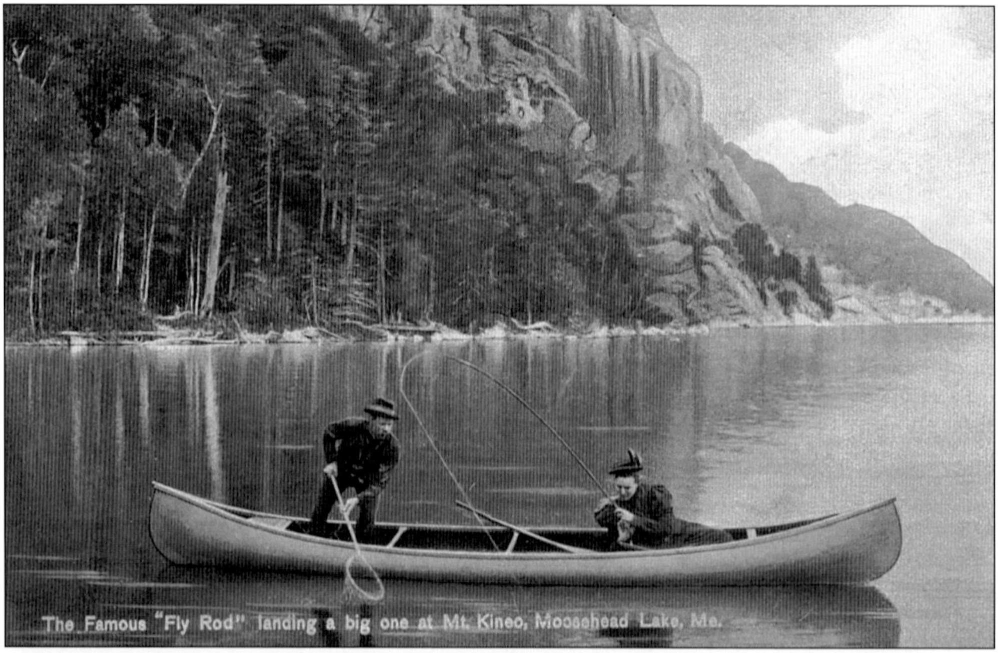

Cornelia "Fly Rod" Crosby was born in 1854. Because of ill health, she was prescribed a life in the great outdoors and so moved to Rangeley and spent her time fishing and hunting. She soon was asked to write sports columns for newspapers and magazines, and the Maine Central Railroad made her the first paid female publicist. She attended many Sportsmen's Shows and spent a lot of time in the promotion of fishing in the state of Maine. She also lobbied for Maine Guide registration and was awarded the first Maine Guide license. She died in 1946 at her home in Phillips at the age of 93.

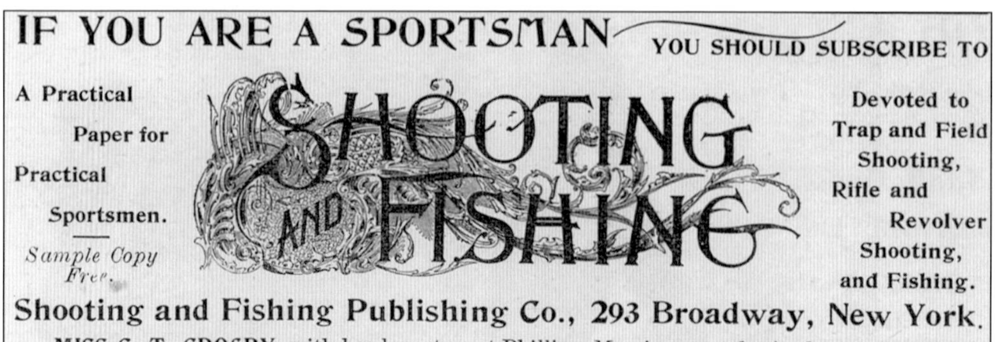

This is typical of the promotional items of the late 19th century. Note that C.T. Crosby is the authorized representative. (From the *Maine Central*, May 1894.)

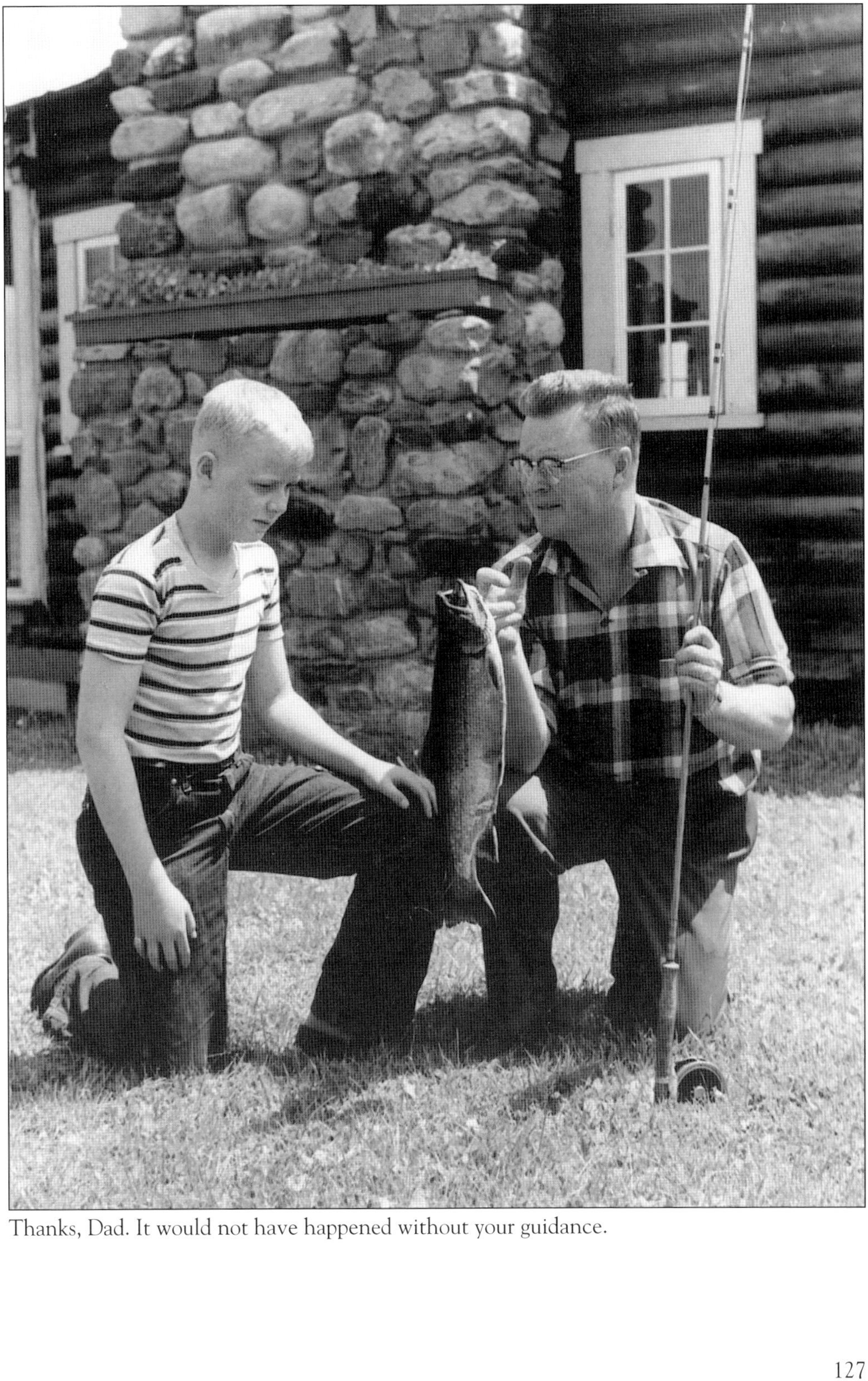

Thanks, Dad. It would not have happened without your guidance.

Bibliography

Audette, Susan T. *The Old Town Canoe Company: Our First Hundred Years*. Gardiner: Tilbury House, Publisher. 1998.

Bangor & Aroostook Railroad. *In the Maine Woods*. Various articles from various years.

Field & Stream. February, 1925 and September, 1925.

Guide to the Rangeley Lakes. Portland: Loring, Short, & Harmon. 1879.

Homel, D.B. *Antique & Collectible Fishing Rods. Identification and Value Guide*. Bellingham: Forrest Park Publishers. 1998.

Keane, Martin J. *Classic Rods and Rodmakers*. Ashley Falls: Classic Publishing Co. 1976.

Maine Central Railroad. *The Maine Central*. May 1894; April 1895; May 1896.

Maine Central Railroad. *I Go A-Fishing*. Portland. 1909.

Merrill, Daphne Winslow. *The Lakes of Maine*. Published by the author. 1973.

Moosehead Souvenir Booklet. A Collection of Articles. 1976.

Warner, Kendall, and Keith A. Havey. *Life History, Ecology and Management of Maine's Landlocked Salmon*. Augusta: Maine Department of Inland Fisheries and Wildlife. 1985.

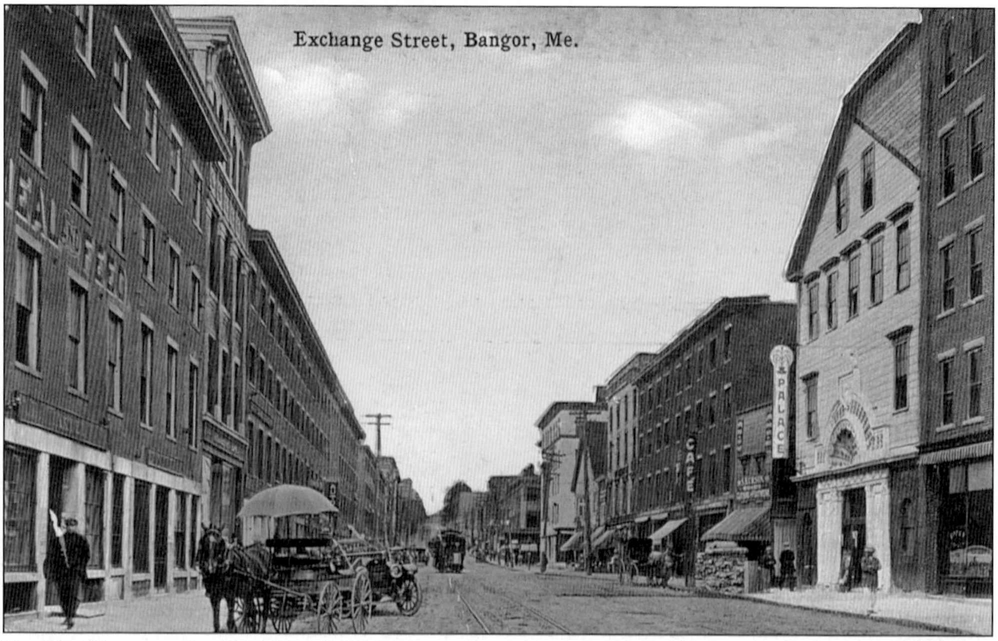

Fred E. Thomas, the founder of the Thomas Rod Company, was born in Newburg in 1855. He left to learn the art of rod building under Leonard in New York. By 1889, Thomas, Edwards, and Hawes decided to form their own company, which later changed to Thomas, Edwards, and Payne. Edwards and Payne left the company after it was located in Brewer in 1898. Thomas went on to build his own little empire, first in Brewer and then on Exchange Street in Bangor in 1902; the location was on the right side of the street, just up from the café sign.

By 1910, the F.E. Thomas Company had become extremely successful and was advertising in many of the major sporting journals of the time. The company produced several grades of fly rods, as well as casting rods and trolling rods for both fresh and saltwater fishing. (From *In the Maine Woods*, 1915.)